WE make our spiritual quest with the clues and the resources life gives us. One of these clues is the people who like us the way we are. In their presence we come to discover who we are and get the strength to be it in those favorable circumstances. So this is the paradox in this system. We need the people who like us the way we are so we can unfold and open ourselves up to that person. This makes it possible to grow and develop—to get rid of some things we are and to change along lines we find we have a natural bent for. The paradox is we need people who like us the way we are so we can become different from what we are. And the beauty here is that as we change, the people who like us the way we were like us just as much, or more, than before.

Fawcett Crest Books
by Jess Lair, Ph.D.:

"I Ain't Much, Baby—But I'm All I've Got"

"Hey, God, What Should I Do Now?"
  (*with Jacqueline Carey Lair*)

"I Ain't Well—But I Sure Am Better"

"i ain't well—
but i sure
am better"

mutual need therapy

---

jess lair, ph.d.

a fawcett crest book

fawcett publications, inc., greenwich, connecticut

"I AIN'T WELL—BUT I SURE AM BETTER": MUTUAL NEED THERAPY

THIS BOOK CONTAINS THE COMPLETE TEXT OF THE ORIGINAL HARDCOVER EDITION.

A Fawcett Crest Book reprinted by arrangement with Doubleday and Company, Inc.

ISBN 0-449-23007-4

Printed in the United States of America

10   9   8   7   6   5   4   3   2   1

This book is dedicated to all those people who opened their hearts to me. Dave was the first one I remember, back when I was seventeen. My wife, my mother, Vince, my children, my aunts and uncles, my friends and my students have all reached deep in their hearts to save my life and give me what I needed. Most of all, one person is the central part of this book. The Arabs say a woman is not just your wife, she is your fate. I am thankful for my beautiful fate.

contents

1

i found
i was not alone

I'm Jess. I have a grave emotional problem. I have a serious social disease—my humanity—and the results are terminal. I think my disease might be the same one you have but I cannot presume to say. That is for you to decide.

I have worked out a system that is helping me solve my problem. The system I have found answers questions I've always had about life. It solves problems I thought I would have to carry with me to the grave. It has saved my life. And it has filled my days with joy and peace.

I thought I was the only one who felt alone. When I wrote my first book I thought if you were brought up right, you wouldn't feel alone, you'd be like the Zulus I talked about. In my first book, *I Ain't Much, Baby, But I'm All I've Got*, I told of the Zulus who showered physical and emotional love on their children. I thought all that love was the answer to growing up without so much pain wondering who we were and why we were here. I think now that I read more into that story than was there. I made it a nice fairy tale. I don't think there has ever been a simple answer to our loneliness. I now believe that everyone feels alone. I believe it is a problem as old as time. It may even be that the problem of loneliness is and always has been the central problem of human existence.

I read a book called *Seven Arrows* by a man named Hyemeyohsts Storm and he gave me a beautiful window into the past. Here, in his book, were the views of a primitive tribal society where they had none of the problems of industrial civilization. And yet the first thing Storm said about the Cheyenne culture was that the one way in which all The People were created equal was in their loneliness.

This statement of Storm's gives me a view of Indian civilization before the white man contaminated the civilization. We are fortunate to be able to reach that far back through the myths and the oral teaching that has been handed down. The Cheyenne called themselves, along with the other Plains Indians, the Crows and the Sioux, simply The People. And The People saw their loneliness as the central fact of their existence. So we have a hint that loneliness is no eighteenth, nineteenth or twentieth-century problem. It is no problem that comes just from the atom bomb hanging over our heads. It is not from the social disorganization that took us out of our communities and threw us into the cities. It does not come from the other things we attribute the problem to, like methods of child rearing, economic inequities or what have you. There is no doubt that all these problems could serve to intensify our loneliness. But when I see that

loneliness as a central force in life went all the way back
to Stone Age civilization, that's far enough back for me.
So now I'm willing to stop looking for answers to loneliness in outward circumstances such as social upheavals.
I'm willing to see that my loneliness is a given—something that is and always has been. When I do this, I can
quit blaming external forces and turn my efforts to dealing constructively with my loneliness.

Storm told me of the Indian's belief in the Medicine
Wheel. This was represented by a circle of stones with
four large stones pointing in the four directions. Each of
the directions had a way of seeing that was associated
with it. The four ways of seeing life on the medicine
wheel were Wisdom which was opposite Innocence, and
Illumination which was opposite Introspection.

The Cheyenne believed that every one of The People
when they were born had some of one or maybe two
of those ways of seeing. But nobody had all four of them.
And nobody was complete in even one of the ways of
seeing life. The purpose of the Indian was to make a
spiritual quest using the clues in his life's vision, his
dreams and the other circumstances of his life to find
out what ways of seeing he had. And then he could
circle the Medicine Wheel and move towards completion
of the four ways of seeing. This was the Indian's spiritual
quest. Every one of The People, man, woman and child,
were dedicated to their spiritual quest.

That sounded beautiful. It was an appealing ideal.
Man was the only creature not born in harmony with
life. His lack of harmony he felt as loneliness. We handle
our loneliness by getting in continually closer harmony
with life. Our aim, which would be shared by all the
people around us, would be making our own spiritual
quests. All things around us could serve as mirrors to

ourselves. We would move towards completion of ourselves as we grew in our given way of seeing and added ways of seeing we had not been given originally.

This all seemed like the typical idyllic view we have of the happy natives dancing in the garden before fire, the wheel and other machines intruded and shattered the dream.

But I don't think life has ever been like that. We always look back on the good old days. But in those good old days, people looked back on an earlier time as "the good old days." These days we're living now will be the good old days for our grandchildren because of the simple delights they remember. Meanwhile, we're dying in agony.

After Storm finished his general coverage of the ideas I have mentioned the remaining three fourths of the book was stories. The story he told first gave me great hope.

The Indians in the village were one at a time going down to the stream. They would see their reflection in the stream and they would speak to the stream of what was deep in their hearts. And that made them feel good. But when they came back to their fellow villagers, they didn't speak to each other of what they had done.

One day, two little children went down to the stream and spoke of their hearts to the stream and felt good. They came back and told the villagers what they had done. And the villagers screamed at them, "You terrible children, you shouldn't do that!"

The children were surprised at this. "You mean you don't do that?" And the adults said, "No. You are terrible children." And they tried to kill them. But Coyote came and saved them.

This was the illustration that was so crucial and so heartening to me because it said that back in those times it wasn't any easier to open our hearts to ourselves than it is now. It is terribly hard for me to be on my spiritual quest. It is terribly hard to have a mirror held up to myself in a relationship and see what I am. And I was glad to hear some other people had problems along the same lines.

So again, I see that this problem is as old as time. The American Indians were frightened just as you and I are frightened. And I see the problem isn't the way we were brought up. I see now that children aren't born strong enough for life. This is something I believe which is very different from what most people believe. They think there is a way you can raise up children so they won't have serious problems. I don't think that will work. I don't think children are born strong enough for life.

Our parents can protect us from physical hurts. But they can't protect us from emotional hurts. As children, we were strong enough for one day, one year, maybe even ten years. But eventually life got to us and hurt us.

We started building a shell and we retreated inside. We were torn between our fear of getting hurt and our fear of showing ourselves. The poet Tagore says, "Show thyself as you are. Stand in the open."

We know that our walls are getting higher all the time as we try to protect ourselves from the additional hurts. But usually we will create our own hurts and our own crises by our maladaptive hiding-out behavior. Or life will hand us a crisis because reality is all around us and we can't escape it. The crisis will show us reality more clearly. We will either use the crisis to grow, or we will run and hide until the next crisis. We were continually hurt and overwhelmed and so our walls got higher and higher. We were torn between our fear of getting hurt and our need to show ourselves, but finally some kind of crisis made us see we could not live this way any more. And of course, the earlier crises had played their part in helping us along the way.

We wanted to come out from behind our walls and start our spiritual quest.

When I had my heart attack at thirty-five was when I finally realized that everything I was doing was wrong for me. I had had some earlier insights into the fruitlessness of what I was doing. A year earlier I had decided I should get out of my advertising business. I wanted to go back to college and get a master's degree in physics, a subject I had loved in college. But I wanted to keep my advertising business going so I could live the way I was doing at the same time I was preparing for a new way of life. I wanted to change but not badly enough to get it done. I was trying to find an easier, softer way. But half measures availed me nothing. My misery got worse and my heart gave way.

So I decided never again would I do anything I didn't believe in. And I committed myself to my spiritual quest in an all out way. I was ready to come out and find out who I was and what I could be—my own spiritual quest.

I started by going deep inside me. One thing about the way I started strikes me as so strange. Instead of turning to formal religion I seemed to turn away from religion as I understood it. I had been in my early childhood a Baptist. My grandpa was a deacon in the Baptist Church. I was never forced to go to Sunday school. I went because I liked it. I was raised in a small community with a great deal of affection from my parents, my relatives and the people in the community. Some people have very bad memories of religion and see their turning away from formal religion as the result of their bad experiences. But

I didn't have any of those kind of memories to blame my difficulties on.

At the university I was a Methodist and later became a Catholic. I had been a Catholic for ten years before the time I had my heart attack. But it is interesting to me that after that heart attack I did not say, finally, "I will adopt one of those previous religions as my own and really work at it." At the most crucial time of my life I didn't think of religion as I understood it then. I had worked at my religions and they hadn't seemed to be able to yield up what I was looking for so desperately. And I had said to ministers and priests, "There's something wrong. I can't make a contact. What is this God you speak of? How can I reach Him?" One of the poor old Baptist ministers referred me to some book by a man named Butler. But I had looked at so many books, I couldn't see that one more would make that much difference.

Instead of turning to one of those religions I had very warm memories of, but not much help from, I did what I thought was a very selfish thing. I looked within myself and said, "What do I believe in? I'm never again going to do anything I don't believe in." I went in search of what I believed. Very, very selfish, I thought. I found out later that it really wasn't.

Who was I going to get to help me in my spiritual quest? Most of you feel as I did that it's a pretty weird society out there. Everybody's insane except me and thee —and I'm not so sure about thee. We can even say about whatever group we're a part of that we're sane but all the rest of those people out there aren't. But I had to have somebody to help me.

Was I going to use the normal people? No. They hadn't seen enough reality yet to break them—to open them up to life. They still thought being normal was good. They were full of phrases like "I'm normal, ain't I?" And when they did something screwy, they justified themselves by saying "Well, everybody's doing it." I was having enough trouble with myself without bringing the whole human race into the situation.

Was I going to work with the crazy people? No. They had seen so much reality that they couldn't stand it. And they were incapacitated by their too close view of reality. A lot of people think that they're in flight from reality. They're not in as bad a flight from reality as the so-called normal people. They really saw too much reality and it broke them down right there on the spot.

Those so-called crazies know very well what's going on. You can take a group of catatonic schizophrenics who crouch in their rooms all day long and get them to come out. All you do is tell them that they won't get anything to eat unless they come to the mess hall. These are people who have been fed for years. Do they starve? No. Within three or four days they show up in the mess hall. They never starve to death. So they are in contact with reality. They just prefer the way they're handling reality to any other ways they have experienced so far. But they are in contact with reality enough to go to the mess hall.

The experiment I refer to was done with people in a mental institution down in Illinois. As a further part of the experiment, these people were later told, "You can't get in the mess hall unless you come at certain times." So they started showing up on time.

Then they put a bunch of buttons along the wall and they said, "You can't get the doors of the mess hall open unless you co-operate enough to get the buttons pressed." So they all lined up in a big line and talked to each other enough to get all the buttons pressed at the same time and they got the doors to open. These were some of the same people who hadn't talked for years.

So sure they're out of touch with reality. But not so far out of touch they can't be reached. They're maintaining sufficient touch with reality to live and no more. They don't want any more than that. The experiment demonstrated the inmates could handle more reality than they had been handling. But those limited new ways of behaving weren't enough to solve the problems of reality that put them in the institution.

Was I going to work with the neurotics? They had seen a little more reality than they could handle but they were willing to work on life. So these were the people who were the most help to me. So I'm Jess and I'm a neurotic. And that always blows people's minds. They thought being a neurotic was something bad. I think it's something good. That shows I'm aware of the problems of my social disease and I'm trying to do something about it.

What's neurosis? I think that's when we don't really know what's good for us or, when we do know, not being able to do it. So it's an inability to see reality or to be able to act on it. Looking back, I can see how powerless I was over many of my emotions and how driven so much of my life was. I had made myself a pulling slave to my emotions.

I thought I had control of my emotions because I decided when I went to the post office. In the important things, my life was unmanageable. I was driven by forces beyond my control because I was so caught up in self-will run riot. To me, that's neurosis.

What's psychosis? I don't really know much about it. I think it's just a worse version of my problem. But I can see I was more dangerous and harmful to the people around me than many people who are locked up.

I will use myself as an example. I will go into more detail later when I talk about my earlier work experiences. But for the moment let me say that I was almost completely out of touch with reality when I was trying to be an advertising agency account executive. I was a complete failure at all aspects of my job but I denied the reality of my failures. I think it is strange and unfair that you can be locked up for thinking you're Napoleon but I could be praised for thinking I was an advertising agency account executive. My way was just as crazy and lacking in reality testing as the guy who thinks he's Napoleon. And I think I was more harmful to the people around me because I pretended to love them when I didn't. The guy who thinks he's Napoleon doesn't hurt the people around him so much because he doesn't pretend to love his family.

I'm not arguing we shouldn't lock up the Napoleon. But we should see we're doing it for our own convenience as much as his. And we're letting a lot of others run around loose who are distorting reality in more conventional ways. When we deny some of these obvious contradictions in life, then we are distorting reality ourselves.

Reality is hard to face. If it wasn't we wouldn't be trying so hard to escape it so much of the time. That's why we need a system that can help us find a little piece of reality at a time with enough support so we don't crumble and run and hide again. My system is designed to do that.

Before we look at my system let's look at conventional therapy. That's for people who feel they can't cope, who want to get well. Sounds great. I don't believe in the distinction, though, between sick and well people. I believe everybody is troubled as we wrestle with the problems of being human—our common shared social disease.

And I don't believe we can ever get well—we just get better.

My disease is terminal, but I can get better and better until the day I meet my higher power—the one who restored me to some measure of sanity.

Another problem I saw was the glaring limitations of psychiatry. The patients don't get much better than the people who present themselves for psychiatric treatment but aren't treated. You put the people who present themselves at a psychiatric clinic for treatment but aren't treated in a separate group from those who are treated. Five years later you look at the group that wasn't treated and compare them with the group that was treated and they seem to be fairly equal in their adjustment. Now I grant that psychiatry might have a little edge. I've used the services of some fine psychiatrists. It's sure better than not doing anything. Two psychiatrists I came in contact with were great men. But I don't have any delusions that psychiatry is going to solve a lot of problems.

I see now that once people finally present themselves for psychiatric treatment they're working on the problem. Once you start working on the problem, you're going to get better whether you get treatment from that guy sitting there in the chair one hour a week or not. You're going to find a number of therapeutic relationships as your troubles get so big you can't contain them any more, so you are forced to share them. Now, like I said, I'd rather have a psychiatrist than not. I always set an extra life preserver on my boat, one more than I need but that's not saying it's all that great.

So the patients don't improve that much and they sit He sits there saying, "Umm" and "Ah." "Very interesting." But then the lonely psychiatrist goes home and kills there telling the psychiatrist of their terrible loneliness.

himself. Psychiatrists have one of the highest suicide rates of any group—the highest in the medical profession. The medical profession is probably the highest suicide group of any of the professions except the members of our oldest profession—the girls on the street. But that's a kind of depressing occupation and it isn't very surprising. So I don't think that psychiatry is a very good system. I had tried it and found it wasn't the system I was looking for.

I saw an interesting thing, though, fortunately, a few years after I got started. Through a lucky coincidence, I had some experience with Emotions Anonymous and Alcoholics Anonymous. Through the twelve-step program, nearly a million alcoholics, neurotics, gamblers and overeaters have cured themselves after everything else had failed, after religion, wives, bosses and friends have given up.[1]

I thought that must be a tremendous system. There are many alcoholics who are told by their bosses, "You either quit drinking or I'll fire you." Some guys who aren't bad drinkers quit. But not the real bad one. He just keeps on. And finally he does get canned. And his wife says, "If you don't quit, I'll leave you." And she leaves him.

He ends up ten years later on skid row breathing fumes

---

[1]For information on twelve-step programs, write:

EA, Emotions Anonymous, Box 5045, St. Paul, Minnesota 55104

AA, Alcoholics Anonymous, Box 459, Grand Central Station, New York, N.Y. 10017

OA, Overeaters Anonymous, 3730 Motor Avenue, Los Angeles, California 90034

There are also groups for emotions calling themselves NA (Neurotics Anonymous) and EHA (Emotional Health Anonymous). Look in your phone directories under EA, NA or EHA or personal ads in classified to see if there are groups in your city. Or write EA for help in starting a group.

in people's faces so they will give him a buck quick to get that stinking breath away from them. So obviously nothing much works for him. And he's maybe about six inches from the undertaker. He's just right for the program.

The AA program wasn't used on the easy ones. It was used on the hard ones and it cured nearly a million of them. And it doesn't cost anything. There are a few small problems because of what people have to do to work that program but it really works. And now that the program is worked out, people don't need to nearly die physically before they are ready to come in. AA is now getting members in their twenties and even some teenagers as young as twelve and fourteen. As well as I can see the AA cure was based on two things. One, we've got to give up our egotism and see we can't do it ourselves. We need help. You know the commercial, "I can do it myself, Mother." That's us. When we are at the center of our world our world breaks down at the center. We are like the old medieval astronomy where they figured the earth was all important so the sun must revolve around the earth. That's a very poor astronomy because you've got to make so many exceptions to the laws you derive from that basic mistake. When we are at the center point, our life breaks down at the center. When we are at the center point, we want the world to get in harmony with us.

The minute you change around and see that you are not at the center, and you step out of the center, then you can begin to find some harmony with life. When we were living in our egotism we sat there behind our walls and said, "How come it always rains on my parade? Today, I'm going on a picnic and I don't want any rain. Tomorrow I'm going shopping and I don't want any rain.

The next day I'm going bowling so I don't want any rain. The next day I'm sick and in the house but I want to see sunshine so I don't want any rain." After about six weeks of us running the weather the earth would dry up and blow away.

Nothing suits us. Finally we get tired of no rain and then just when everyone else wants a clear day, we decide we're tired of sunshine and we want it to rain. We want to hear a little rain on the roof. But everybody else is out on a picnic. So nothing ever suits us when we're at the center. Everything is an insult to us and it's only one out of a hundred things in life that are satisfactory, if that.

But the minute we get out of the center and we start to break down our egotism, then we have a chance. And that's the first step of the twelve-step program. They admitted they were powerless, that their lives had become unmanageable, and I sure could see that I was powerless, that my life was unmanageable. I wasn't addicted to alcohol, I was just addicted to work. And work is a very socially acceptable addiction in this dumb society of ours. If I would have died with that heart attack, people would have said, "Wasn't that guy a great man? Look what he did for his family. He left them all that insurance and that big house. Oh, isn't it so sad that our hard workers have to go first?" Isn't that weird? Here I was insane and people didn't see it.

I knew of a guy who had a heart attack at a young age like me. He hadn't been home but three nights in the last thirty-six because of all his clubs, associations and good works. It's like the question, "What did your daddy do before he died?" "He just sat up in bed, went 'Aughh,' and died." And that's what this old guy did at the age of thirty-four. He and I had the youngest heart attacks in our crowd. Quite an accomplishment. The only thing is he didn't make it. I hope he had a lot of chance in that last few minutes of life to make his spiritual quest. It's a short one, but I know he did the very best he could. We all do. We can't ever judge another's spiritual quest. But I'm sure thankful I had more time. An old priest believed that the time of death for each one of us is when our soul is at the ideal point for us. From all the times death has turned me away I can see my soul sure isn't ready.

Another thing we do when we admit we are powerless and helpless, is we become willing to give up our surface relationships. Montana is the "Howdy" state. You walk down Main Street in Miles City and if your hair ain't too long everybody will say "Howdy" to you. It's "Howdy there." Real friendly. Twenty years later you are seeing the same cat on the street and he's still saying, "Howdy." Really friendly. In twenty years he's refused to tell you anything more than "Howdy." And that's why Montana has one of the highest suicide rates and one of the highest divorce rates in the whole country. That's what that beautiful isolation and alienation does for you. Fantastic. A lovely way to live. "Oh, cordiality is so lovely. Oh, I've got a lot of friends. I can meet a man on the elevator and talk to him five minutes and he's my friend." That kind of friendship does so much for you. "Oh," I tell you, "love 'em and leave 'em, that's me. You ought to thank God I was there for five minutes giving you the gift of my beautiful personality. I was really with you, man. I forget what your name was and I forget your story, or anything about you, but it was really important to me. Oh, unbelievably important."

Well all that's a lie. A dirty, rotten lie only we won't admit it. Is that lie going to hurt the other guy? No, not

much. But it sure hurts me. It is very hard on us to live
in cordiality with a group of people for thirty or forty
solid years and never tell them any more than our name,
rank and serial number. That says, "I don't trust you,
man." You say, "How are you?" And we all say, "Just
fine." But some of the times we ain't fine. Ma just died.
And we just got caught with our hand in the till at the
bank and they're about to can us. So that ain't fine at
all. That's terrible. But we ain't going to tell him. Because he's a very virtuous man. He must be because he
never told us he did anything wrong.

So these cordial relationships are a very terrible thing.
When we give up our surface relationships with bar-
tenders then we can go in search of real relationships.
What is that real relationship and what does it do? It
gives us the answer to our loneliness and that is real
communication. Where do we find real communication?
At the start we find it with people where we see our
mutual need for each other. The beginning of life is with
people where we see our mutual need for each other.

Okay, but this is contrary to what most religions seem
to teach. They seem to teach that you've got to be nice
to everybody. You've got to love everybody. Well, I can
see that perhaps someday, I will be able to love everybody, but that's going to come later—much later. And
it ain't going to come ever until I can learn to love, first
myself and then secondly, two or three people.

It's like you might hear some guy say, "I'm going to
take up mountain climbing." You say, "You are." He
says, "Yeah, I'm going to start by making the southwest
ascent of Mount Everest." "You aren't going to do any
mountain climbing before that?" "No, sir! I'm going to
Nepal tomorrow and do the southwest ascent." Wow!
Supreme arrogance.

That's what a lot of people are doing when they say, "I'm going to love my enemies first. After I get them well-loved, I'm going to love my friends. And then when I finally get that done, I'm going to love myself. Because I'm naturally a generous outgoing person and I believe in spreading it around."

Well, let me get out of his way. "You go right ahead, man. You are welcome to your way. But please warn me when you're hitting town because I want to get out of there." I can't stand the pain of being around someone who thinks like that. I have a different program. I have turned his program upside down.

When I become a mountain climber the first thing I'm going to start working on is a flight of stairs. Then I'm going to progress slowly, very slowly, until I'm confident I'm ready for the next stage. I don't believe in psyching myself out on something real important like that. Because this is life or death I'm talking about. This is no parlor game. So I'm going to give myself every advantage. Every chance I can I'm going to take the easiest possible way I can find. That's hard enough for me. If you want to take a harder way, that's beautiful. I'm glad there are people like you around.

I'm going to make my spiritual quest by paying attention to the clues life gives me. The most precious clue life gives me are those people who like me the way I am. And believe it or not there are a few. I ain't everybody's cup of tea—but thank God I am somebody's cup of tea. And there doesn't have to be many who like me because I don't need a whole bunch. I need five friends, a wife and some kids, my family and with that I've got an awful good start. So I can screen a lot of people to find those who like me the way I am so I can be free to become something different and better than I now am.

Bozeman has 20,000 people and if I only need five, well that means a lot of people can decide they can't stand me and I'm still all right. I've got no problem. Because all I need is five, and who are those five? They are the five whose faces light up when they see me. Once we start looking we all know who those people are. The sadness is so often they have been standing at our elbow waiting for us to realize they love us the way we are. But we haven't been paying attention to them because we've got our eye on the gal who owns the ranch or the one who's got those flirty eyes or something like that.

To the gal at our elbow who's waiting to love us, we say, "Not you, honey, you've got a wart on your nose." Well, maybe she's got a wart on her nose, but she's got the most precious thing in the world for me: a warm heart for me. She likes me the way I am. And she hasn't got any program for my improvement.

The only one who has a license for my self-improvement signed by me is my wife. I know there are other people who have long programs for my self-improvement. They occasionally come up and wish them on me and go into chapter and verse on how I should improve my grammar, my dress, my sloppy enunciation and all of my other low moral qualities. Those people want to read that list to me and then go into a detailed explanation of how I can correct myself. I always plead a dental appointment. "I'm sorry, man, much as I'd love to listen to you, I do have to move on. Much as it pains me to leave you I have to move on."

"But wait a minute. I haven't got through improving you yet." And I say, "Sorry, man, it's just going to have to wait until a later time." That's the way it goes. You can't do every good thing in life in one day. That's not the kind of communication that can save my life.

I call the process I'm talking about mutual need therapy, because it's based on the real communication that can come when we find people where we have a mutual need for each other. That real communication is my therapy.

What's therapy?

Therapy is not sick to well. It's not sick to normal. It's us getting better—the spiritual quest. I think maybe everyone needs this kind of therapy but I can't judge for you. I see therapy as very similar to physical and occupational therapy. It makes you better. Who among us couldn't benefit in some way from physical therapy for a weak arm, leg or other part of our body?

My oldest daughter had cerebral palsy when she was born and right at two she started physical therapy and later speech and occupational therapy. She had many years of it. She's twenty-four now and has been supporting herself for the past year working in the old people's home. She does a beautiful job working around the patients. She is in a job where she is able to excell. I never thought I would see the day not only that she would be self-supporting, but that she could excell at something and know that she is good at it. She is good at it and those old people love her. I couldn't last there a day. It is even hard for me to go and visit her there at work. And she learned to ski. It took her a long time, but she made it down the hill. Now she can ski Sunnyside with us.

So therapy is getting better. Janet had therapy in her school but her therapy didn't stop there. Now her job and her work are also her therapy. Therapy is learning new behavior through understanding, through changing our attitudes and through experiencing and practicing new behavior. And then we keep on practicing the rest

of our life. Therapy is like ski instruction. We help you
get rid of fears, get new understanding, give you new
experiences of what you want to do. We give you drills
to practice the new stuff. And we give you methods to
diagnose your skiing so you can find out for yourself
when something starts going wrong again. But you never
finish learning.

When Jean Claude Killy came to the United States
after his three Olympic gold medals, he had some new
things to learn. He hadn't skied our kind of powder much
but he learned how and he really enjoyed it. A few years
later he learned parallel slalom on the pro circuit. That's
a very different thing from regular slalom because you've
got the distraction of the man skiing alongside you. As
great a skier as he is, he never stops learning. And this
I see is what therapy means, a continuous program of
learning and understanding and changing our behavior.

What's mutual mean in mutual need therapy? Mutuality
is when we find someone who we like and who likes us
just the way we are. Neither of us have any plans for
improving the other person. We feel good when we are
with them. Mutuality is made possible by our diversity.
Each of us are so different. But once in a while we find
someone who likes our particular set of differences. Why
did God make such a different bunch? That's so there
would be some other nuts just like me. There is a small
chance that a few of you who are reading this book are
just as crazy as I am in my way. If I were a resident of
your town, you and I might get along beautifully. And we
would be friends. You might occasionally ask, "Why do
we fit together so well?" And the answer is, "I don't
know. That's just the way it is."

I used to want everybody in the world to be just like
me. Then I realized what an awful world it would be

if I got up some morning and met nothing but a succession of Jess Lairs through the day. I'd commit suicide by noon. The terrible boredom and monotony would kill me. Think what an awful doom that would be. The people I'm talking about who like me the way I am aren't like me. They are very different from me but they like me the way I am.

One gal told me, "You know I read your first book just after I tried to commit suicide. I saw your arrogance so clearly in that book. I saw I was just as arrogant as you are but if there is a place for someone as arrogant as you are, there must be a place for me, too. And you gave me such hope." Another guy was sent my first book by his sister. He was in Leavenworth Penitentiary for a rather serious offense. He wrote back to his sister and she sent me the letter. He said, "Sis, it's spooky. This guy is just like me." I took it as a compliment.

I got a letter from a guy who was in Warm Springs, Montana's state mental institution. He said, "Jess, I got hold of your book in the institution and I realized I had a chance." That was a compliment because it says there's somebody else out there whose face is going to light up when they see me and that's what I need to save my own life. And I don't need to see a lot of them.

What do I mean by need in mutual need therapy? What's need? I'm not talking about a dependency, I'm talking about a need. We need food and water, but we don't think of ourselves as having a dependency on them.

A good distinction here is like we see in the gal who comes to me and says, "Jess, I've got to get Willie back. Willie left me. I've got to get him back."

"Does he want to come back?" She says, "No. He says he hates me. How am I going to get him back?"

"Let him go. There's a thousand guys who would like

a gal like you." "But I want Willie!" she cries.

She's got a dependency on Willie. That's probably one of the reasons he left. What's a need? That's very different. I have five friends. I need them. But if all five of my friends by some unique set of circumstances moved out of town tomorrow, I've got some people around me who might like to spend more time together than has been possible because of my commitment to my five friends. They would be my new five friends. They could never replace my present five friends, but they could do many of the things for me my five friends now do. So I have a need for them, but not a dependency.

A beautiful illustration of that is in Kahlil Gibran where he speaks of a marriage of love. He said that is when two people don't lean on each other but they stand independently like two trees side by side with their leaves touching. That's an ideal relationship. That's not a dependency relationship, it's mutual need therapy.

Where the wrong kind of need for us is satisfied, that's bad. It's like our sick games. If I go to the wrong places to have my needs satisfied I feel the pain afterwards. My wife's saying for this is so useful. "They charge too high a price for a drink from their poisoned well."

When I have lunch with my friend, Jerry, frequently he says afterwards, "Thank God you had lunch with me today, Jess, because you have calmed me down so beautifully." Well that wasn't my intention at all. I went to lunch with Jerry because I wanted to have a good time. And I wanted to talk about interesting things. I never know what it's going to be but I can count on talk about interesting things with Jerry.

When we see that we aren't the center of the world and start looking for what is we start on our spiritual quest. We can't get in harmony with life when we sit at the center because we *aren't* the center of this world. The minute we leave the center, then we have a chance to read the clues and to find how to be in harmony with life.

What kind of world is out there? Is it screwed up? I used to think it was. My students used to raise this question and it's implied in *I Ain't Much*. . . . They would say, "Hey, Jess, it's unfair what you're doing. You're telling us that there's a better way to live but we've got to return to that same terrifying, horrifying world. You're doing a cruel thing sending us out there with these illusions and false hopes you've given us."

I didn't have a very good answer for them. I thought they were right. All I could come up with was a lame excuse: "Well, at least you're prepared for it and you know it's going to be there. So you'll be able to deal a little better with it. And you can pick and choose the best parts."

But what I see now is as I've gotten more in harmony with life in recent years hardly anything bad ever happens to me any more. What does that say about that terrifying, horrifying world? It says I caused almost all of my own troubles. What little trouble I still get now is very simple to bear. So that ain't a horrifying, terrifying world out there in reality. It is for us only because we make it so. We sit there in the center of our own narrow little world so limited in our own thinking and fears that we bring about the very things that we fear.

One of my young friends, a gal about twenty-six, was telling me she and her husband wanted to move. They needed a twelve-foot Hertz truck. He's a real, hard-charging guy. He called the Hertz rental system in Bozeman. They didn't have a twelve-foot truck. He blew his stack because he didn't want to pay for a twenty-four-foot truck when a twelve-foot would do. He was a man who was very careful with his money. His sanity doesn't mean very much to him, but his money is real important. Finally he got himself quieted down a little bit. He and his wife realized they were fighting the world. They realized there must be some kind of solution.

The minute they started getting halfway calm, the guy said, "Gee, I wonder if they've got a truck over in Belgrade." It's a town that's a fantastic distance from us. It's eight miles. They called over to Belgrade and the guy said, "Well, we've got an eighteen-footer over here." The two thought about it and realized it was a lot better than a twenty-four-footer so they went over to look at it. It turned out the guy had measured it wrong and it was a twelve-footer.

You see how we cause our own trouble? We lie down on the floor like a little kid kicking our heels in a temper tantrum because we can't get our way and we block out any possibility of anything good happening to us. We have tunnel vision because of our anger, fear and anxiety. We've got ourselves 100 per cent blinded, insulated and protected against anything good. And then we say, "That's a terrifying, horrifying world." Yeah, it looks like it is but we caused it. "Well, when am I going to stop causing it?" You're going to stop causing it when you want to stop causing it. Until then you are welcome to what you're getting.

Jim, a friend of mine who is in AA, was trying to get a drunk to try the program. The drunk didn't know whether he wanted to try it or not. Jim told him, "I tell you what I'll do. I'll give you this guarantee. Try our program for thirty days. At the end of the thirty days if you aren't satisfied we'll give you back your misery."

That's a beautiful way of putting it. As long as you and I love our misery we're going to have a lot of it.

That's pretty awful to see in ourselves. That's one of the things I have found my mutual relationships show me. They are a mirror that helps me see into myself. And most often at the beginning I didn't like a lot of what I saw. That's why this kind of therapy isn't ever going to be all that popular. It ain't ever going to be a mass movement and a mass therapy because it has some very unpopular principles, like we cause most of our own misery. You ain't going to sell that real well. But that's too bad. I need a system that will work for me, not one that's popular.

We make our spiritual quest with the clues and the resources life gives us. One of these clues is the people who like us the way we are. In their presence we come to discover who we are and get the strength to be it in those favorable circumstances. So this is the paradox in this system. We need the people who like us the way we are so we can unfold and open ourselves up to that person. This makes it possible to grow and develop—to get rid of some things we are and to change along lines we find we have a natural bent for. The paradox is we need people who like us the way we are so we can become different from what we are. And the beauty here is that as we change, the people who like us the way we were like us just as much, or more, than before.

I can illustrate this principle very simply for you by asking if you have some other person who, when you're with them, makes you feel like you're ten feet tall. That's who to start with. But you know what I can tell you about that person? You know what you're doing? You may be going to that person some but you know what I'm proposing? You go to them about every day at first. "Oh my God!" you say. "Why? I should only come on that person by accident. Sure they're the greatest person

in my life. Sure they make me feel like I'm ten feet tall.
But I couldn't make myself feel good—every day. That
would be immoral! Feel good every day?"

Now if you have five such people and saw each of them
every day, that means that five times every day you'd feel
good. "Oh, my God, that's really disgusting. I'm a puritan,
man, and I know that the more I suffer the higher place
I have in heaven." But I've got news for you. There is a
small possibility that when we get to the end and if we
are judged and if we go beyond into some other state,
which I leave up to your own speculation, I can't conceive of a higher power who takes anything away. I
think we might be given some additional things. But I
can't see a higher power that would take anything away.

Furthermore, it is very possibly a long time until that
day. There is a very good chance that you and I might
not die tomorrow. There's a very good chance you and
I will live on—and on—and on. The trouble with this life
is it's so damn daily. For most of us there isn't a quick
death rushing the barricades being a cheap hero yelling
"Viva la France" as we hurl ourselves at the bayonets
and die with a bullet in our chest. That's the simple, easy,
quick way to go. But not very many of us are going to
go that way. Almost all the lovely young people in my
classes are going to end up as old people like those in
the home my daughter works in. They've got an awful
lot of miles they've got to travel in between. And if those
are pleasant, beautiful miles it makes a much lovelier trip
for you and me than if we're miserable all the way.

If you want to be miserable all the way go ahead. I'll
see your miserable face on the street in Bozeman coming
towards me and I'll brace myself to smile and say
"Hello" so I can avoid being part of your misery. Because
I don't want to play the misery game any more. There's

enough real misery in store for me so I don't need to look for any additional misery.

Often a big source of misery for us is our past and this is why we need to make a break with it. We feel we didn't get what we wanted or needed or expected. So we keep going back and back. Very often we are tied to our parents or some previous situation that didn't meet our needs. We keep going back in the vain hope the situation will finally yield up what we have so long wanted and never gotten.

The answer is no way can it. We need to see that our parents and the other people in our past did the best for us they could. What they didn't give us weren't things they maliciously withheld from us, they didn't give us those things because they didn't have them to give.

I am a limited father to my children. I gave them what I could give them. I did the best I could. I would hope that they could walk away free in the knowledge that I did that. And that they would have compassion for me. And that they would have the same compassion for me that they will hope for from their own children. I am a limited human being and I did the best I could.

Until we have compassion for the people in our past we are not free of them. We are either tied to them in conforming to them in the vain hope we will someday satisfy them and they will think well of us and give us what we need. Or, we are tied to them by rebelling against them. "I'll show those so and so's." That rebellion ties us to our past as much as our conformity.

We need to go and get our needs met where they can be met and how they can be met instead of expecting everything from each person.

That is why it is so important to pay attention to the clues life hands us on what we are and how we can have our needs met, instead of ignoring them as we are doing such a beautiful job of. There were all kinds of people standing around at my elbow who wanted to love me. And I said, "No, not you, not you. I want you." That's a terrible thing to do. Now I pay as close attention as I can to the people who want to love me. I don't care whether they are short, fat, skinny, or have warts on their nose. Whether they are twenty-six or ninety-two, if they like me the way I am, they've got the most precious thing and I'll go right for them.

I'm a man in a desperate situation. I'm a man who nearly destroyed myself for lack of real communication and real relationships. So now I'm going to go out in life and get what I need. A lot of the people I'm getting it from say, "Jess, you're saving my life." And I say, "That's fine, but that's accidental, because I'm here frying my own fish." That's what mutuality means.

In a way, I'm a cheater. I don't live life the hard way. If you want to, you're a tougher person than I am. Just like on the ski hill. I've got the best equipment, good boots and the finest instruction. I cheat. I don't ski on those old wooden army skis I used in 1946. I don't do it the hard way. Some people make it a point to do it the hard way.

I want everything in my favor, especially in life like this where I'm in such desperate circumstances. If the life of my family were at stake I would use everything to save them. Well, the life of my family and my own life is at stake in this matter so I'll do anything to save us.

When I'm able to be myself with a few people—my five friends and my family—then I'm more able to be myself with some other people. Whatever comfort, hope or ideas you may be getting from this book, whatever what I say may mean to you, most of it comes because of my wife, my children, and Vince and Jerry and Dave and the other people who have so lovingly given me what I needed. What you see in me is what they made it possible for me to be. And because I was able to be it with them I am now able to be it with you for a little while.

I have done a little traveling to speak to various groups. I have found it to be wrong for me so far, because if the people around me gave me this thing, it doesn't make any sense for me to be on the road 90 per cent of the time. That would say I don't need them any more and I sure do. And it says to them, "Okay, you guys have played a part in my life and you've given me the most precious thing there is, now I'll go and fly." No way. Commitment is crucial. It is the most crucial thing there is in a relationship. This is why the love 'em and leave 'em I do out on the road I have come to see can be so wrong. On a one-night stand on the road I hold out to people the most precious thing there is or the illusion of it and then I pull it away. It's like a summer camp romance. You're making love as the calendar slowly moves towards that day. That's no way to live. It's nicer than nothing, but it isn't as good as the real thing is. I think the real thing is where you're making love and you know it will go on and on and on. That's what commitment means in a relationship.

I don't care if you stand on a mountaintop and say, "We commit ourselves to each other in front of this mountain and all this sky." That kind of commitment will work better than any kind of religious ceremony I've ever seen without a sense of commitment. The point is the commitment.

As we spend more time with the people who like us

the way we are, we change and become more like what we are ideally capable of becoming.

What's here for us on this earth? I used to think we had to put up with this misery and sorrow until we got to heaven or some kind of hereafter and I didn't believe in it very much and I sure wasn't anxious to get there. I now see that on this earth we can have serenity and abundant living, find out who we are and get the courage to be it. We can even become some things we aren't now. So growth means adding some things to ourselves, getting rid of some of our defects of character and deepening some things we have.

That's our spiritual quest. I hurt you when I attempt to meddle in your spiritual quest. I help you when I concentrate on my own spiritual quest. All I should ever do is simply tell you how I'm doing. That's simple to say but it's the hardest thing in the world to do, to keep my nose out of your business and my grubby little finger out of your life. Because each and every one of you are so beautiful—just the way you are. The only problem is that so often you and I can't see that. We think there is something wrong with each of us. But there isn't anything wrong with us. You and I are lovely people. I could love you just as you are. You could love me as I am. When we each see that then we can start the loving— and the living. They're the same thing.

2

examining
our relationships

Now we need to examine our relationships to see how much mutuality there is in them. There is so much lying we do to ourselves about our relationships. My students so often claim, "Oh, Jess, I live in such a groovy world, I love everybody and they all love me." I think there is a chance some of these students are lying to themselves. I have done a lot of lying to myself and I'm still doing a certain amount of it. It's like the question of "How strong is my left arm?" It has been broken three times and it's a very weak arm. Now I can lie to myself that my arm is strong. But say a car falls on my son. I have to get that car off him or it will kill him. Then I find out that my left arm is not a strong arm. That's reality. In the same way we need to look at our relationships as realistically as we can.

I feel the strength of our relationships has a lot to do

39

with our desire or lack of desire to live. I had never heard the expression "one-car accident" until I came to Montana. A one-car accident is often just a quick way to commit suicide. They talk about this being the "Howdy" state. This is a state where people are outwardly very friendly, but there is often very little depth to that friendship.

Now, there are some very friendly people in Montana, but there are an awful lot of very, very frightened people. But as I mentioned in the first chapter, just saying "Howdy" to those frightened people doesn't make them want to live. So one day they finally get out their gun and blow their brains out. Or they get in their car and put it right off the road into the bridge, into the creek, into the cliff. So one-car accidents aren't just a result of Montana's poor roads and drinking drivers. It is a socially acceptable way of killing yourself.

When you don't want to live any more and want to put your wife's nose right into it, you walk down in the basement and blow your brains out while she's at home. When you don't want to live any more and don't want to rub somebody's nose in it, you get in your car and you put it off the cliff. And they say, "Gee, he must have gone to sleep at the wheel."

Suicide is the ultimate sign of a lousy relationship. I think that other signs of lousy relationships are things like poor health, heart attacks, even cancer. There is some evidence that in prehistoric tribes there was not very much cancer, if any. When we know the effect that the mind has on the body, it isn't very hard to see that a troubled mind can weaken the body and cause all kinds of physical troubles. And you can all see that some people look twice their calendar age while other people look half their calendar age.

You know those two masks on theater programs, tragedy and comedy? Remember how the tragedy one has the terrible sad face with deep lines of sorrow and anger? Well, you see people on the street with faces that look like that. You can't help wonder how long it took. How many millions of sad looks and miserable looks does it take to force your features into that kind of a mold? It is a mold that has never seen a smile.

All of these things tell us what our relationships are really like. There is a doctor who has the idea that having sexual intercourse is a great way to lose weight. Well that's beautiful, but the fact that a woman is heavy often comes out of a difficulty in the sexual relationship. In some respects her fat is a way of running away from sexual relationships. By telling a person to have sex relationships to get rid of the weight, one shows he doesn't have much understanding of what caused the weight in the first place or compassion for the woman or man who is fat to avoid their sense of sexual inadequacy.

This is not a perfect world. None of us are going to have perfect relationships. But we need to get as good relationships as we can in all areas of our life. The better relationships we can have in one area, the more they feed over and bleed over into other areas. So we surround the problem. Maybe there is some crucial relationship in our family we can't seem to improve. But we can surround that relationship with good relationships that just kind of overlap into the problem area.

So let's take a good look at my relationships. At the time I had my heart attack I was thirty-five years old. I had people in my life who were great for me: my wife and some friends like Jim Larkin. I knew some who were kind of average people for me in terms of relationships. They were the kind of friends you make fairly easily.

Then, within a few years, in a new place, you quickly make friends like that again. I also had some people who were very lukewarm in the relationship, but there was at least a fragile connection. And then I had the last category. There were people who were actually wrong for me but I mistakenly thought I had a relationship. The terrible sadness was I put all these relationships, good, bad and lukewarm, under the same category. Every one of them I called friend. I wasn't able to feel the difference between the good and the bad relationships.

Say we had all the big mountains of the world lined up in a circle around our valley here. Over there is Mount Everest, the tallest mountain in the world. Next is Mount McKinley, the tallest mountain in North America. Beside it is Mount Whitney, the tallest mountain in the United States. And then our mountains, Blackmore, Mount Ellis, Green Mountain and some little hills. Say I call them all Mount Everests. That's a lack of ability to see the difference in things just like my inability to tell my good relationships from the poor ones. But even worse, my inability to see the differences in quality was a terrible lack of respect for the good relationships in my life.

What kind of an awful feeling does it give you when you are the most trusting friend a person has, yet they say "Yeah, you and my other friend, Pete." But you know Pete hates your friend. He bad-mouths him every chance he gets, and yet your friend says to you "Yeah, you two friends of mine, you and Pete." You just want to kill that dumb so and so.

Now, are my relationships going to flower in this kind of terrible confusion on my part? Of course not. No way. Because I'm automatically suppressing them. And I'm blind to the differences between my friends and my enemies. So I can't tell who tears me down or who lifts me up. And I can't build my good friendships and stay away from the bad because I can't tell the difference.

Before my heart attack, when I was so stupid in my relationships, I had a weird way of deciding who to have coffee with. I would go right down the row of offices. On Monday I would have coffee with the guy in the first office. Tuesday I would have coffee with the guy in the second office. And through the week I would continue down the hall. And the next week I would start up where I left off.

That's how stupid I was. I would go to lunch with a guy who was trying to sell me something. No wonder my digestion didn't work so good.

Since my heart attack, I don't think that I have been to more than two business lunches. They stand out so because I have become so used to something different that I could hardly stand them. Now anytime a salesman says "Hey, I will buy your lunch," or "Let's go to lunch and we will talk over this business thing," I say, "No way. Any business we have to talk over we will talk over right now or sometime during the day." If it isn't important enough to make some time for during work hours, then it isn't important enough to bother with.

So who do I go to coffee with every morning? Simple. I go with Jerry Sullivan every morning except when Sullivan is not available for coffee. Then I go with someone else who is high on my list. And there are guys that I ain't ever going to get to. I will even go by myself and pick up whoever I can find over there before I will ask some people to coffee.

Now, am I showing some terrible disrespect to those guys I don't ask? Absolutely not. It's the kindest thing in the world I can do to those guys. I'm leaving them alone. I'm letting them go to coffee with people *they* like.

Look what happens if I pick out one of those guys down the row and say I should go to coffee with him. "It is my Christian duty to go to coffee with him. My political duty, too. He might vote against me in the next faculty meeting." So I ask him. But look what he is thinking: "Oh, no. Here's Jess Lair. I have to go to coffee with that idiot much as I can't stand him. It's my Christian duty and Jess might vote against me in a faculty meeting." So we go to coffee together and we sit there hating our time together and I come back to work in my office and wonder how come my stomach feels so terrible.

What happens when I go to coffee with Jerry Sullivan? Jerry will blow, "Jess, I just said this terrible thing and that person will never speak to me again. I lost my temper and it was just awful." And I say, "Oh, Jerry, you are always saying that. But people keep appointing you to their dumb committees and stuff like that. You're a liar, Sullivan."

"But you should have seen what I did," I tell him. And he says, "Shut up, Lair." Then he tells me about his kids and I tell him about my kids. And we just talk on and on, see. Having a good time. So we go back relaxed and feeling good.

When I was teaching full days, who would I go to lunch with? I would go back to get Sullivan. Now I would be a little careful not to lay this on Jerry too strong, so sometimes I would hang back and see if Sullivan came to me and said "Hey, Jess, where have you been?" By stepping back, I would give him a chance to help set the pace for our relationship. And it gets nicer and nicer. In a way, it is really strange because Sullivan and I are such very, very different people. I can't figure out why he likes me. But I know why I like him.

I think love is telling how it is with you in your deepest heart. Jerry and I do that. Much of it is unspoken or just hinted at, yet we get the point loud and clear. But I'm not going to tell Jerry Sullivan I love him. He would shoot me.

I know, too, that our relationship could create some problems for Jerry. A couple of times I have talked to him about it. "Hey, Jerry, look, here is this whole department of yours and you and I are going out to coffee so much." He just says, "Hey, look, Jess, don't worry about it. I will balance it out." In fact, when he got that department head job I said, "Hey, Sullivan, are you going to be so busy you aren't going to have time to have coffee any more?" He said, "If that job keeps me that busy I'm going to get rid of it."

What I have discovered in the last few years is how much I took mutuality for granted—so much that I overlooked it. A while back I realized that a fellow professor and I always had lots to say to each other when we met. So I've started making sure we meet more often rather than leave those meetings to accident. Now we are starting to play a much bigger part in each other's life.

The clues we get aren't always easy to read or figure out. There was another professor I ran into often. We also had wonderful warm conversations every time we met. So I started calling him and asking him to lunch and coffee. I asked him to call me. But he never did. Finally I had to stop because I didn't feel comfortable being the only one who took the initiative.

I have found that when I talk about mutuality in relationships it drives some people crazy. They don't like to hear me say "Unless there is some kind of mutuality in

the relationship, get out." They say "Oh, I couldn't leave
Joe Doakes alone. If I wasn't nice to him he'd have nobody in the whole, wide world."

See how egotistical that is? It says, "I've got the pattern
for the whole universe. And God that I am and great
magnificent, kind, loving person that I am, I can just
barely stand to be with Joe Doakes. So it's obvious that
if I can't stand to be with Joe Doakes, nobody else could.
If it wasn't for my pity for Joe Doakes, no one would
ever talk to him again. So it is my Christian duty to
make sure that Joe Doakes, much as I hate him, gets
taken to coffee by me at least once a week." If you went
and asked Joe Doakes about this he would say, "I wish
that Jess Lair would just leave me alone."

That little example tells much about the way our relationships are, too much of the time. When I tell you
to examine your relationships, look for some real depth
in some of them. And look for mutuality. It usually hurts
to look honestly at our relationships. And it makes some
people very angry when I tell them how I question myself
about my relationships so I can pay closer attention to
them. "Am I layin' my trip on this guy all the time? Am
I always the one who is saying, 'Hey, come and go with
me?' " If I am, that's an awful bad sign.

I know a man who draws all of his friends from the
upper reaches of the Bozeman social register. He has
never told me of a poor friend. All of his friends have
incomes above $50,000 a year. Now, how come it just
happened that the kind of people he grooves on all have
high incomes? How come he doesn't like any poor
people? That's strange, the way it works out for him.

It is like I say to my students: "I need you." And
during the course of the quarter a certain few of them
come toddling through the door. But I'm always alert

to watch for something crucial, and that's this: The students who need me back had better not have anything in common about their exteriors or I'm in trouble. If they are all girls, I'm in trouble. If they are all guys, I'm in trouble: What am I doing to the gals? If they are all pretty, I'm in trouble. What kind of message am I sending? If they are all short or all tall or all fat or all skinny, it says something about me.

I have my own automatic test for beautiful people. A beautiful person is someone who likes me. So whoever walks through that door, "Hello, gorgeous!" But they better be a variety of shapes and sizes, and sexes and ages. And thank God, they pretty well are and more and more so all the time. So there had better be mutuality and there had better be diversity in externals. Take a good look at relationships.

Mutuality has nothing to do with age. Anna Pearl Sherrick retired as head of the nursing department some years ago so she must be a little older than me. Every time I see her, I feel good. My students are less than half my age, yet some of them I seemed to like immediately and instinctively.

One of my students is a startlingly beautiful girl who has been a beauty contest winner and a fashion model. I really liked her a lot but I was suspiciuos of myself. I was afraid my liking for her was because she was so pretty. But one day as we were walking back from class together I realized she really wanted to be my friend. I saw that while I tried not to be prejudiced against a girl because she was fat or had warts on her nose, here I was prejudiced against a girl because she was beautiful. So I decided I was willing to let her be my friend.

Recently she came to see me just before graduation. After we had talked awhile, she looked at me very strangely and said, "Jess, how come you like me so much?"

In a way that's a very funny question. For a fashion model to ask an old beat-up college professor why he likes her so much, is almost ridiculous. But not really. I've had lots of beautiful women in my classes. Many of them I wouldn't go out of my way even to say "Hello" to. So this girl's question was valid. Why did I like her so much? I told her I didn't really know why. I had always liked her just the way she was. I never had a thought about how she could be improved. It was not her appearance I liked, but the person behind the pretty face. And she realized that was why I liked her and it was why she liked me, too.

In the past three years since she was in my class, I haven't talked to her more than ten times. But we are close friends and we will be no matter how infrequently we see each other in the future.

This is the way it is for most of the students I learn to know well. We are close while we are together. And we usually stay that way despite long separations and big distances.

This is another sadness here and that is the fact that you and I have a lot of preconceived notions about who should be our friends and who shouldn't. Some of our friends had better come from what a snob like me thinks of as the lower walks of life. Of course, the distinction is artificial but it's one I'm very aware of still.

Families are a problem, too. We can't have good mutual relationships with everyone in our families. We think, "We have to have a good relationship. We are blood! We just have to have a good relationship!" It doesn't work that way.

I have five children. I thought, "Boy, I'm going to

have a great relationship with all five of those kids. Now I see that they are individuals and I'm going to have five different relationships." But because of my egotism I had those exalted notions of the way it was supposed to be, and they are so hard to get rid of.

How about our neighbors? Well I'm certainly going to have a good relationship with my neighbors. "I'm a good neighbor. I'm a good little Christian. Love thy neighbor. The guy on either side of me." Funny thing. I'm not necessarily going to have one unless they want to have one with me. It has to be mutual, you see. So we will just have to throw away our preconceptions of the way it is supposed to be. My neighbor can't be an enemy of mine or it kills me. But he can't be a close friend unless we can find a way we can fit together.

When I started looking at the friends I really had, I saw I had another problem. I felt so inferior, I couldn't have any friends who were anywhere close to me in terms of income or accomplishments. I had a tough time accepting that. I came to see that anybody near me in income or accomplishments scared me. The only people I could be friends with were people I could look down on. But how could I really be friends with someone I looked down on? I had to face this sad fact about myself. I said to myself, "Jess, you dumb jerk. Why is it this way?" And my answer was "I don't know why it is this way, but it is." Okay. "What are you going to do about it?" Simple, tiger, you take what you can get. And you do with it what you can.

I have seen that as time has gone on that problem has disappeared somewhat, so more and more the people I am friends with are spread out through the income, occupational and social levels. To me that is a comforting sign. Some of the people who are my friends now are

in more conspicious positions than I am, so a lot of
my insecurity has evidently gone away. But boy, it didn't
used to be that way at all. I couldn't be a friend to
someone unless I felt drastically superior to him. And
like I say, that is a kind of a sick friendship, but it is
better than none. Because being completely without friendships doesn't warm your heart at all.

What I want you to do is mentally to go through your
list of people you call friends, including relatives. See
how much mutuality there is. And where it is. Look at
your relationships and look for the Mount Everests in
those relationships. Look for the special relationship that
really lifts you up and sustains you and then spend a
lot more time in that relationship. It is precious. It will
lift you up and sustain you far more as you devote time
and effort and appreciation to that relationship. And, as
you show that person you really appreciate a Mount
Everest when you see one, you will find the relationship
will quickly improve.

Now anyone who doesn't appreciate a Jerry Sullivan
when he meets one, I can see now, is really foolish. If
I get credit for anything, it is for appreciating a few
good people like him. But this is so hard to do because we
need all of our deceptions. We need to see ourselves as
"We are a person with a lot of friends."

Kidding ourselves about how many friends we have
hurts us in a lot of ways. Like I said earlier, it mixes
the good relationships in with the bad ones. That hurts
the people who really like us because they see that we
don't appreciate what they really mean to us. But our
deception hurts us in a worse way. Until we start concentrating our time with the good relationships we can't get
much out of life.

It's like trying to live on a very thin soup. There's a

lot of water, which is the bad relationships or those that just don't do anything for us. And there's very little meat, which is the good relationships. When I cut out the bad and the indifferent relationships, the soup gets thick quick. It's almost all meat. And so no wonder my life gets happier and richer.

But, simple as this idea is, I have lots of trouble getting it across to people. When I get as specific as this, they really fight me. They argue that their job is to love everybody, to have good relationships with everybody. If they don't get along with some people, they had better learn how to fit together with them.

I see two flaws in that argument. The first is that we can't be in relationships with the whole world or even a small part of it. We can be in relationships with only a very few people. So what's wrong with concentrating on those who are very clearly our cup of tea, those people who really like us the way we are?

I think the deeper flaw in the argument against a few relationships comes from our fear of being close and the self-knowledge that it brings. It is hard to see that we just have a few friends, and even those relationships aren't very good. Worst of all, we then have to face how we have neglected the few good friends by confusing them with our enemies. And as we concentrate on those few good relationships, we have the terrible pain of seeing how little we bring to the relationship. No wonder we want to throw things back into confusion and chaos and shout, "Go away from me with your foolish talk of a few friends. I have lots of friends. Ask anybody about me and they will tell you, 'Jess Lair has a lot of friends.' "

I was telling one of my students about this book. I said it's an awful simple idea for a whole book. She said, "Yes, Jess, it is a simple idea, but it is very hard to get

to that simple idea." I know that's true for me. It took
many years and lots of pain before I would look at the
simple truth about what my life had been, why it had
been that way and how it could be different.

One of my students told about a gal who at one time
shared more than she wanted to share so then panicked
and escaped from the relationship. She ran away. I had
a bad situation like that a while back too. Partly it was
my mistake because I pushed it too hard. This person
said, "I have something I need to talk about but I just
can't talk about it to you, it will hurt too many people."
And I said, "No, you need to talk to me about it." And
he said, "No, I can't." So I said, "Sit down." I reached
down into my deepest heart and told him of three or four
things about myself that had been hidden from everyone.
I was opening my heart. I thought that it would help
him open up. And it did. My action forced him to
reciprocate with what was in his heart. But I made him
go further than he wanted to go. So I didn't help him,
I hurt him. And he has avoided me ever since.

I think the difficulty came because it is just like forcing
a flower in a hothouse. When we force the flower open
we are not sensitive to its natural development. In a
mutuality relationship you start out feeling your way,
opening yourself a little. The other person opens himself
a little in response. So you just gradually go deeper and
deeper together, you see? You keep in touch with each
other and you are as sensitive as you can be to the needs
of the other—and the fears of the other about openness.
But it's hard to be that sensitive and much of the time
one of us in the relationship has gone farther than was
appropriate at the moment. A good example of something
that wasn't smooth was in a class of mine where a group
of people really opened their hearts to each other, all of

a sudden. Most of the people in that group felt a warm and moving closeness for a matter of two or three weeks. But then some of them started building up their walls again. They couldn't stand living out in the open. The group experience had given them more openness than they were ready for and could stand.

But like I say, this isn't perfect. I'm not asking for a perfect system. I'm just asking for one that works—better than what I had before.

I would hope, too, that as you examine your relationships you would be able to identify at least one relationship that is a very destructive relationship in your life. Someone you thought a friend may actually be very hard on you. Just say about him, "Hey, Jess says that I don't need to see him any more. Somebody else will have a chance to like the poor guy if I leave him alone."

On the opposite side I know that each of you will find at least one person who is a candidate for a Mount Everest in your relationships.

In my experience the problem is not a lack of people around you waiting to love you. The problem is our lack of willingness to open our eyes to all the people who have been standing at our elbow waiting for us to love them.

"How come," a student asked, "you haven't mentioned anything about the external threats to a relationship that can destroy a Mount Everest-type relationship. To give an example. You have a close relationship with a friend. All of a sudden your job is on the line. You're going to get fired. All of a sudden he is gone as a friend."

Something like this can really test a relationship. But I've got a pretty good idea now about my relationships because I'm paying so much better attention to them. I know Sullivan is not going to cut and run on me. In fact, if I get into any kind of fight at the university, there is nobody I can think of I would rather have on my side. And he is going to be there nine out of ten. Sure there is a chance I could lose. And I told Jerry, "If you ever end up on the opposite side of an issue from me, whale away. Because if you are on the other side I deserve what I get." I can blow it and be on the wrong side of an issue. And if I blow it, I want Jerry to be on the other side.

My student still was not satisfied. He said, "There are many times these relationships are very close. They may be close for years and years and years." I know exactly what he spoke of. A lot of times that is a sign I didn't pay attention to that relationship. I thought it was closer than it really was. Much of that came out of my own need for self-deception.

I used to be in that situation. I would have what I called good friends who would do some terrible thing to me. My point is there really wasn't a friendship there. I just called it one out of my ignorance. Looking back I can see that the problem was my deception of myself. I needed the idea that I had all these close friends. And I actually harmed that other person as well as myself by calling a relationship close that wasn't.

It wasn't that he sucked me in and got me believing in him, then pulled the rug out from under me. I did it to myself.

Now that I don't need this deception of myself any more, those old problems aren't there. There is no way someone can pretend to be a friend of mine and carry it off. Now that I'm paying attention, I can tell when there is really something between us and when there isn't.

For a goodly number of years now I have had a few intimate friends I could trust. And not once have those friends broken that trust.

Many people tell me this isn't possible. They say I'm living in a dream world. Well, I've lived both ways, without friends I could trust and with friends I can trust. I have found it can work for me.

A good example of how I used to need to deceive myself about the closeness of my relationships was a situation that happened some years ago. I thought this guy and I had a fairly close relationship. We were going along just ducky. But all of a sudden, pow, he pulled three or four rugs out from under me in a row. And as near as I could see he didn't even know he had done it. I stopped everything and took a long, hard look at our relationship. My wife and I talked about what was happening. I was able to see a lot of things I hadn't noticed about our relationship. He and I were both talking big about how close we were and we had both been fooled by it, because we wanted to be. But when a problem came up, we weren't able to live up to our own talk. He was also blind to the consequences of his actions. The things he had done blindly and hurt me with were symptoms of what he was doing to other people, too.

I considered telling him what was going on. But the fact his blindness was showing itself in so many ways was a sign to me he needed his blindness for a while longer. He was in the same situation I was in before my heart attack made me willing to open my eyes to what I was doing. Light without love is a bad deal. I would be in the position of giving him way more light than he wanted or could stand without enough of the love needed to take the sting away.

When he doesn't need his blindness any more, he will start seeing some of those things for himself. This is why I see confrontation between people as often being rather harmful or at least not productive. Sure, I can give someone some information about a problem he has that can give him an insight. But that's pushing him. It's like forcing the flower. When he is ready, he will seek an answer and it will be lying right there ready for him. Only a very few of the changes I have made have come from other people's insights into me. Almost every one of the changes I have made came about because of someone's acceptance of me as I am. In the beautiful warmth of that acceptance, I wasn't being pushed to change. So I was able to change because it was something I wanted to do that wasn't forced on me.

The way I handled the problem was I did for my friend what others have done for me. I accepted him the way he really was rather than the way he said he was or the way I wanted him to be. The changes caused a lurch in our relationship but it was soon over and we are on a sound, solid basis with each other now enjoying as good a relationship as we can enjoy.

But the most important point was that I was able to see, "Hey, Jess, you're lying to yourself. Let's put this relationship back where it really belongs." Now the relationship is growing again. A lot of the problem had come out of my own self-deception. I was reading things into the relationship that weren't there because it pleased me to think of myself as such a groovy person who could build lots of groovy relationships quickly with all kinds of people.

Can you always be analyzing your relationships that closely? No, that's dangerous, too. Too much analysis destroys the very thing you want to build. If I've got four or five relationships and one blows up on me, so what? I still have three or four left. If you sit around being paranoid about your relationships you're whipped before you start.

The key to building these relationships is to see that you can't have a lot of close friends and that you can lose them. It is water over the dam. But what counts is we had better learn from our mistakes instead of just repeating them.

A guy I know went through a period of grave personal difficulty with a divorce. He felt that many of his friends were going around lying about him. We had been very close for two years so I could talk to him. I said, "What does that tell you about your ability to tell who your friends are, tiger?" You learn from a mistake. We need our mistakes, don't we? I know I need my mistakes. I need them skiing, for example. Some of the falls I take help me learn not to make that particular mistake any more.

We are talking about getting a little better at something than we already are. What is it worth to you? Is it worth the price of this book and your reading and thinking time to get a little better at being friends? Is it worth your time to have a little better sense of who your real friends are so you can spend more time with them? And so you can stay away from some of the losers or klinkers in your life? I know what those things are worth to me. They are making my life more enjoyable every day. Now I'm happy to get up in the morning because I'm interested to see what nice things are going to happen today. That's a feeling I never thought I would find.

How many of us are personally strong enough to look at these things? I don't know. Like I say, I'm not teaching and writing about these ideas for you as much as I'm doing it for me. The only thing I know is that I'm working on these ideas in my life just as hard as I can. I'm not talking about something out on the edge of life. This is right in the center. This is where most of my thoughts are concentrated during the day.

And I don't need to be concerned about all the people in the world. I just need to find a handful of people who are dying to have Jess Lair in their lives and then I'm on my way.

Is a close personal friend to me someone I can bare my soul to? Yes. But I can bare my soul in different ways to different people. Most friends I can bare only part of my soul to. I do have one friend, though, I can tell anything to. There is nothing I have ever done that I couldn't tell that one and know I would get complete acceptance. But that deep a friendship takes years of searching to find and develop.

I have found a number of people I could tell how I felt about myself and the things I have done or still do. I'm finally at the point where there isn't anything about myself or anything that bothers me that I've done that I haven't told someone. So I have the beautiful feeling of knowing that there isn't anything in my life I haven't been able to say to some other human being.

Notice I'm not talking about confessing to a priest or asking God to forgive me. That's just fine, but this is different from that. This is telling another person, whose face you can see, the deepest and darkest things about yourself. I felt some of those things I had done were so awful that any person who heard me tell them would run from me in horror. But the person I was telling them to never felt they were so bad. That was why it was so important to me to be able to see the faces of the people I was talking to instead of being in the dark like in confession because the expression on their face gave me the most beautiful reassurance in the world. I wasn't an awful person, in fact I was quite ordinary.

"Do we need to be aware of what a friend can take?" Yes. We need to know what he can handle and what he can't. Like Jerry. Once in a while he has to say, "Jess, let's not talk about that any more. It's making my head ache." He's very kind, he doesn't hit me in the mouth. He just smiles and tells me, "Hey, Jess, let's cool it."

How many close friends can you have? Two, three, four? One of my definitions of a close friend is a guy who is around when you need him. And it isn't because you called him up, he is around because he is your friend. I don't worry about any jam I get into. I know I will be having coffee with Sullivan or seeing Vince or Dave. Or I will see Rolf or Kenny. I don't have to go look for them. I have somebody handy. There are many other people around who are just checking with me to make sure everything is going well with me. If they see any sign I'm in trouble, they come running. One reason this is so crucial is that when we are in trouble we are least able to ask for help. This makes it extra important that our close friends come to us often just as we are going to them often.

How do we get better at relationships? Like anything else, it's just practice. Have you ever skied? Remember how slippery those skies were at first? They were going ninety-six ways. Do you know why? You and I were *sending* them all those different ways. Before we could even begin to learn to ski we had to relax enough so we were not sending our skis off in so many different directions. We needed our mistakes. The worst thing I can do for somebody is to say "Okay, I have told you how it was with me, so you don't need to make any of these mistakes. In fact, if you make these mistakes, I will be offended. You will show that you are a lousy student."

It is a terrible thing when we say to our own children "You can't make any mistakes, because I don't want you to." We defend our request by saying "Oh, it would hurt you too much." But what we really mean is "It would make me look foolish in the eyes of my neighbor and myself, in my own egotistic conception of myself as a parent." Who in their right mind could possibly pretend that their kids aren't going to make mistakes?

We want the neighbors' kids to make mistakes, but not our kids. We justify our attitude on the basis that we don't want the little dears to get hurt. Baloney. I'm worrying about my kids' hair length because of what the neighbors are going to think about it, instead of the fact that it is too long. I like the looks of long hair. What we're really worried about is what people will think of us because of what our kids do. And as far as pain goes, we can't spare our children all pain. If we try to do that we have to wrap them up in cotton and put them away in a box. In the process of protecting them that much we inflict the worst pain of all on them which is complete control of them by us.

You have a right, each of you, to your mistakes. And one of the biggest faults I have in my teaching is I don't want any of my students making mistakes I have made. That doesn't make any sense.

So we are going to get a little better. We practice. And the more we are willing to get just a little better, the faster we will get better. The minute we want perfection we kill everything. I ain't much, baby, but I'm all I got. I ain't going to do much, baby, but it is better than nothing. The minute we think of ourself as some exalted, perfect person, we are in trouble. No way are we going to get anything done. All we need to do is admit "Hey, I'm not some exalted, perfect person, I'm just a finite human being, just a dumb Norwegian." That isn't much but it is something. And that's an awful lot better than nothing.

A lady asked me, "Is there something wrong with you if you are content with one close friendship?" I told her that was up to her to decide for herself. But the idea of just one close friend really scares me. Not because of the chance of losing that friend but because of dependency. If I have just one close friend there is a real danger I won't pay enough attention to the clues that tell us when we should be together and when we shouldn't be. We would get a dependency for each other like you do for alcohol or drugs. I talk about needing people— and I do. In that sense I'm dependent on people. But I'm not dependent on any one person. It is like Jerry's house of many pillars he talks to me about. If you take out one of the pillars the roof still stands.

Another problem about just one friend is, why be so exclusive? If that one friend is really a friend, I can't help but create a few other friendships just by being me. But often our one close friend is not a friend. He is like the guy I ran around with in high school. We weren't friends, we were just clinging to each other in our desperate need. It wasn't until later that we found we didn't even like each other.

Many of my students use the "one friend" argument to avoid these ideas. They say "I already have a friend, I don't need to think about what you are saying." But if they truly are a creative, outgoing personality, they will reach out and be friends to some of the people around them instead of being so withdrawn and wrapped up with their one friend.

As for me, I have a different view. I'm like a man down in the ocean. My ocean liner went down. I'm trying to assemble enough boards that are floating by to build me a life raft to get up out of the water so I can live. In that predicament, there is no such thing as having too many boards. You send some more boards by my raft and I will pile them on there, because you never know when the storm is coming. And I dearly want to get into the current and start navigating towards shore. So I want the nicest, biggest raft with the most rope and the most boards and the most conveniences.

I have come to see that I was in a desperate situation but I was too dumb to see it. I used to look at other people and say, "Thank God, I'm not as bad as they are." Or I would say about some former alcoholic, "Sure, I would do something if I ever got as bad as he was." But then I saw the light. Most people don't live long enough to get that bad. They die first.

I looked at my own situation. I had so screwed up my life by the time I was thirty-five years old that I wasn't doing anything I believed in. And I had far and away the youngest heart attack in my crowd. How much worse can you get than that and still live? I finally saw the truth about it. Now I don't deny all the time and wait until the house is half burned down before I stop denying and call the fire department. Now I can smell smoke and I get help right away. Then I look to see what caused the fire and fix that.

So I now say about myself, "I have never seen anybody in worse shape than I was." Once I saw what a desperate situation I was in, I started paying attention and being very careful, just as you would do if you were down in the ocean, alone.

Not only does paying attention to my relationships help me live longer, it makes my days far different than they were then. Then I was bored. I was looking at the clock. "Won't the clock ever roll around?" The days were empty. Because the days were empty the years seemed to flash by. Now my days are so full. That clock just seems like it is whipping around. But there are so many beautiful things happening in a day that the years seem like they go on forever. It is an altogether different dimension than I have ever experienced before.

But those days before, they were so empty of bright moments. Now I find myself having five to ten good things to think about in a day. Maybe it is just some elaborate kind of self-deception. I don't think so because a few people I deeply respect as being good at this process are saying, "Way to go. You are doing great, Jess." I will trust my life to those people because I can see in their lives the thing I am looking for. I see serenity and I see abundant living in those people.

I grant that in a way I am overstating my reaching out. But my coronary personality is still very much with me. And also, I am overstating the case as a way of trying to make my point. But again, is there any one of you who wouldn't welcome one more deep, mutual relationship? Is there any one of you who couldn't make room for one more really fine, warm relationship where you really are able to be yourself and see yourself in that relationship? Is there any one of you who wouldn't welcome another intimate friend you could trust completely?

But however you answer the question you are still faced with another crucial question. "Is there any way my relationships can be improved? Can they get any better, so the love that comes to me through them is deeper and richer, and flows out more into other areas of my life, into my family and into my work?"

Like Freud said, "There are two things a mature person should be able to do: To love and to work. But because our work should be done out of love, there is only one thing a person needs to do and that is to love."

Right now, I'm in the fortunate position of teaching because I want to. So I lecture and teach only in the situations I want to. I'm on two years' leave, but I still have office hours and go over to the university to see my students and my friends. And I teach when I want to, usually without pay. So when I find myself getting impatient with some class, I have to stop and get hold of myself and say, "Hey, Jess, you are here because you want to be. Why not act like it, huh?"

"How much time," a young teacher asked, "does it really involve to have a deep relationship with a friend? If you have a deep emotional relationship with a good friend, why do you have to be with this individual constantly? The friendship is there and it doesn't take a lot of time, that's the way I see it anyhow."

This was a good question because it strikes right to the heart of what I'm trying to get across. There is all the difference in the world between what he is talking about and what I'm talking about.

I know the kind of relationship he speaks of. These are the relationships I used to call friendships and while I still recognize the friendship that is there, I don't confuse it in my mind with the deep, mutual friendship and love that can save my life.

Say this person we call friend is in the same community with us. Look what we are really saying about him when we don't see him often. We say, "You are my good friend. But your friendship and love is not important enough for me to see you often. I am so busy." Or, "I have other friends more important than you."

We can't lie to ourselves about our relationships. And we can't lie about the messages we send others by our actions. I have many, many people who think I am their friend and in a way I am. But here is the message they send me. They say, "Jess, I love you so much. But I have to go away now. I will be living over on the other side of Bozeman two or three miles away, so I probably won't see you much any more." And they are right. They don't see me much any more. Yet they go on saying, "My good friend, Jess."

That isn't a deep, mutual friendship and love as I see it. That is simply a potential friendship that goes undeveloped. When Vince Lombardi was dying of cancer, Willie Davis flew from Los Angeles to Washington, D.C., to spend three minutes with Lombardi. That is the kind of friendship I'm interested in. That's the kind that warms my heart and saves my life.

The people who are really my deep, mutual friends are too important to me to leave seeing them up to chance. This is what is so sad. Until we realize these things and give importance to them, our life is like an ocean liner without a pilot. It goes lurching around the ocean occasionally bumping into something good.

I don't believe in that. I'm spending each day of the rest of my life with the people who really love me and need me back. I'm not going to leave the most crucial thing in my life up to chance.

Once I have identified the five to ten people who are really crucial to me and who lift me up, I just make the route among them like a farmer milking cows.

They give me so much. When I have had a loving contact with one or two people like this in a day, then there is a chance I can reach out my hand with love and friendliness to some poor stranger. But the law is receive and respond. I have to receive first. I can't give away money unless I get money first. I can't give away love unless I get some first. Some people want to argue that they get all their love right from God. That may be but sometimes I wonder because often people come to me about a person who says that and asks me, "Jess, what can we do about Sister Mary? She's hurting everyone she touches."

So the problem in my life before I saw these ideas was that my "friendships" were my way of lying to myself about my relationships. There was the possibility of a deep, mutual friendship there, but it didn't mean anything really until I was willing to face the truth about myself and the relationship.

A common question at this point is: "What about all my friends in other cities who are far away?" Yes, what about them? Either you or they sent a terrible message. "As much as we mean to each other we are going to move away or we aren't going to do anything about the distance that separates us."

You say, "But that isn't the message I sent. It is impossible to be together for some reason or other." No. Not impossible. It was our choice to part or stay apart. When I moved from Minneapolis to Montana the message I sent to all my friends there was: "I don't love you enough to stay." While I still have friends there, it can't ever be the same. A few of those friends I see or call every time I'm in town. But that isn't enough for my definition of a deep, mutual friendship.

I'm not in that herd any more. I have to face that. It is the handful of deep, mutual relationships in Bozeman, Montana, that are saving my life today and making me much less the frantic individual I used to be. It is my deep mutual friendships here that make today a joy and give me a peace I never knew a nut like me could have.

So I don't want to kid myself about something as important as this.

Some of the people I tell these ideas to don't think

they amount to much. The ideas seem to them so simple and they have felt the results so seldom. Yet when I ask my students if they have at least one person in whose presence they feel they are very special, most of them raise their hands. But when I ask if they make a point to be with this special person a lot or just leave meeting them up to accident they agree that they leave it up to accident.

What I'm talking about here is taking this process out of the hands of chance, developing a few deep mutual relationships and making them a big part of our everyday life instead of an occasional, accidental encounter.

It all sounds so simple. But it isn't. It's the hardest thing I have found for me and the people around me. It's because our relationships require people who are reasonably happy to be what they are—you and me. It's amazing to me how hard it is to be me. That's why I need the people whose faces light up when they see me.

3

finding the people who like us the way we are— mutual need therapy

Now that we have taken a look at our relationships, it's time to think again about what it is we're after.

As I mentioned, my problem was I couldn't tell my good relationships from my bad ones. And I didn't realize how my poor relationships were hurting and frustrating me. But worst of all I refused to see the difference in my relationships because I needed the idea I was such a great person and was right for everybody so obviously all my relationships had to be good.

Now that I've tried to see my relationships more clearly and honestly, I have realized I ain't everybody's cup of tea. I can face reality more. And I now try to make a more honest attempt to look at the state of each of my relationships.

We are told we should love one another. And there is no question in my mind that is true. But there is now no

68

question in my mind that being able to practice love for everyone is an ideal that very few people can come close to. But more to the point, even if everyone else in the world is good at loving, I know I'm not. And I've got to start at the bottom where I am and gradually work my way up. I see now that until I can learn to love myself and a few people around me, I don't have much chance of truly loving my neighbor or, hardest of all, my enemy. That will come later—much later.

Many of my students wanted to tell me how much they loved me. At first that was nice to hear. But as time went by and nothing came of that love, I found I couldn't tell the difference between those who said they loved me and those who didn't. Now I don't see that cheap talk as loving. If I love someone, I want that person to be able to tell I do. If they can't tell I love them, then I don't want to kid myself about the love I think I'm showing them.

I think we need to learn to distinguish between love and everything else. And, of course, we can do this only if we are willing to get rid of some of our egotism so we can look at ourselves and life more as they really are and stop denying reality. The question of denying reality raises another problem. A lot of people want to argue about what is reality and what is truth. I don't want to argue back any more. When someone asks me "What's truth?", I know from sad experience they just pretend to ask a question. What they really want is an argument. I don't want to argue. I left the debating society a long time ago. I'm trying to save my life, not argue.

I know philosophers have had lots of trouble with words like truth and reality. They are abstractions and ideals that can't be reached. I know that. It's like which way is the wind blowing from? You can't ever tell exactly.

But you can come close enough to fly your kite. And that's all I want to do. I want enough truth and reality and honesty in my life so I can live better than I did yesterday. And by seeing truth and honesty and reality in my relationships, I can see a lot of things I wasn't able to see before and life is working better for me. Sure, I will never know ultimate truth and ultimate reality, but that's fine. Sure, some of the things I today think are truth will turn up false, but that's okay, too. Because I'm not seeking perfection. I'm just trying to get better. And I'm happy to leave those arguments to the philosophers.

So please understand me when I speak about looking for truth and reality in our relationships. When we seek truth and reality, that's what we will get. More truth and more reality than we had before. And it will be enough for the moment. In fact, once we earnestly start asking for truth we will often get more truth than we can stand.

When we truly look at our relationships we see what puny and limited lovers we really are. So then we can see we must give up the deceit of loving everyone. What are our relationships with people going to be like? I've found I can divide my relationships into four levels:

The lowest level is the people I can't stand. There is something about some people that just sets me against them immediately. In some cases this ripens into a strong dislike. This is how I feel about them. I don't defend the feeling, it is simply how I feel. The problem is that my dislike for these people hurts me a lot more than it hurts them. So I'm trying to get rid of those feelings or moderate them in such a way that they aren't so harmful to me.

When I hate my neighbor, I have to carry that hate

around inside me. It's just like carrying strong acid in the palm of your hand. The acid eats a hole right through your hand. The same with my hate. It will kill me emotionally and it can kill me physically. I can't explain very well why hate kills me emotionally but I've seen that it does. That's why I want to get my relations with these people I dislike up to the next level which is courtesy and respect.

Courtesy and respect is the minimum level for the relationships in our lives; we owe it to everybody. Some of my students argue that courtesy and respect isn't enough. They think we owe people more than that. I grant we do. As I said before, my hope is that someday I might truly be able to understand and practice loving everybody. But I'm so far from there that right now I'll settle for being able to treat everyone with at least courtesy and respect.

I know the people I dislike and treat poorly would really appreciate courtesy and respect from me. It would be a lot more than they're getting from me now.

The third level up the ladder is acceptance. But most of us have a problem when we say we can accept someone. What we really mean is: "I can accept you but I have plans for your improvement." A lot of people talk their acceptance but I don't see or feel much warmth in it because it is a very begrudging acceptance. In fact, I have heard many people say that when they say "I accept you," it doesn't mean "I approve of you." To me that isn't worth a lot. It is better than courtesy and respect; at least a part of us is seen as desirable, but not all of us. I see the third level of acceptance as a complete acceptance of the individual as he or she is. I have no right to approve or disapprove. That kind of real acceptance has some warmth to it. I know because I've felt it.

The fourth, and the highest level of human relationships as I see it, is where you are valued as you are. That's when a person's face lights up when they see us. This is the crucial clue to mutuality. It is the behavioral measurement of mutuality in your relationships. You have a real basis for mutuality only with those people whose faces light up when they see you. And they haven't got any plans for your improvement. They are happy with you just the way you are.

There was a student in the class I presented this book to who grasped what I was talking about the very first hour. He liked me and he liked what I was saying. I told him our feelings for each other were a good example of what I was talking about. We had the mutuality which would be a good basis for a deeper relationship. I told the students in class how I felt about him. I said, "With old Monty, here, I have nothing in mind that I want him to do differently. I like him just the way he is. If he has some way he wants to improve himself, fine. But I could even add the caution 'Monty, go real slow because I don't want you to disturb that beautiful personality. I don't want you to change too many things about you, because you might change something precious and we would lose the Monty we know and love. So please be careful about any self-improvement programs you embark on, Monty."

That is valuing a person as they are. That's the highest level. Okay, that brings you to a very difficult assignment I would like to give you. I want you to do some thinking. I want you to come up with some names of people whose faces light up when they see you.

When I tell you to look for mutuality, I want you really to see people's faces and to read them totally. I don't want you just to pay attention to their words. I want you to watch their faces and their bodies, and everything about them. I want you to read the whole communication instead of just their words. Recognizing mutuality comes out of really reading people. Look for the face that lights up, and the person who just leans towards you. There are all kinds of things that say mutuality. These are the signs that give us the very precious clues. When a person really wants to be with us they are more animated, they are happier, they talk about happier things usually, although they can talk about a few problems, too. The opposite response to us is a very mechanical kind of talk, standing at a distance, fidgeting, wanting to get away from us quickly.

As I say, sit down and figure out who values you. Even more important, as you go through your day look for those people who value you who you weren't even aware of. Now if you come up with a hundred people who value you, there's something wrong with your eyesight. You are an egomaniac. How about one or two? That's what I understand. I'm looking for one whose face lights up, whose face beams when they see me.

I saw an example of this recently. I was walking down the street with my two oldest sons, each about six feet two or three and good-looking devils. I was walking down the street with them a few months ago, one on either side of me. We kept seeing all these young gals coming towards us in the fifteen to twenty age range. I never knew there were so many teeth in the town of Bozeman. Wow!

There was a college gal who was an advisee of one of my fellow professors down the hall. All I had ever seen from her before was a small smile and a nod. But my oldest son was up to my office visiting me recently.

She looked into my office, saw him, stopped and gave us the biggest, warmest "Hello" I have ever seen. That's the expression I mean.

Then the next thing you have to look at is the hurt part. We see there is mutuality—the basis for a deep friendship. But we have to face the question in us: "What part do we play in these people's lives, what part do we let them play in ours?" And: "Isn't there some way we can let them play a bigger part in our lives so we can let them lift us up more in the special way only they can do?"

Somebody who values us has the most precious thing in the world for us. It is just like a gas station for our car. What is more crucial to keeping your car going than gas stations? And nothing is more crucial in my life to improve my whole spectrum of relationships.

I didn't get to have lunch with Jerry Sullivan the other day so I picked him up for coffee right after my two o'clock meeting was over. I plan a whole bunch of things during the day where I will be in the company of people who value me. Other people who value me come into my life each day in the normal process of living. But I'm not ever going to count on accidents. That's the way I used to run my life, by accident. I just let the good people in my life come into it by circumstance. Well, that's really dumb, isn't it? If you see how much you need those people and if you see what they do for you, you should take care of those encounters with them. You shouldn't leave running into them up to accidents. You can't make a long trip by car without a group of gas stations spotted along the way.

Deep mutual relationships give me the strength to accept more people. They give me the calm and self-respect that helps me move more of my relationships out

of dislike up to courtesy and respect. And from courtesy
and respect into acceptance. Most people are working this
problem the other way. Instead of spending lots of time
loving the easy ones, they are struggling to love the
hard ones. I don't see that as productive. To me, I
think I had best start at the top and work down.

Not only do deep relationships give me the strength
to do these things I have mentioned, but they give me
something even more crucial. As friends really value me,
I'm able to see deeper into myself. It is like the sun on
a chrysanthemum bud. What does it look like as a full
flower? There is no way I can tell unless I get the sun
of mutuality on that chrysanthemum bud. The deeper my
relationships are, the more I am open to myself. This
helps me discover who I am. The more I discover my
uniqueness and individuality, the more I discover the
power and glory and majesty that is me. This, then, is
me working on my spiritual quest. But you and I aren't
going to find out how great we are unless we get with
enough of those loving people each day for a long period
of time. And unless we stay away from the people who
are wrong for us. They make our little flower start closing
right back up. There are enough of those people who
come into our life just accidentally without going out and
subjecting ourselves to them on purpose.

I hope you realize how horrible an assignment I have
given you. I have asked you the most awful question
there is in the world, which is to look honestly at the
quality of your relationships so you can honestly see what
you have and what you haven't got in the way of relationships.

Aren't there some people who value just about everybody, whose faces light up for just about everybody?
Maybe there are some people like that. For them there

might be mutuality with almost everyone. But mutuality isn't the relationship. It is what a real deep relationship must start from. I won't have a deep relationship with every one I feel mutuality with. The mutuality we feel can make our lives more enjoyable but unless we go deep with a few we won't experience what I see is there to be experienced. But we can't go deep with everyone we have mutuality with. There isn't enough time. In a deep relationship there is a commitment to each other that is like a good marriage. I have a commitment to my five friends. Each of them knows I will regularly come into their life. And I know they will regularly come into mine.

But I can't regularly come into the life of a hundred friends. There are many people now with whom I have a deep mutuality and a deep communication when we are in contact with each other. But unspoken between us is the knowledge that we won't be in close and continuous contact with each other because of any number of reasons: distance, circumstances we can't change or simply the fact that each of our lives are pretty well filled with the few especially deep relationships we now have.

Take Bill Oriet. He is a guy I have always wanted to hunt elk with. I'm probably never going to be able to hunt elk with Bill for a simple reason. The first guy who ever started hunting elk with Bill is still hunting elk with him. Also, Bill has three boys who are now hunting with him. So he isn't going to have room for me. I will just hunt elk with someone who needs me to hunt elk with them. Now Bill's face lights up when he sees me, there is mutuality there in the special sense of the word as I use it. I always get a special welcome when I go to his house, but he doesn't really have room for another deep relationship in his life. He has as many as he can comfortably handle. Not very many people are that fortunate, but some are.

So in these deep relationships, first there has to be a mutual valuing of the other person as they are. Second the two people have to want to play an important part in each other's lives.

When I call this process mutual need therapy, I'm not thinking up something that didn't exist before. What I'm trying to do is uncover principles of life that are operating here in Bozeman and the rest of the world. I'm trying to uncover the principle of life that the good-living people I've seen use to make their lives so productive. I'm trying to uncover the principles of life that I need to make my life much more productive so I won't be so likely to want to die of a heart attack. Because when you are happy, they can't hardly kill you with a bullet. When you are unhappy it is so easy to find a way to die.

So sit down in a quiet place and do some meditating. Start naming names to yourselves and look at your recent experiences with each of them. Has that person really shown that they want to be with me? Have they taken the initiative very much of the time or has it always been me? Is it a relationship that depends mostly on circumstance? You see how crucial circumstance is when you quit a job and go to another. Nine out of ten of the people you thought you were close to never take the trouble to spend a dime to call you up. "Oh boy, I got beautiful relationships out of that place. I was in a beautiful set of relationships."

There was a guy I worked with in Kansas City many years ago, who I thought I was close to. Over the years I think I have written the guy at least five times wanting him to respond. He never did. I finally got the message. There was nothing there, or there was very little there.

Now, out of that whole set of relationships that I made during that year in Kansas City in 1952 there was only one where anybody took any initiative at all to ever see me. Okay, they weren't very good relationships. That's sad to look at, but that's the way it was. We are talking about reality here. Because it is only reality that is going to make us a better teacher, a better liver of life, a better husband or wife, mother, father, friend.

Many people think the kind of openness I'm talking about in a mutual need relationship is like those unfortunates who tell us all their troubles. There is a big difference between telling your troubles and talking what is in your heart. When you just tell your troubles that doesn't do anything for anybody. I can tell you about how right now this spring my wife has a bad back and my horses are skinny and there is mud in the corral. That doesn't mean anything. But when I tell you how I blew it with a student in class yesterday, that's opening my heart. That's not telling you my troubles, it is telling you about my feelings and about myself. When we tell of our troubles we are just talking about outward circumstances. There are all kinds of people in this world willing to tell us their troubles, their circumstances, but there are precious few people in this world willing to tell us their feelings. Yet when we can tell them our feelings and they can tell us their feelings, all of a sudden we aren't alone any more.

This emphasis on relationships is, to me, the crucial difference between my first book and this one. *I Ain't Much, Baby—But I'm All I Got* was a book on the psychology of the self. In this book I'm still talking about developing the self, but the development of the self comes out of the relationship. The relationship is the basis and then out of that come the other things.

So how do you tell a mutual relationship? You tell it by seeing that you are valuing each other exactly as you are—with absolutely no sense of anything you would like changed about the other person. Is this idea any good for you? Find out. Are these relationships all outside the family? No, I want you to look at all your relationships, outside the family and inside. Hopefully, for some of you our best mutual relationship will be a husband and wife relationship. Where a marriage relationship doesn't seem to be as mutual as you'd like, building some mutual relationships outside the family can be a way of making the marriage relationship more mutual or at least more tolerable while you are waiting for it to improve.

Doesn't our sense of what is important in life depend partly on how badly we have been frightened or hurt by life? I think so. Then we tend to be more honest about ourselves. This is the big advantage I have over most of you. I nearly died three times. Each of you have had some things happen to you that shook you up enough to make you more honest. The more times this happens, the better. Disaster shows us the truth. We will deny reality until the last possible moment. But reality keeps intruding. Life gives us bigger and bigger blows until we pay attention. I had to nearly die three times before life could get my attention.

But if all of us don't need to make all the same mistakes, there is hope. Each of us doesn't need to make every mistake there is to be made. I have seen I can learn some things from somebody else's experience. If that's so then there is a chance that this book might have some value.

So think on that. Identify these mutualities and go to these people just as much as you can. See what happens. See if they lift you up. See if going to them lifts you up. See if going to them helps calm you down so you see a little more of yourself. See what you get out of the deal. And then see what the consequences are in your life because of spending more time in those relationships.

When you are in the process of looking for mutuality you are going to see some lack of mutuality. You are going to see some people you didn't really like and you didn't know it. And you'll see they didn't like you and you didn't know that either. See if you can identify some of those in your life and stay away from them for a while.

As near as I can see, my egotism is the biggest problem in my relationships. I would decide who I was going to have a good relationship with and then I would close my eyes to all the evidence to the contrary. But I was in complete control, I thought. I would choose my friends. I would decide what the quality of each of my relationships would be. But with my giant-sized ego in charge, I was picking my friends based on their appearance, popularity, money, social position or their usefulness to me. It was like I was picking my friends cold-bloodedly as adornments to me. They were my personal jewelry.

Is it any wonder then that most of the people I thought were my friends didn't really care for me that much? And that some really couldn't stand me? Why should they when I approached the process of friendship like buying a piece of jewelry?

Now I've turned that whole process upside down. As much as I can I let mutuality decide who my friends will be. So far mutuality doesn't seem to be anything I have much control over. I try to make sure that the only control I use now is to follow up on the mutuality I find. And of course I'm limited in this by the number of relationships I can handle. But I can still recognize the mutuality that is there even though there is no way to act on it further because of the extent of our other commitments. I find this issue of commitment to be a very hard one to handle. It may be that I'm confused and wrong-headed and will later see that. But I think my problems and other people's objections to commitment come from a different source. I think that commitment to a relationship is the hardest thing there is. We don't seem to be too frightened of relationships. But when we raise the issue of commitment in the relationship then I see the hackles rise. I'm not talking of marriage here. I'm talking about commitment in the relationship. Marriage is just a special case of that broad class of commitments.

My own relationships are a good example. Here life has given me relationships like Jackie, Vince, Dave and a few others. Those relationships are what, deep inside me, I always wanted. In my earlier years I never dreamed I could have such things. Now that I've got what I never dreamed I could have, why would I want to put them down and go looking for something better? What could be better?

I tell my students the story of the young guy who goes to the dance and meets the pretty red-haired girl who just loves him and she's the only child of a father who owns a big ranch. If that young guy has any sense he will get her out of there before she finds a better-looking guy. But most of us make the mistake of saying, "This is a great dance. If I can do this good this early, maybe I can do better. I'll put her aside and see if I can find a prettier girl with two ranches." And of course we fail and go home alone.

Why do we do such things? The explanation I come up with goes back to why we are afraid of relationships. I think it is because of our fear of self-knowledge. We don't want to face what we are. We don't want to find what's deep within ourselves. We don't want to see our imperfections. A relationship is threatening enough. But when you add commitment to that relationship, it is really a problem to us. But I think only with a sense of commitment can the deepest relationships flower and develop fully. So out of deep relationships and out of commitment comes our spiritual quest where we discover what we are and get the courage to start being it.

A part of us wants that benefit of deep relationships. But another part of ourselves runs in horror from it. Carl Rogers says that an advantage of encounter groups is that it trains us to make deeper relationships more quickly in this present world of fast-changing relationships. But who sets that pace? Who makes today's world transient? We do. I think we move so much because we want to run away from permanence and commitment. In every town and city in the United States there is a sizable minority of the people who are permanent residents.

The fact that I was so crazy I would move across half the country just because I got a new job at $500 more salary a year doesn't mean everybody's that crazy. What I told my friends by those moves was "You're very important but I have to go." The further I get away from those years, the crazier I see I was. And yet, at the time, that passed for sanity with me and the people I was leaving. They all believed it, too. That's the kind of people who lived with me in those suburbs. Knowing what I know now, I couldn't stand to live in a suburb. My college students argue that everyone's that way. I disagree. I think it is just us dissatisfied people who think what is important is to go to college and be somebody. We already are somebody. But we don't see that.

Another thing that's so weird is it doesn't bother me

that I've made lots of commitments to things and ideas and they are commitments I fiercely defend. It doesn't bother me a bit that I have made a personal commitment to Chevrolet cars, Remington rifles, Fenwick fly rods, my political party and various philosophical ideas. So why should I resist making a commitment to something much more important—to certain people.

Whatever the reason we run from commitment, I believe it is important. There are few people now in my life I have a commitment to. If you ask them "Do you feel Jess has a commitment to you?" I think most of them would feel that I do.

That commitment has a great benefit to me in what it does for my relationships. But it is also a limitation in that I can't make a commitment to everybody, just to a small number of people.

I have found the woman I want to spend my life with. I helped create the children I will be committed to for the rest of my life. I have chosen this community and the people in it as the place I want to make my life. And I have made a commitment to my five friends.

A psychology is a system of controlling behavior. In my case I'm looking for a system that will give me better control of my behavior by enlisting the help of some resources outside myself. I found I couldn't do it alone. I'm offering my psychology to you to see if it can help you. So give it a try and see if it works for you. I can make it work for me, at least I think this is what is working for me. Other people tell me they can make it work for them. But you have to judge for yourself. Try it out. Concentrate on driving your little car into gas stations that say "open" on them instead of stations that say "closed." And don't worry about the people you are leaving alone. They are right for someone else, not for you—but for someone else. We will go deeper into that later.

4

living
mutual need
therapy

One of my students and I were sitting in class one day trying to top each other in saying nice things about each other. And she said, "This is kind of a mutual admiration society, isn't it?" Our usual response to something like that is, "Oh no. No." Or, "That's awful." And that was my first response, too. But then I realized what we were doing was really good. "Yes, it is a mutual admiration society. And I need all of it I can get."

If any of you have too many friends who make you feel like you're ten feet tall, okay, you're very fortunate. But my day is not just all filled up with people who want to really listen to me and care for me and say great things to me. I'm still meeting some people who seem to be bent on cutting me down to about six inches high.

I had an interesting set of experiences the day before the class. My wife and I had a beautiful morning together since I didn't teach until afternoon. We were sitting out in the back of our house. I had just bought my wife a lovely gift. It was equivalent to $10,000 in value. What it was, was one of these tables for the yard with an umbrella on top of it. This is most every girl's dream, I realized. It's like a canopied bed for the bedroom. And I was wise enough to act intelligently when she said, "Hey, Jess, what do you think about getting one of these from Sears?" I said, "Get it." You know, occasionally I do the intelligent thing. So she was feeling like a very rich lady.

We were sitting out there drinking our tea and watching the horses in the back yard and it was real nice. There was a small note of discord because the horses had been on the lawn and there were some horse dumps around. Still fresh. So I got the shovel and put those a little further away. I didn't put out too much effort, but it helped. So we sat there having a really beautiful morning. Then I left for school.

I was living the abundant life. I was really on top of the world. Actually, what I was doing was floating on a romantic, sentimental pink cloud. And, of course, I should have been smart enough to know that this was a bad sign. When you are really high, a low is just sitting about six inches from you. And what it is, you cause your own low because you are as blind in a high as you are in a low. That's why I like my highs to be quieter so I don't get so blind and make so many mistakes. So I got careless. I was walking out of the Student Union about 3:30 that afternoon. I was having a pretty good time, but I was still real careless and not paying attention.

Standing out in the front hall was a student of mine from a couple of years ago. She was really taken by the ideas we had talked about in class. She was eighteen or nineteen then and so now she was about twenty-one. When she was in my class she was a discussion leader for me for a quarter or so. And she just raved at that time about how great my ideas were. But since then each quarter she has grown increasingly more aloof. Her greeting has gone from "Hi, Jess!" and the big turn-on to a cool "Hello there." She was standing talking to some guy. She looked lovely. She had a sleeveless dress on and she gave me a real warm greeting. She's a cute gal. So I just moved over to her and put my hand on her bare shoulder and said, "Hi! How are you? It's good to see you." And what I really meant was, "It's good to see you smiling at me again." But she turned cold and pulled away. "See ya. Okay. Go ahead. We'll see ya."

I felt like a dirty old man, and very low. I could have crawled under a snake and had room to fly my kite. I imagined all kinds of awful things and wondered what was going on here. I felt just terrible.

I spent a lot of the time that afternoon and evening trying to get my serenity back. I kept saying to myself, "Jess, are you going to let this twenty-one-year-old girl take your serenity away from you? Is it that fragile? Is it that much up for grabs that whoever wants your serenity can grab hold of it and take it away?"

I spent a lot of time trying to get my serenity back. I must have thought about it a hundred times in the course of that evening and the next morning. Just after lunch I talked about it to a fellow professor, a guy I could be honest with, a guy I really admired. We laughed and it really made a big difference to get it out in the open.

Then, I went to my behavior modification class. The class had gotten to the level of cordiality in about the first week or two. And it stayed at the level of cordiality up to the sixth or seventh week. But then the class became more and more aware of the opportunity they had to know each other better and yet they knew they wouldn't do anything about it. They realized "Hey, we can go further than this. There is something that Jess can teach us, but we don't want to learn." And that became more and more apparent to them. The class resorted to just frantic talking to each other in this false kind of jibber-jabber we do when we know we should be doing something else. They were threatened by facing themselves and were ducking and running just fierce. And here we were on the last day of class. I was going to cancel the class out that day but I thought, "No. I'm going to tough it through. I'm going to be whatever kind of teacher that class wants me to be as much as it is humanly possible to be." But I nearly blew it. In the middle of that class I almost exploded. I wanted to scream, "Look you dumb jerks, why don't you get your heads out of your lies and face the music of what has happened here, which is I reached out my hand in love and friendliness to you cats and I offered you me. And you just went, 'Yuck.' And I feel terrible."

But Vince says you don't do things like this. When we reach out our hand in true love and friendliness, it ain't a deal. He says, "When I'm dependent on results it doesn't work." He said, "We must not be dependent on results." We know that almost always some people will respond but we can't ask or expect people to respond to us, which is being dependent on results. We need to be willing to play the odds and get the three out of five. And we need to realize that a whole group can choose not to respond as occasionally happens to me. But that's life. And it means we can't kill those people with our eyes the next time we see them. Wanting to kill them means being dependent on results, you see.

I got through the class, but it was a strain. I was sitting in my office afterward hurting from the experience and the strain when a woman came to my office to interview me for a story. She asked me a question about spiritual experiences and their behavioral consequences. In other words, if you have a spiritual experience, what behavioral consequences do you see? I spoke from my heart on the matter.

I've seen a lot of people have spiritual awakenings and I have seen the immediate lift that all of them get. I guess everyone who has a spiritual awakening that I know of has an immediate positive reaction from it. In fact, they feel some very physical things. And you can see the effects in their lives for a period of time, for a day, a week, a month, six months. But as near as I can see, unless you do something to sustain that, it will die out.

You can get the spirit but you can also lose the spirit. So what I told her is, "Yes, I see an immediate behavioral change in everybody, but I think the only people who have a continued and improving behavioral change are those people who work at it along the lines we are talking about here, continuously and with as many people as they can muster." Our discussion was going along great. She was really fascinated by this because she had seen some of this in the circles in which she travels.

I mentioned another thing I had noticed. People do one of two things, typically, when they start having trouble living out their spiritual awakenings. They may fall off their mountaintop and because they see themselves then as an outcast and being ostracized by other people in their group, they just drop out. They don't think they are fit for the company of these so-called friends of theirs, these perfect people on this spiritual

mountaintop. Other people handle trouble in their lives
by denying it. They say, "Things are beautiful with me,"
even if they aren't. And those are the two most common
reactions I've seen to trouble in their lives.

Only in cases where a person is around good teaching
and people who will support them instead of tearing them
down are they able to stay with the spirit they initially
have. And they need to be willing to submit themselves to
that teaching and to reality, which is ups and downs.
Reality is that in any twenty-four-hour period I will do
some good things and I will do some awful things. Reality
is recognizing the cruddy things I'm doing and admitting
to them and just smiling to myself about these signs of
my humanity. This is my human imperfection and being
spiritual doesn't mean being perfect. It means making
progress but it doesn't mean being perfect.

Things were going along beautifully in the interview
with the lady and I was supposed to leave in about two
minutes. All of a sudden she said, "What bothers me
about this one group of people, the Full Gospel Businessmen downtown here, is some of them are very rich
people. And I've seen a lot of poor people and I've seen
a lot of suffering and poverty." I said, "What are you
getting at?" She said, "Well, you know, why don't those
people do more than they are doing for those poor people,
really do something?" The tone of voice in which she
asked the question and what I thought was a smug, self-
satisfied expression on her face hit me like a hammer.
I blew up inside and I threw questions at her like arrows.
I said, "What right do you have to judge someone else's
behavior? Their behavior is their problem. You're also
putting all your emphasis on material things. Most of
the rich people I've seen have been just as miserable as
the poor ones." But I was making the same mistake I was

accusing her of. In my anger at her I was judging and condemning her. We ended up with a hassle before I finally got out of there.

These are the moments when I blow it. I've told you so many times I'm in this world to try to survive. And yet here I was twenty seconds away from finishing that dumb interview in my fifteen minutes of allotted time so I could pick up my daughter and I ended up throwing half an hour down the drain fighting with this poor woman. So, what I ended up doing was to get very tired because fighting takes a lot out of me.

This is why I say it is so crucial to have people I can go to and restore my serenity—our mutual admiration societies. The more of them the merrier. I know some of the grief I got from the young gal I touched on the arm I probably deserved. Some of the trouble I got into with the lady I got mad at I probably deserved, in fact, I know I did. But I don't like to see myself doing too many of those things. I usually don't have a couple of them that close together, that bad. To me this is where mutual need therapy is so important. I still manage to screw up plenty during the days. So the warmth and closeness of some mutuality helps take the sting out of a troubled day and it makes a good day better. So how many of the good things do we have built into our days, plus the ones that are going to happen by accident? Like the next day I wasn't going to be able to have lunch with Jerry Sullivan so I gave some thought to putting some nice things in the day. I was going to go to see another man for a while and he and I get along great. So that would be pretty good, but it wouldn't be the same as the warmth and ease Jerry Sullivan and I have. I saw I had better build something in the day ahead of time and then

I would also get the luck of the draw on the rest of the day.

Many people want to argue that I overstate the seriousness of life. They say it ain't that hard. Well, that isn't what my eyeballs tell me. I'm not the only one who gets into trouble all the time. I see a lot of other people who are living life like these two moments I had. They have a lot of those during the day. Then they go home and beat up on the wife and the kids, and the dog and anything else within reach. And they think that's normal. But I've seen enough now to know that may be what we call normal, but it isn't the way we have to live. A friend of mine, Ed Halvorson, expressed this problem so beautifully in the first two lines of a song he wrote:

> Has life become like a shoe that pinches
> Is living just a matter of dying by inches?[1]

So often this is what people mean by normal; it's dying by inches. On the surface they say things are fine but just get them a little drunk and you find the bitterness and resentment just below the surface. Such a person thinks you're normal if you're not committed to a mental institution.

As part of my improving my sanity I'm learning to avoid those extreme emotional highs I had yesterday morning. Whoopee! Ain't I got abundance! That's unreal. That's the roller coaster. You go way, way up and then you go down so fast. I used to think highs were great. I now see that I'm as blind to the people around me and as destructive in a big high as I am in a depressed low. Neither highs nor lows have any serenity in them.

[1] © 1974 by Ed Halvorson, Bozeman, Montana.

Serenity is more just being real calm. It's even. It isn't high and it isn't low. It's just even.

One of my students had this to say: "A point I've got out of what you've said is to pay more attention to what I do. I used to come home from school and I would nag a lot. Now I find myself saying, 'Wait a minute. Hold back and look the situation over.' And I find myself enjoying my family much more. I don't know whether to attribute this to the class itself or maybe these ideas have always been in me.

"I think probably one of the most traumatic experiences I ever had was last year, when our third child was born. We found out two days after he was born he was mongoloid. That was hard for my wife and I to face, and the usual emotions came out. I started to feel pity for the boy and his unhappiness when he grows up. Then all of a sudden it changed and I started feeling sorry for myself.

"One day my wife and I were sitting down and talking about this. All of a sudden it dawned on me he is my boy. I'm part of him and he's part of me. He will never ever be as intelligent as I am. But I can make him as happy and intelligent as he possibly can be. And that was what we were looking for. I think what happened to me there was I finally understood him and what's going on. And I understood people instead of thinking solely of myself. And I began to look at other people. And as was pointed out in class time and time again, it's fine to talk here in class, but do we practice it at home? This is really the crucial point and I think, at least on my part, I might not be even 50 per cent doing the job, but at least I feel the job is beginning to be done and I'm beginning to grow and understand other people."

He was right. No one needs to put these ideas in you;

they are already in you. But this book can help uncover
these ideas in you. Every person in this whole world is
a magnificent, splendid person full of the power and
glory and majesty that is them and uniquely them. So we
aren't putting anything in anybody. We don't need to. The
marvel is already there. The spirit you need to start you
on your spiritual quest is already in you just waiting. It
is the uncovering of it, the revealing to ourself that is the
very heart of what we are talking about here. The point
of this book is we need mutual relationships so we can
have mirrors that let us see ourselves. We can't discover
ourselves sitting alone on a desert island because we don't
have a mirror.

You can meditate alone about your relationships with
other people and learn from them. But if we dropped you
on a desert island, after you had meditated up to a certain
point and used up your past accumulation of relationship
experiences, you couldn't go past that point. And particularly you couldn't do this if we dropped you on a
desert island at twenty, or eighteen or sixteen. You could
go very little distance because you wouldn't have had
many experiences to learn from. You and I can't make
our spiritual quests without other people.

A mutual relationship, where there is real mutuality, is
like a very clear mirror in which we see ourselves
revealed in a deeper way. Consequently, when we go back
into that relationship, we can go deeper into ourselves
and it is a deeper relationship and it is a clearer mirror
and we can see further into ourselves. And it is a spiral
that takes us deeper into us ourselves and our relationships. But there is absolutely nothing other than illumination that is added to us by the other person. There doesn't
need to be. And it is only, in my experience, in the

mutual relationship that this happens. And not in what we call cordiality.

Now, cordiality is fine. It makes our day go along more smoothly. I'm not putting down cordiality. But we can spend our whole lifetime in cordiality and just wither up and die five minutes later. That's why we can move and not have a friend left behind that cares about us for more than two letters. Many of my students say I make too much out of the benefits of relationships. They say, "I've got relationships and they aren't doing for me what you're talking about." I think that's because all there is in those relationships is cordiality.

It was like that class I talked about a few pages back. Cordiality is a nice social lubrication. But a continuing cordial relationship offers more and more chances to be personal and to open ourselves up. When we refuse to give of ourselves and just continue the cordiality, there is a deep hurt there. Behind our smiling and warm conversational exchanges, there is this ice-cold unspoken dialogue that knows each of us is refusing to go deeper into the relationship that has been made available to us. We know that each time we had a chance to get closer, we turned it off with some funny remark or superficial chatter. Cordiality is just treating people with courtesy and respect but that's just one level higher than dislike on my four-level scale.

Now that I know what warm relationships can do for me, cordiality not only doesn't help me, it is a hurt. That's because I'm so aware of our joint refusal to go deeper into what is offered us. I don't see that a cordial relationship does anything for either of us. In a way, it can make our loneliness worse because it may seem to us that we are in a relationship yet nothing is happening. That's why it's important to understand that cordiality is no help to us in the sense I'm talking about relationships being a help.

How do we keep increasing the mutuality in our lives? We increase it by seeking and finding mutuality, finding mutual relationships where we can talk about things in our deep heart, not necessarily constantly, but occasionally and as often as we need it. And because those people aren't around us just exactly when we need them, we better have enough. So many people want to say, "Well, Jess, I've got one mutual friend or I've got two. What do you expect?" And the answer is again, how in the world can you have too many where there is deep mutuality?

To have deep mutuality there doesn't need to be this other thing in a friendship which is that continual relationship. You can only have a few what you call close friends. But you can have mutuality with a lot of people where you can speak your heart to them even though you know that you aren't going to play a close and constant part in each other's lives. In the class I taught to the teachers, there was a lot of mutuality, but we weren't necessarily going to be frequent associates. Since the class ended, the mutuality that was there between us hasn't gone away, unless we wanted it to, unless we got frightened by it and decided to batten up the hatches.

Here I want to warn you again that most always you and I will run from the very closeness we need so desperately. Even those who claim they want it often find out that after they experience some closeness they want to run and hide. I've seen this happen constantly with the closeness that we experience in our classroom. Typically, I find after six months to a year some of the people I was close to can only manage a very feeble greeting when they see me.

My college students are fairly free to reflect how things really are in our relationship because they are not so concerned with faking it, especially because they aren't contemporaries of mine. While we were in our class together they came out in the open for a while. But it's like getting caught in just your Jockey shorts. You don't like it that way so you start getting some clothes on again and covering up. There are very few people who are willing to admit their fear of closeness. So when they pull away they can't admit to themselves what they are doing. But if we want to find more life we can't lie to ourselves like that about something so important in our lives.

 • If you come out in the open with people and find you need to hide, do what you can do, do what you have to do, do the best you can do, whatever that is. But be aware as much as possible of what you're doing instead of playing some sick game and calling it closeness. I've got some sick games I play. When I catch myself playing them I ask myself: "Is that the best that you can do? Yeah. When you going to get better? I don't know, I hope it is soon. As soon as I can manage. When are you going to give up those sick games, you dummy? Well, I'm working on it. Well, that's not fast enough to suit me! Sorry."

I'm trying to be more aware of my sick games. I'm trying to realize I'm going to play them until I get better ones to take their place. I think the more honestly I admit to what I'm really doing, the faster I will get rid of those sick games by getting good games or no games to take their place. So we need a tremendous dosage of honesty with ourselves. And again we can bring that out in each other, too. I can come to Vince and say, "Hey, Vince, I ran into this situation." Then Vince can say the good things, and he can say, "Well, how about this, Jess? How about that. How come it worked out that way?" And I can say, "Well, Vince, I wonder if I didn't do such and such?" "Well, whatever you think."

Okay, that's being honest in a very nice way. But that's a precious thing. A lot of people want to come up to me and say, "Be honest with me, Jess. Tell me this or that." No way. They haven't earned honesty. They wouldn't appreciate it if they got it. They would hate me for it. They don't want honesty. We have to really earn honesty. Vince once made a comment to me: "Jess, I've got a hundred people I can go to if I get screwed up, who will be honest with me." Now that's something. You just don't build relationships like that over night.

In keeping mutual need therapy going, you need to develop those mutual relationships and go to them. I see with many of my students we have developed some mutuality. They see what our relationship is doing for them. But because of their fear or just because they take this precious thing for granted, they tell me, "Oh, Jess, you really do so much to lift my spirits, and I really feel so much better when I talk to you." I'm sure it's true. I can see it, too. But what have they done about it since then? Absolutely nothing. They walk away for good from something they see as valuable.

What if I drew you a map to the Lost Lady gold mine and told you exactly how to get there? "You go two miles that way and a mile this way and four hundred yards up the valley and then you come to a lone cedar tree. Right there at the base is where the gold mine is." But you take the map and just throw it in a dresser drawer. Yet you claim, "I always wanted a gold mine. I wish someday I could have one." And the map to your gold mine is sitting unused in your drawer. That's weird, isn't it? But we do that all the time.

You have met a lot of people you really groove on and you haven't done a thing with them, have you? You don't separate the wheat from the chaff, and see that you can do something about it. Why leave it up to accident where the good things and good people have to come into our life only by chance. If you say you like someone, really enjoy them, then it's simple. They live three blocks that way. And would they be happy to see you? Of course they would. It's dumb not to do anything about this stuff. It is dumb to be sitting there broke when you've got a map to a gold mine sitting in your dresser drawer.

I learned a lesson like this about fishing when I first came to Montana. Before when I would fish a river, I would very carefully fish out all the water. Lloyd Rixe took me fishing one morning. He started fishing at 7 A.M. because he had found that's when the fish bite the best. He led me right to a big deep pool and we each caught two or three trout. Then he walked a hundred yards upstream to the next good hole and we caught some more fish. We walked right by lots of water I would have spent hours fishing. By nine o'clock, when the fishing slowed up, we each had ten nice trout to eat.

Lloyd wasn't fishing much differently than I was but his secret was he fished when the fish were biting best and he concentrated all his time on the good spots and skipped the poor ones.

The analogy between fishing that way and mutual need therapy is a close one. We all have some mutual need therapy in our lives. But we are leaving it too much up to chance. There are some things I can change. I can have lunch today with anyone I choose. I don't need to wait until I run into Vince or Jerry by accident, I can go see them as often as I want.

Most of the trout in a stream are in the big deep holes.

Same with the stream of life. Most of the good things for us and our spiritual quests are with the people who like us the way we are. Once we see that, it is simple to make sure we spend some time with the people who love us and avoid spending a lot of time with the people who want to change us. The analogy breaks down in one way: What is a good, deep hole for me (a good person for me) isn't good for someone else. A lady came to my office to talk to me. But she soon got nervous because she was afraid she was taking up too much of my time. I pointed out in the hall and said, "You don't see any line out there do you?" Vince and Jerry are two of the wisest men I ever expect to know, yet people aren't lined up waiting to see them.

Since I said this book to my class, I have taken two years's leave and I can see so much difference between the days I had then and what I have now. These days I'm home most of the time. I go over to school two days a week to have lunch with Jerry and have office hours to see my friends. But when I'm at school I run into some of the people who can't stand me and who I have trouble with. It is inevitable we see each other because of our jobs. Each time we come in contact with each other we can't help but be painfully aware of the years of difficulties between us. There are other people at school who I don't have trouble with but we haven't chosen to do much with all the opportunities we have had to be a part of each other's lives. I find these contacts are difficult for me. I see now that I'm away from those contacts on an everyday basis, how much they used to pull me down. That was why the contact that would lift me up was so much more important to me then. It is still important to me now in a positive way because of the enjoyment and value I get from it. But when I was at

school every day there was a repair function that isn't
so necessary so often now.

"Maybe the reason we don't reach out to the people
we have mutuality with is because we think, 'Well, I'd
really like to hunt with Bill Oriet, but he doesn't need
me!' "

Right. He has his hunting partner. But I can go with
him in other ways. I go out and have coffee with him.
I know he needs me to have coffee with him. That's
just putting yourself down if you go across the board
and say, "I'm sure no one would want to see me."

When I reach out to someone in love and friendliness
I often find it isn't love and friendliness I'm offering.
It's a deal. I'll be nice to you if you'll be nice back.
That's not love and friendliness. So I need to see that
the odds are about three out of five. Say I reach out five
times. One of the times is to Sullivan. Another time is to
somebody else great. And the third time is to another
good person for me. Then I reach out to somebody like
the girl I mentioned where I couldn't handle her response.
And then some stranger walks into my office to interview
me and I have a bad time. If I'm going to be put down
because of those two, look what I say about the three
who said yes to me. I say in effect, "You don't matter
to me enough to make up for these other two. You three
who are such a big part of my life, you aren't that
important. You aren't big enough to make up for those
two really small incidents." You see how that puts down
the greatness of the good people in my life? "You're not
enough. I've got to have them all." Or because some
one person disagreed with me, I'm going to sit around
and nurse my wounds. I'm never going to reach out
again.

Now, one of the things that makes these rebuffs so hard

to take is there's always an element of truth in them. When they hit us and hurt there is often an element of truth in that for me. I was afraid the gal I touched thought I was a dirty old man. Yes, I am partially a dirty old man. A friend of mine and I were having coffee when a very pretty young girl walked by. It was a warm spring day and the juices were flowing. All the girls were running around without any clothes on. And it was giving us old guys a bad time. He said, "Oh my God, Jess, I don't know what I'm going to do." And I said, "I don't know what I'm going to do, either. We will just have to sit here and maybe hold hands."

So that's what makes something hurt, when there is an element of truth in it. If that gal were to say, "Get out of here, Jess Lair, you are the laziest person in the world," I would have just said, "Yeah, I sure am," and yawned. That wouldn't bother me a bit because I know I'm the furthest thing from lazy and she is going to have trouble finding very many people who agree I'm lazy. So, if she were to say, "You're lazy," that wouldn't hurt because there's no truth in that.

It was the same problem with the gal who interviewed me on the spiritual experiences. I let her put me in a situation where I was at my worst, where I was cutting down other people. I got up on my high horse and was cutting down these people who won't give of themselves where I'm such a fantastic guy and I give of myself all the time. Everybody knows that. I'm just such a sweet person. So I'm mad at her for something that I've got a lot of in me.

I've got a part of me that is a real loser. I'll come right up close to something good for me and I'll find some way to screw it up. I used to be such a loser I could find a way to screw up a free lunch. When my first book was coming out and some other good things were happening, my wife said, "Jess, don't you lose. Don't you blow this." And, of course, it was easier not to because it was a more natural thing than many of my phony attempts at fabricated accomplishments in the past. Before I tried to make success out of nothing. So far, despite so many very good things that have happened to me, I haven't really gone off on the pink cloud of illusion for more than a few hours like I told you about the other morning when I was sitting in my back yard drinking tea playing the part of the colonial planter.

One of my students told this story: "Just this week I had the girls in my class stay and eat lunch with me. They're six and seven years old. We were sitting out on the lawn and they all gathered around me and were eating lunch. But two of them went a distance away to be by themselves. I said, 'Sarah, I guess that you just don't love us any more.' And one of the little seven-year-olds who was sitting by me said, 'Well, what about all of us who do love you?'" That's our immaturity and egotism showing. Those who love us aren't enough. We want everyone to love us.

I think when we think of the psychology of the victim, it is a pretty awful thing. When I want to cry, "I'm a victim, man, I've been had," then all I need to do is think about a few of the wives of alcoholics. Once in a while there is the woman who marries an alcoholic so he will beat on her, and she can run to the ladies downtown and show her bruises. "See, I'm being beaten up." But I know what can happen when that guy gets sober. Often she leaves and marries another alcoholic. But that tells me she likes to be beaten. That's pretty sick. And there's some victim in all of us. We've all got a little touch of loser. Once in a while we will have the misfortune, or perhaps the good fortune, to see it.

I learned a lot from that incident with that gal I touched inappropriately. I thanked God for the teaching. You say, "Does all teaching have to hurt?" No. Not all teaching. But we need our mistakes. That's one of the ways we need to learn. We don't need to make the mistakes. But there are certain mistakes it seems each of us need to make before we will find the truth. And they are different for each one of us. So thank God for the teaching. What a sad thing it would be if we weren't taught anything. Or what a sad thing it would be to make our mistakes over and over again. I see a guy at the university doing that. He keeps making the same mistake over and over again. I think something is happening to his mind because I knew him five years ago and he was so different. Now, five years later, he is rubbing everyone around him the wrong way. I think I have a pretty good idea what it was that happened to him. But he isn't seeing his mistakes. He is making a lot of them but he isn't seeing them. I know from what I knew of him before, he had the kind of insight and understanding of the problem to do something about it. So it is his blindness to his own mistakes that is such a terrible difficulty to him now. We need our mistakes.

Another way to look at the process of mutual need therapy is in terms of energy. Where do we get the energy we need to live? Freud believed man was born with only so much psychic energy or emotional energy. When that was used up you had had it. He was proposing a closed system of energy. Seyle has a theory of stress. He thinks man will stand only so much stress. When you're working happily at something you like to do, that isn't stress. When you're working unhappily at something that's stress. Or when you're loving unhappily, that's stress. Whenever you're doing something you aren't in harmony with, that's stress. Seyle says that there's a limit to how much stress a given organ can take. When that limit is reached, then that organ dies whether it is a heart or kidney or lung or what have you.

I think there are some notable exceptions to those ideas. When Vince was forty-five years old he crawled upstairs on his hands and knees to a second-floor AA meeting. That was twenty-four years ago. Vince is getting younger by the year. He is sixty-nine now, his youngest boy is about six. He seems to me to have gone from a situation where his life energy was almost completely depleted to where he has more energy than he is using. His organs must have been almost gone but they have rejuvenated. He is quite a guy. When we talk to Vince my wife just marvels at what a handsome guy he is and the tremendous vitality in him.

His heart stopped a few years ago. He had to go to the hospital with heart trouble and while he was there his heart stopped. They got it going. In just a couple of days he was up and around talking to the other alcoholics again. But he is so serene. One of the biggest dangers I see in a heart attack is the terrible emotional reaction that a person has, the fear he's going to die. I think that's probably more killing than the heart difficulty itself. I know Vince's heart was damaged enough through those fifteen years on skid row to be a kind of a limiting factor but even that has to be reversed an awful lot. A lot of damage to his heart and organs has been reversed by the vitality and the abundant living and the serenity that he has experienced since then.

So I don't think it is a closed system. I think that it's an open system: The happier you are the longer you live.

Now there are some people who are miserable and live a long time, too. All I see there is a testimonial to the fact they've got hellish strong constitutions because most miserable people manage to die or kill themselves.

"A lot of the things you've told us to try are things that make us more aware of what is going on in life," a student said. "I got to thinking about this. A lot of people know they are unhappy. Things are going bad. But it is amazing how people can hurt from this."

How do you mean?

"Well, when you go to a course like this, you get a chance to discuss the other end of things that happen in life. And so you kind of get a picture. But the people who have not done this, or maybe not had the opportunity to do this, their interpretation of things is different because their exposure has been a little different."

This is another reason why it is so crucial to find mutuality, to have intimate friends we can trust, intimate friends we can say anything to. It's like Vince says, "Jess, I can get up a conversation on money twenty times as I walk down Main Street. But you try to get into a conversation about spiritual matters as you walk down Main Street. You've got a tough time finding that person who you can talk to about the kind of ideas we've been talking about here. You need a special kind of friend to talk about the spiritual side of things. Man is one but he has three sides to him. He's got his body, he's got his mind, he's got his spirit. This is what I see watching alcoholics. Unless they have a series of spiritual awakenings, they can't get long-term sobriety and serenity.

"No power on earth can get you sober. And most alcoholics have tried every power on earth. They've tried drugs. They've tried doctors. They've tried hospitals. They've tried health cures. They've tried travel, psychiatrists, psychoanalysts, psychologists, ministers. They've tried everything known to man. Finally, the doctor says to them, 'You're going to die in a year. Nothing on earth can save you.' And they know the truth of that. But a power higher than earth does save them when they finally admit they have a problem and ask for help."

Most every AA who's got long-term sobriety admits to a spiritual awakening which is a change in his personality. Now by spiritual awakening, I don't mean you have to have a vision or hear voices. What I mean by spiritual awakening is a change in our personality. As I see it, once we get out of the center and stop trying to make life revolve around us, then we accept that there is something else besides us. Once we do this minimum step, the acceptance produces a change in our personality and we are a different person in that small way. If we do our part and keep supporting that difference, we will be different all the rest of our lives.

It has been three years that I've been working on the ideas in this book. I first said these ideas to my class of teachers in the spring of 1973. But now, as I finish writing them up, I'm starting to think about a new book on our relationship to some higher power that will deal with what we can truly change and what only our higher power can change. My old ways was to try to run everything and try to change everything. I was trying to change my personality and the personalities of everyone around me and reform society. Thank God I couldn't do that. If I could change a personality, think of my ego. So the working title I've selected for my new book is *Jess, You Ain't the Doctor*. It will tell how I found I had to put the spiritual side back into my personal psychological system. I'm not talking about religion. I'm talking simply about a belief in any power outside ourself—God as you understand Him.

To my mind the sadness of psychology is that it will not admit the spiritual side, generally. But by psychology's own definition, which is the control of behavior, you have to admit the spiritual side because there are a million alcoholics who are recovered. They control one of the most difficult pieces of behavior to control, which is alcoholic addiction, through a spiritual awakening. If you ask most of them, "What is the one thing that made you sober?" they would say, "I had a spiritual awakening." So this controlled their drinking. And yet, psychology is saying, "Well, we won't admit that into psychology because it doesn't fit our ideas of what should be psychology." Well, there is not supposed to be a conception of what should be psychology. If it works, it's psychology. It doesn't matter if I use cheese cake to hold up a bridge. Somebody says, "You can't hold up a bridge with cheese cake." I say, "Well, you drive your tractor over my bridge." He drives his tractor over my bridge and the thing holds up. I say, "Okay. Cheese cake will hold up a bridge, won't it?" And the guy's got to say, "You're right."

I don't care how we think things should be. It's how they *are* that counts. The thing about alcoholics that is so beautiful is that they can tell clearly if something is working for them or not. If it is working for them, they are sober. If it isn't working for them, they are drunk. Most other behavior is far easier to fake. So many people lie. A lot of people go through encounter groups. They tell me for years afterwards, "Jess, I am a magnificent, beautiful individual for my experience." I want to say, "You can't prove it by me, tiger. You are the same cat that went away. And if you're such a magnificent human being now, how come these people around you are coming to me and saying, 'What are we going to do about this guy?' "

It is very easy to talk this stuff, but it is so tough to do it. And the only test of our doing it is what we do with our hands. I don't care how you talk in the long run. Talk is the first step to action, but it isn't action. But what I want to see is, I want to see that action. I want you to tell me about what you did.

Many of my students give me this baloney about, "Oh, Jess! Your ideas are so great." I want them to tell me what they did. And preferably show me. It's like Eliza Doolittle in *My Fair Lady*. She is yelling at this guy, "Quit singing me all those songs and reading me all this poetry and telling me your heart's on fire. Show me. Show me now." Yet he keeps on with his dumb talk.

One of my students said, "On a lot of the problems that everyone faces, the problem itself is basically very simple. At the time, we didn't have to go out and do some real complex thing to get rid of this problem. But why is it we try to make things so complex when the answer to a problem is a very simple solution?"

"It's just like, why do you work more than you should? Because you need it. You need your work to run away from the problem. I think all of our escapes are used so we won't be aware of our imperfections. Now you say, "Well, we all are aware of our imperfections." Are you? Okay, speak to me of them, now.

"Okay, but then that's right back to the simple truth, isn't it? It's not a complex truth."

"Yes, it's a simple truth. But simple doesn't mean easy. This simple truth about ourselves is the hardest thing there is. That's why you've got to keep things stirred up. You've got to keep a big cloud of dust in this area or you're going to see the truth.

"I'll go along with that. What we are talking about is simple but people make it complex to cover it up. That is why I feel that the primitive tribes are very modern."

Yes, that's right. And we have lost a lot of the seeking of truth and spirituality that is in most every so-called primitive civilization. We are the savages. We came to this land and claimed it for ourselves. It was already somebody else's land. Just because they weren't using it the way we thought they should, we said we would claim it. That's like a Sioux going to England today and claiming that land for the Sioux nation to be used in common by them. Only a supreme egotist would do such a thing. Yet that's what we did here.

We worry about preserving a Stone Age civilization that was recently discovered in the Philippines. Or we worry about preserving some endangered species of animal. Hell, we killed off hundreds of small Indian civilizations. We killed a million to two million Indians with guns, disease or starvation. And we did it with a Bible in one hand and a smoking gun in the other. That's an example of our spirituality, our oneness with all God's creations. There are just a few remnants of Indian civilization left in the central plains where enough Indians survived to carry on part of their culture.

Vine DeLoria, Jr., a Sioux, said, "Our ideas will overcome your ideas. We will cut the country's whole value system to shreds. It isn't important that there are only 500,000 of us Indians . . . what is important is that we have a superior way of life. We Indians have a more human philosophy of life. We Indians will show this country how to act human. Someday this country will revise its constitution, its laws, in terms of human beings, instead of property. If Red Power is to be a power in this country it is because it is ideological . . . what is the ultimate value of a man's life? That is the question?"

Pearl Buck said the Chinese spent half of their educational time teaching children how to get along with one another: half of their time was spent on human relations. We don't do that here. We are seeking money, power, glory. That's why we need so many psychiatrists. That's why people are so screwed up. Our society is out of joint. Okay, I'm not saying that the Chinese society is all that perfect, but I think societies go through periods of evolution and get to be in real good shape and we see this in the rise and fall of societies. I think that our society is really screwed up. I think we are producing a lot of material benefits. We have our tremendous freedom. But some of that goes right along with our desire for loneliness. In a way we have a mutual pact, "I'll leave you alone if you'll leave me alone." That's the kind of freedom that's a little too much alone to really fit the needs of the individual. I'm not saying that our society is all bad. But I think that our society is somewhat out of joint. I wouldn't want to call this the Golden Age of any civilization.

To me, when you look at the broad sweep of time, I think we will find some way to get our society back into better joint. But am I going to sit around and wait for that five hundred or one thousand or five thousand years to pass? No! I'm going to do something about it right now. That's what I've been doing. So I've got a fine society of friends here in Bozeman, Montana. It's a beautiful thing. And it's getting better every day.

I have a slogan for you so that you will remember to keep it simple. It's KISS. That stands for Keep It

Simple, Stupid! Or KISMIF, Keep It Simple, Make It Fun.

"I read a story about a lady who had a problem," one of my students said. "I can't remember what the problem was or anything, but she went to a psychoanalyst. He told her what was wrong and how to get rid of the problem. And so she did it and got cured. But the story made the point that had she gone to a psychologist or a psychiatrist, they would have told her that it was an entirely different problem and this is how you would get rid of it. If she had done that she would have been cured. If she had gone to a minister, he would have told her that it was this problem. It said the point is that the lady needed something to believe in, in order to do it. And she could get rid of the problem herself."

I object to that view of life on these grounds: that is, it suggests that our problems are too much from our own perceptions. There's a great deal of that often in our problems. And often we just need reassurance. Usually, though, our problems come from being out of harmony with the laws of life. And the laws of life aren't different for each of us. And so the answer from any one of those experts that lady consulted is probably substantially the same. So often when I am talking with somebody who is very troubled, I will say to them, "Hey, I bet your husband or wife has been trying to tell you this for twenty years, haven't they?" And they agree. So I don't see that any solution drawn out of a hat will solve a problem. That's chaos and confusion. I believe there is an order and a lawfulness in life. If there wasn't the ideas in this book wouldn't work consistently as they do for so many of us. Saying any idea works equally well is just another attempt to use confusion to run away from what is simple.

I see that there's a great deal of harmony in the things that different viewpoints are saying to the same person rather than a great deal of difference. The view previously mentioned that anything will work tends to confuse the picture. Vince knows where the center of the earth is. By paying attention to people like him, I'll get closer to the center.

This is one of the other reasons you need an intimate friend who knows more about life and the laws of life than you do. That's a sponsor. I've got some sponsors. Vince, Jackie and some others. I go to them when I've got a question. You know what I do when I ask a question? I listen very carefully and I don't argue and I don't interrupt. Now a lot of people ask me a question and before the words are half out of my mouth they start arguing with me, or they start telling me why that's dumb. They don't have an understanding of respect. I'm not speaking of blind unquestioning obedience. I have a ski instructor I never argue with because he's proven to me he can teach me and others to ski. I respect him completely in that area. My sponsors have shown me they can teach me the things I most want to learn, how to live. So they have earned my deep respect. When they speak, I listen. I don't argue. I listen. Some things I can't understand yet. But I just wait because I know that later on those things will be said again and then maybe I will be able to understand.

5

living alone
with reality—
the spiritual quest

We have been talking about mutual need therapy and how we need to look at our relationships. Always the central point is seeing if those relationships are doing something for us. But we spend most of our lives away from the warmth of those mutual relationships. I see now that how well I do when I'm alone lets me know how well my mutual need therapy is going. My loving contacts with my family and my five friends and others who love me give me the fuel to let me be alone in a good way. Before it was often hard for me to be alone. But I very seldom get that nervous feeling when I'm alone any more. We also feel alone in a crowd when those people are strangers to us or don't want to open up to us. Again, I find I can be fairly calm in those situations.

Our friend Snoopy in "Peanuts" was having a terrible time sleeping one night. He just couldn't sleep. And he was tossing and turning on top of his doghouse wrestling with some really grave problem. Finally about sunup he got to sleep. Then two of the kids walked by about ten in the morning and saw Snoopy asleep. One of the kids said to his buddy, "Wouldn't it be great to be a dog and sleep all the time?" After they had gone by Snoopy just opened one eye and said, "Except at night!"

Do you always go to sleep just when you want? Do you spend a night of blissful sleep with no nightmares, no wakeful times, ever? Do you wake up peaceful and happy from your night's rest? Do you just automatically do that every night? If you don't, then I've got some company. Of course my wife gets mad at me because I've got about ten times as easy a problem as she has. But nevertheless, there aren't very many of us who don't have some of those dark nights of the soul. In the middle of the night you wake up and all of a sudden something that you really screwed up on the day previous or sometime previous rises up to haunt you. And it is so big in the middle of the night. To me it's ten times as big a problem as it ever is the next morning. But the fact that it isn't going to be so big the next morning is of little comfort in the middle of the night.

To me the real test of living alone with ourselves is how we do in the middle of the night. If we can solve that problem and get that handled and answered, then we have got the answers to those smaller problems in life like when you show up for the dental appointment and the dentist says that it will be six hours before he can see you. You don't dare leave because it might only be ten minutes. You haven't got any place to go so you just sit there.

Or maybe you are just semidepressed, having a bad day or struck by that sense of your own aloneness. And no matter how close you are with the people around you, there is no way that they can ever get inside your skin. One of my students said, "Jess, it seems like we are doomed to spend our life in our iron shells, tapping in a crude core to one another." That is one rather negative way to look at the limitations of human communication. But that *is* our dilemma. What are we going to do about it?

I see that we have just two choices. First, we can try to escape from life in some way: business, sports, alcohol, drugs, power, interfering in other people's lives and calling it helping. These are the most common escapes from life. Pretty soon we use the escape so much we are addicted to it. Then we have another problem: our addiction. But finally reality has a way of breaking through and letting us see how unreal our escape is.

I was addicted to business and making money so I could impress others. My life became more and more wrapped up in my work. It became my god and was the first priority in my life. All other aspects of my life including my wife and children were subordinated to my work and the opinion of some nebulous "others." To watch me, you would have thought the whole world depended on the way I worked.

Even before I had my heart attack I began to see the futility of what I was doing. I started to want to live instead of escape. I wanted my work to be a means to an end instead of an end in itself. But it took the shock of my heart attack to clear the blinders from my eyes. Then I could see my escape was destroying my life and I decided to find out what I believed in. I wanted to find what kind of life was right for me. As soon as I asked myself what I believed in, I found I didn't know. So I had to go looking for something without knowing what

I was looking for ahead of time, only hoping that when I found it I would know it.

So I had to live without the clear direction my escape seemed to give me. And I had to live without all the confusion and activity my escape provided me. It was like being lifted out of a circus and set on a desert island. It got real quiet quick. But I had to live with that quiet and avoid escaping again. The living alone with myself was the hardest at first. Each day it got easier as I got over the withdrawal of having the excitement and confusion of my escape out of my life. I offset part of this by going back to school and doing some things outdoors. But those were milder escapes and they didn't become addictions.

All this time I was slowly learning to reach outside myself for help in finding out who I was and what I believed in. It took me a long time before I was able to have a good relationship with a person—to get an intimate friend I could trust. But fumbling as my early attempts were and poor as the relationships were, they were much better than what I had before. What I had before was false so it gave me nothing. Any honest attempt gave me something. So feeble as my beginnings were, they were a start. But all that time, I had to live a good part of my life alone with myself. And the hardest times to handle were in the middle of the night when I would wake up with some problem eating at me.

I was talking to my friend Vince the other night. What Vince does when he wakes up in the middle of the night is he says to himself, "Hey, this is great. I've got some time for meditation. I can meditate on the truth. I can reflect over my day or the events of the past, and think and meditate upon the truth. Why didn't the situation I was in work the way I thought it should? Or, how should I have handled some certain problem?" I can give you a really good example.

My son and I loaded the trash barrels into our horse trailer and headed for the city dump. We were driving across the East Gallatin River on the road to the dump at ten minutes before 6 P.M. One of the men from the dump flagged us down and said, "The dump's closed."

I said, "Isn't it supposed to be open until six o'clock?"

"No! A quarter to six it closes."

I said, "I thought it was supposed to be six o'clock."

"Well," he said, "it is just two minutes to six anyway."

I said, "No my clock says ten minutes to six and it is always right. I've got an Acutron. It is always within thirty seconds of the exact time."

"No. My clock says two minutes to six."

And I said, "Do you want to bet?"

And he says, "Well, it doesn't make any difference because by the time you get up there it would be two minutes to and it would be time to close anyway."

So I said, "Okay."

He went on his way and I turned my trailer around. One of my sons was with me who has a personality very much like mine, feisty and mean as hell. He said, "Dad we should have got him."

I said, "Turn the radio on, Mike, we're going to find out what time it is." The "Call-in Show" was on.

Mike said, "That doesn't end until six o'clock, Dad."

And I said, "I know." And I could see that there was quite a bit of time left on "Call-in." So we started back towards home and I said, "Mike, I'm going to get him. City Manager Fryslie and Mayor Sedivy are people I know. We're going to put a complaint in on that man."

We went back up the canyon. When I got home my wife was mad about what happened. She said, "Why don't you call Harold Fryslie right now?" I wasn't going to disturb him at home. But then I thought, "I will dial Harold." The phone rang once and I hung up. I said to myself, "No way. This is dumb. I will go back to the supper table and wait until morning like I should." That evening as I was driving into town to my class I could see my cool was part blown. I told them of the incident and the thought came to my mind, "How would Vince handle this?" Now this is meditating upon the truth. How would Vince handle this problem? The answer is simple. "There is another day and another time. Forget it." Many times I have left my work early the same way he was doing. If I had unloaded my stuff I would have held the man up well after six. I really had nothing to be mad about. So there is another day and another time. Forget it! But how can you forget it when your guts are boiling like Old Faithful Geyser? And the answer is, you forget it. That is meditating upon the truth of your life and right principles so you make a wise decision. You see, I hadn't done anything yet. After I had a chance to think about it, I realized I wasn't going to do anything. The next day when I went back to that garbage dump I saw that man and I just smiled and said, "Hello." And I silently told myself, "I hope he is as happy right now as I someday hope to be."

That's one of my biggest problems. I see somebody else do something that in my great judgmental role of being God I find distasteful. What they are doing seems to me to be going against the laws of life as I see them. So I have found that simple sentence is one I can say to myself that is better than anything I've ever heard before. I have found myself using it a lot since I came across it: "I hope that other person is as happy right now as I someday hope to be!" I hope the very best things happen to that person instead of hoping that the worst things happen to them.

"How can you be honest and say that?" one of my students asked. She said, "I would have wanted to dump the garbage on him." One of my other kids said, "I would have dumped that garbage right at the entrance to the dump."

I said, "Then we make the problem worse. And they've got the police after us. So we have created additional trouble."

I find what is so important to see is that all of us have our bad times. When we catch someone at their bad time or doing something they know they shouldn't they are going to react poorly just like I do when that happens to me. So if we wait for some other later time, there always will be an improvement.

That waiting is part of Vince's answer on how to end depression. I used to have depressions that would last a week. They would paralyze me. I had advertising deadlines facing me where I had to act but I couldn't. I would just sit at my desk cleaning out my desk drawer. Or I would wander around downtown supposedly doing something but actually just terrorized by what would happen if I didn't act. I made lists of what I had to do that day. But I couldn't do the first thing on the list. That went on for day after day. I couldn't figure out what was wrong with me.

I can see now what was wrong. I was working at something that I was deathly afraid of but I didn't even know it. I knew I was a good advertising man yet I was still afraid of advertising. I spent five years being afraid all my clients would leave me. Logically I knew my work was good but my emotions didn't understand logic! Feelings aren't facts. Feelings don't have heads. They were frightened. The problem was made worse because of my blindness and being always so overtired from my anxiety.

What's interesting is I still do the advertising for one of those accounts. The president is a good friend. Some of my other clients were good friends, too, but this man makes it so easy to do good work for him. And I love to write advertising about hybrid corn. So I see myself enjoying this one little part of advertising and doing very well at it. But with all the experience I've had, I know that if I went back to those other accounts, I would still be frightened. If I had to do that work or starve, I think I could manage to handle my fear now, but it would still be hard.

The writing and teaching I do frightens lots of people, especially the way I go at it with no regard for any of the conventions and accepted ways of doing things. But I can take some lonesome position way in center field all alone and not be bothered by it a bit. The feeling I have is "So what if other people don't see it this way. I do and I'll act on my belief." Looking at it objectively it would seem that logically my advertising recommendations would be much easier to defend because I had years of good training at the best of agencies. But I think logic isn't the answer. Writing and teaching are right for me so I feel confident in them. Advertising wasn't right for me despite the fact I was good at it.

These are the things that are happening in our minds as we struggle with ourselves and self-knowledge. The long depressions I used to have are almost completely gone now. I'll get a small, short one once in a while, but Vince tells me how to deal with them. He says we should measure our depression by saying to it, "How long are you going to stay?" And then Vince says, "I stand pat." He says, "Things are always changing." That depression has to end sometime, that's what he means by measuring it. So the pressure is going to go away because things are always changing. When we know things are changing, we know our depression has to get better, at least a little bit. This is meditation on the truth so we have wisdom.

What wisdom means is making wise decisions. Now this has nothing to do with intellect. There are a lot of people with a lot of intellect who have no wisdom. Like Vince said, "I had only a sixth grade education. But that was all I needed. If I would have needed more, I would have got more." But here he was quoting parts of the Bible by chapter, and Gibbon's *Decline and Fall of the Roman Empire* and various philosophers. So he isn't just a sixth grade educated person. That is where his formal schooling stopped, but he has learned a lot since then. He is concerned about having wisdom so he can make wise decisions. And, of course, that comes from meditating on the truth.

When we meditate on the truth, we get an idea and we try it out against life to see if it works. If it does, we've got something that we have proven for ourselves. A lot of people tell you how things will work according to someone's theory. But I've seen the evidence that most psychological theory is based on and I'm not impressed. Most theories I've seen in psychology aren't soundly based. So I'm uninterested in most theory. What I want to know is what did you do and how did it work for you?

One of my students said, "I have such a vivid memory of the bad things that happen, each one of them. Even though you wait and you meditate on it, it takes a certain toll out of you every time you do it."

Yes. It is hard to meditate on the reality of your life.

But if you measure your progress, you can see that each time you get better at handling problems. As I work on these ideas, five years from now my hope is that when I run into a man who closes the garbage dump early and says, "We are closed for the day," I can smile and say, "Okay, I'll see you tomorrow. I should have been here a lot earlier than this anyway." Or, even better, I'll see that I'm crowding time by going so late and I'll stay home and go the next day.

"That could be called being a coward, too."

Or being intelligent. Or, let's put it this way, I'll call it anything you want to call it, but I love it. If two people get two shots at me a week versus ten, I love it. Because that means that I've got only two to handle instead of ten. And out of two of them I've got a chance of handling maybe one of the two halfway intelligently.

Why? The worst thing in the world we can do is ask why. Because we are never going to know why. Asking just puts us down and makes it worse. The best thing in the world to do is accept it. Everything changes. That wheel is going round and round. The merry-go-round goes round and round. If we miss the dapple gray horse all we do, instead of crying, is just stand there and wait, then pick up the dapple gray on the next time around. Everything changes.

A lady was telling me how hard it was for her to be stranded for a day in a blizzard. This is where Vince would say, "Well great, I have a chance to meditate." How often have we said, "I wish I could have sixteen hours just to myself." Vince said, "I can sit in a place and maybe for an hour or two I will just turn my mind off, make it blank." I asked him, "What is the point of that, Vince?" He said, "Oh, nothing, but when you can do it, that shows that you have enough control over your mind

that your confusion and scattering of thoughts is pretty
well gone." What he is talking about is a lot like the
Eastern people talk about in transcendental meditation.
Vince just turns his mind off for a while. He will do whatever he wants to do. So he is not at the mercy of the
world. Nothing can happen to him. This is what serenity
means.

Now the fact that a man in our town has achieved this
is really striking to me. Sure it is striking to me that some
men in the Bible were able to meditate like this and
achieve the serenity he talks about. And it is interesting
that some of the great figures that we know of were able
to do these things. But to me it is hopeful that a person
living in this town can. And even more crucial, he can tell
me how he was able to do it. So this is the extreme of
serenity and peace and the abundant life when you can
live alone in the dark times of the day or in the night
serenely and happily.

When we are living with ourselves, what is it that guides
us? Here is where the Indian story of the spiritual quest
comes in. I believe that central and primary task for each
of us is to make our spiritual quest. No other person
can make this quest for us. No other person can even be
a reliable guide. All another person can tell us of is their
own story and the principles they see as important in any
spiritual quest.

While it is very hard to talk about what goes on inside
ourselves, I see two voices inside me. One voice is the
voice of self-will and egotism. This was the voice I had
followed. I wanted to go into advertising and make a lot
of money so I could show people I was something big.
I wanted to be an advertising agency account executive
because I presented a good appearance, loved to talk and
be in center stage. I wanted a big office, a big house, a

fancy car so people would see I was something. That was my voice of self-will—the big I.

My other voice was a deep inner voice that's hard to name. The real me is one name for it that is accurate but I don't like the words "being real." They have been badly abused, partly by me. But it's probably still one of the best words to describe what's really me, the deep me the true me that when I'm living that part of me, I'm in harmony with life. It's me. And at first it's a very little me because it's a voice that's been listened to so little.

The spiritual quest, as I've seen it, is learning to hear the deep inner voice and saying no to the self-will. This means facing life directly instead of using some kind of money, power or glory ego scene as an escape. This is our life's work and we get closer as we go along. Each of us has been given different resources to work with. As I see it, all we are accountable for is what use we made of the resources we were given. I can't judge another's spiritual quest. Considering what they were given, they may be making much better use of their resources by just staying alive than I'm doing with what I was given. And I see now I was given a great deal.

My only task is to take what I was given and do with it what I can. When I first started this spiritual quest, I tried to do it myself. Then I found I couldn't do it myself. I needed some power outside myself—the warmth of a mutual relationship where we could truly communicate with each other because we saw our mutual need for each other.

When I gave up on being able to make my spiritual quest without any help outside myself, I surrendered. I surrendered to my need for some other people to help me. And I had to give up on my self-will as a guide and go to that deep inner voice inside. That voice of the deep me doesn't tell me what I should do to please others or what I ought to do to make myself look big. It tells me what to do that's right for me.

I find that my deep inner voice tells me to do things that put me in harmony with the universe, so what's right for me in the long run usually works out to the benefit of the other people around me.

In medieval times, the astronomers figured the earth was all important so the sun must revolve around the earth. But with that false belief, there were all kinds of things in this astronomy that didn't fit their system. When the radical notion that the earth revolved around the sun was introduced, it was scored as against God's will. But it sure cleared up a lot of questions the old astronomy couldn't explain. And it wasn't against God's will, it was just against the egotistic twist men had given to their interpretation of God's will.

I see life the same way. Before, I had myself as the center of the universe. I looked on the world in complete immaturity. Why wouldn't it give me just what I wanted? Nothing much suited me. As I said earlier, I wanted the sun to shine all the time. I only wanted it to rain when I got tired of sunshine. That might have been a nice world for me for a while but I would have killed all the crops.

The way I saw it, the center of the whole world was my own navel. And, of course, nothing worked.

Now I've seen that none of us is the center of the world. The world turns in complete harmony. The only question is, will I work on my spiritual quest and learn to live in harmony with that world and its universal principles or not?

Imagine that you and I came here from another planet

and we were taught to operate an automobile but we
weren't taught any of the traffic laws. Imagine the trouble
we would have. Think what chaos there would be for us.
But look what would happen if someone told us just one
thing: All those other drivers are following a set of rules.
Knowing just that, it wouldn't take us long to figure out
what the rules were. And we could do pretty well.

But now, imagine being told one more thing: All
drivers, including ourselves, have grave emotional problems which most of them control very well most of the
time, but some can't control well at all. So when one
of the driver's grave emotional problems is showing they
forget about their driving and could kill us. Knowing
that, all we need to do is drive defensively. We can have
a beautiful time driving as long as we keep a weather
eye peeled for the person who might accidentally kill us
and our family.

In the hands of a good defensive driver, an automobile
is a thing of joy and beauty. Good defensive drivers have
put on a million miles of driving without an accident.
Some of us can't drive across town without rumpling a
fender.

We can carry defensiveness too far. We can be so
defensive because of the seeming chaos in the world that
we refuse to drive. This is the person who gets hurt in an
early attempt to love and vows never to risk loving
again so they won't get hurt. To avoid hurt, they guarantee the biggest hurt there is which is complete loneliness.

If we are going to make our spiritual quest we have
to go out into life and take our lumps as we learn to live
in harmony with life. And we need to see that everyone
else is doing the best they can on their own spiritual
quests. I know it sure doesn't look like it. I spend so
much time yelling and screaming at other people for

not doing what they should. And they are often yelling
and screaming at me for not doing what I should. How
much better it would be if each of us minded our own
business, our own spiritual quest.

I have found another thing that is like the spiritual
quest of the Indian. As a proceed on my spiritual quest
I go along looking for clues and trying to follow my inner
voice. All of a sudden, I find that some part of my
personality has changed. I spent twenty-five years as a
salesman, advertising man and teacher trying to be a
person my students would like. All of a sudden, one
year ago, I walked into my classroom and realized I didn't
need to do that any more. I was going to be me and let
the chips fall where they may. Some of my students who
had been in some other classes of mine before thought I
was a better teacher now for my change. I know it sure
made teaching less painful and troublesome.

I was stingy with spending money for my wife and
children. I would buy them big things like skis, horses
or motorcycles. But I wouldn't give them fifty cents. All
of a sudden, about a year and a half ago, that changed
and I started handing out the spending money without
begrudging it.

So I have seen that by surrendering to the harmony
of life, life can go along more smoothly and I can be
given some qualities on the medicine wheel that I was
not given originally. These changes in personality I see
as spiritual experiences or spiritual awakenings. They are
so exciting to me because I had always thought the best
I could hope for in life was to get through life with what
I had. I now see that some of my personality problems
can be removed from me when I'm ready to give them up
and don't need the sick games they produce any more.

These ideas I have just mentioned are very different

than anything I used to believe in. They are hard to explain partly because I don't see and understand them that clearly yet myself. But what they add up to for me is that I'm not in charge of the universe. I'm not God. I'm not running things. "Jess, you ain't the doctor." That's what Vince said to me as a caution to work on my spiritual quest and stop trying to run other people's spiritual quests for them.

I have to say something to those of you who are by now screaming at me for not using Christian terminology and a Christian framework for what I'm talking about. I'm using the American Indian perspective on the higher power for a very definite reason. Christian words are loaded with emotion and associations that are often very hurtful to me and many of my students. I find almost all my students are spiritually hungry. As long as I stay away from too much God-talk or religious language, my students are happy to talk about spiritual things all day long.

Some people are offended by my refusal to use God-talk. One of my students asked me if I was a Christian. I told him, "No, but I'm working on it." In my understanding, a Christian is a person who, when you look at them, you can see Christ in their lives. I have seen people I felt were Christ-like Christians, but that's nothing I want to claim for myself. If someone else wants to claim it for me and say they think I'm a Christian, I'll thank them for the compliment.

But this student felt I was wrong by not saying I was a Christian. He wrote me a note saying he wanted me to say it to the class. I thought later that if it was such a good thing to say and so important, why didn't he say it?

The whole point of this discussion is that if my navel isn't going to be the center of my world, then what is?

I have seen that the minute you and I get the center of
the earth outside ourselves into something else, things
go better. Our center or God can be a belief in one
other person, a small group, nature, order in the universe,
whatever is your understanding of God. Your understanding of God can work for you. The God that people
have waved in your face to frighten you and coerce you
can't work in your life.

Once we get the center of the universe outside ourself we can start to live in some harmony with life. And
once we start to find a God of our understanding, we
have a higher power that can be of some aid to us in
guiding our spiritual quest. Once we get our heads out
of our navels, we can see life so much more clearly.

So this is the heart of learning to live with ourselves.
Lombardi said his priorities were: 1. his God, 2. his
family and 3. the Green Bay Packers. Where did Lombardi fit in there? In Lombardi's case it was more obvious
that he fitted in with God. But it's true in our cases, too.
Until we find a God of our understanding and find our
relationship to that God, I don't think we can be any
good to our families or to the rest of life.

I've never seen a person who didn't have a God. What
our main priority is, that's our God or gods. My old
main priorities or gods were money and my recreations.
Nothing could interfere with my job or opening day of
hunting and fishing season. I thought any man who was
home with a sick kid on an opening day was stupid,
hen-pecked or a poor manager.

When your God is like mine, money or the opening
day of hunting season, that's a very limited God that
won't do much for you in your life. The God of my
present understanding has a lot of power and brings about
a lot of good things in my life. But some of the things in

my life are still so important that I feel I can't leave them in God's hands. I have to handle them. I just know that if I don't handle them, they won't be handled right. So I haven't given up complete control. I know how foolish it is not to give up control but I'm still working on surrendering control and I will be working on it for the rest of my life.

As I go through my day, my most common problem with myself is to know which voice I'm listening to. Is it the voice of self-will which tries to build up myself? The big I? Or, is it the deep, inner voice that's trying to make its spiritual quest? The inner me? One way I've found to tell the difference between the two is in their results. If the particular action that results gives me peace and comfort, then it's the deep inner voice talking. If the action results later in pain and sorrow for me and others then the voice was probably self-will.

If an action brings me more in harmony with the world, then I experience the fruits of that harmony. If an action is self-willed and self-centered then that takes me out of harmony with the world and I experience the disharmony that results.

When I speak of living in harmony with the world, I know that many people think that's bad. They think the world's a terrible place and they want nothing to do with it. I think the world is a beautiful place. It is only my lack of understanding that keeps me from seeing all its beauty.

Some person, in his own fumbling attempts to work out his spiritual quest, may be harming a child. I know of a nun who broke a pointer over an eight-year-old girl's back because she stepped out of line to get a drink of water. How was that beautiful? If what she was doing was a mistake, she was simply using her precious right to be wrong. Or, she might be making very good use of her very limited resources. Nothing I can do can make that nun be different or make the little girl not hurt from that. "Jess, you ain't the doctor." All I can do is what I can do. Which is to make that today with that little girl be as good as I can make it. If I'm distracted from today by the memory of that yesterday then I make the yesterday happen again in some new way because of my momentary blindness to life and that little girl.

Life is the ceremony. I used to think religion was the ceremony and life the problem. I now see that life is the ceremony and religion is often the problem.

When one of my brothers and I come together in our mutual need for each other, God as I understand Him can't help but be present. When I turn away from my brother saying I don't need anything in this world, I think I'm in trouble. That way it's like I'm sitting in my room watching an evangelist on television with the door locked to keep all those noisy people from interfering with my piousness.

Some people criticize the mutual need idea because they don't think there is enough service to others in it. I can't see that. "How can I be of service to another and at the same time say I don't need you?" You need me but I don't need you. I am the giver and you are the receiver. I don't want to give things that way and I don't want to receive anything in that spirit.

6

communicating
our whole hearts

Before we go into more depth on building better mutual relationships, we need to look at our communication. I used to think communication was my words. I now see that my communication is everything about me: my clothes, my facial expressions, body movements, touching. All are part of my communication with the world around me. My words, which I used to think were the biggest part of my communication, I now see are just a small part of what I communicate in a situation. We need to step back and take a complete and total look at what we communicate.

Most of us argue that we are misunderstood or that our communication is faulty. I have come to see that as a terrible self-justification—a big lie. I find I communicate perfectly. I just won't accept the communication I'm sending. I want to argue, "How could such a nice guy like me ever send a bad message?" But I'm doing it all the time. One of the biggest problems is my words seem so innocent. But my tone of voice, my expressions and my body are sending an altogether different message.

I have come to see that we are beautiful communicators. All we need to do is honestly face what we are communicating and that tells us what we are in that situation. Once we face reality we can do something about changing what we are—and by changing what we are we will change what we communicate.

Body language is hard to figure out for that reason. Body language is so complicated that I don't think we can send signals on purpose. The only way I think we can send body language is from the inside out. We've got to feel the emotions. Only then will our body be able to begin to find ways to telegraph the new emotions we feel. But one of the problems is we are so inhibited. I told my class that I suspected many of them thought they were sitting there pretty joyful most of the time and interested and concentrating. But there were a lot of times I looked around and saw faces that looked awful sad to me. Now I'm sure many of my students would say, "Hey, my face isn't sad." I wanted to say to them, "Are your hearts happy? If they are, please notify your faces." That's true to a degree. But if our worried face is grooved so deep in us, it's hard to change that face even if we do feel good inside. We can't just paste on our Brownie smile. So one of the ways to telegraph something really accurately is to have the feeling very big. The bigger the feeling, the more you telegraph. In my experience, when you are first working on this, you don't telegraph a very high percentage of what you feel. It takes a long time to get more expressive and more out of your box.

Here is where our language comes in and is so important. Listen to what happens now as I switch language on you: The existential and humanistic psychology which is presently under discussion can have important consequences in producing a more adaptive and fulfilling lifestyle. The nature of the phenomena that we are trying to observe is that of human interactions and human interrelationships. Many psychologists have studied these phenomena and proper credit should be given to the appropriate researchers.

Look what happened. The minute I got overly conscious of my language, the minute I started speaking in very careful sentences my communication went to hell. I didn't understand how crucial this was when I said my first book to the nurses five years ago. I told them, "Get rid of your fear of the language. Free yourself from those restrictions that the English teachers of the world and the social strictures have put on you. Get rid of them." When I came to write my book off the tapes, I couldn't see how that made any sense in terms of self-acceptance. So I left it out of the first version of *I Ain't Much*. . . . It wasn't until I revised *I Ain't Much* . . . two years later that I saw language did have a vital place in our lives because it is part of our expressiveness. "How in the hell can we communicate ourselves to another person if we are so inhibited that we won't let our face show it, we won't let our language show it, we won't let our body show it?" It seems to me that in expressing something to somebody else, those three things are very important. One gal student wanted to drop my class. I said, "Fine." It was about the first week of the course and I encourage people to drop out of class if it isn't right for them. She said, "You're a doctor, aren't you?" I said, "Yes." She said, "Well, could you tell me why you speak so poorly? I'm going to be a fifth grade teacher. If I spoke like you it would be a terrible influence on my children." I said, "Honey, don't you worry. With that stilted language of yours there ain't nobody going to pay any attention to you."

I told her the story about Mark Twain. Mark Twain used a lot of profanity in his speeches. This embarrassed his wife a lot. One night they were getting ready to go out for a speech. As she was tying his tie she uttered a long string of profanity at him. He just looked at her and said, "Livy, you've got the words, but you ain't got the music."

You see, when we are trying to speak correctly and there ain't no such thing, our language gets stiff and artificial—we lose the music. The English teachers are trying to pull a fast one on us. There is no such thing as correctness of language. There are simply things that different people say and do. Churchill hated the rule that he shouldn't end sentences with prepositions. All of our great speakers did some things that people don't regard as grammatically correct. Like Will Rogers. He said, "A lot of people who ain't saying 'ain't,' ain't eating."

Language is a living thing. You never think of holding up a mouse and saying, "Is this a correct mouse?" That mouse might have a much more pointed nose than many mice. It might have a tail that is a centimeter longer than the average mouse tail, but you don't say, "Is it a correct mouse?" It is a mouse. Every word in the English language is there for a purpose. It is there because it means something to a number of other users of the language. When you and I come to use a word, we don't come to use that word until we know that there has been some degree of mutual use of that word. We know it is reasonably appropriate in that situation.

This is why new words work themselves into the

language. The Russians, for example, have no words that are the counterparts of Mr. and Mrs. They have comrade, which sounds too political. They have another word which is too formal sounding for familiar usage that was used by the nobility in the time of the Czars. They don't have those words so their language is in trouble. Because of their political upheaval, they had to throw out that old formal form of address and they haven't replaced it yet. So their language will have to change to find new words.

The English teacher constantly wants to roll our language back to thirty, forty or fifty years ago. She is going to decide just exactly how far back we all go depending on her age. Furthermore, she is going to decide which of the different usages of that period she likes.

For example, we used to say, "We went clean through town." Educated people North and South said, "We went clean through town," instead of "clear." Now, in the North, we have switched away from that and we say, "We went clear through town." In the South, though, people still use "We went clean through town" and don't think of it as an uneducated usage, where in the North it stamps you as an uneducated person. If we are going to roll our language back fifty or so years, then we've got to roll it all back. We've all got to go back to saying "She went clean through town." "Well," our English teacher says, "I don't want that usage. I want to use the more recent version of that. I don't want to go back to the old usage. It isn't refined enough to suit my ear."

So what you find is, she wants to be a dictator of our language. She wants to fix our language at some particular time and then she is going to be the judge. We can't do anything unless we call her up on the telephone and say, "Hey, do I have this expression or that expression just the way you want it?"

Meanwhile, our linguists like Arthur Sledd and Bergen Evans, the top mucky-mucks in the language, say that what she is doing is crazy. That doesn't bother our old English teacher. She refuses to listen to the authorities of the language. She wants to be the arbitrator of language because she wants to use language like they do in England as an instrument for achieving social status at the expense of somebody else. She wants a situation like in *My Fair Lady*. We can use our language like that to achieve social status. But the minute I start using my language to raise myself up socially, look what I tell you. I tell you of my hate of what I am and my fear of you. But the English teacher doesn't understand that. She doesn't see that her own need to climb up a step on the social ladder is the reason she is distorting the language.

She justifies herself by saying someone needs to stand for virtue and truth. The poor thing doesn't know enough about language to realize her beloved Shakespeare was one of the biggest inventors, borrowers and changers of words our language has ever known. He had no respect for the established order. All he had was one of the best ears of all time for the music of our language. He did things with our language that had never been done before. Yet our English teacher thinks she is being true to the spirit of Shakespeare by protecting the language. She's wrong. She's violating part of the spirit of Shakespeare that led to his power.

Our English teachers aren't the only ones using language to improve their social status. A lot of us who sit in those English classes bought the same deal she did. We wanted to rise a step in the social ladder, too. So we wanted to learn to speak English. Mark Twain argued that we speak American, not English, so the classes should be called American.

Our linguists agree that we must not use our language to achieve social status. When we try to use our language to achieve social status, we freeze it into classes as it is so much in England. If you talk an Oxford dialect, it makes a difference for the whole rest of your life in the amount of money you can make and in the social circles you can travel in. My language isn't that way. If I cave in to artificial language strictures, then my talk shows it. What sense does it make when I'm trying to communicate my heart to you for me to speak in an artificial and stilted language? When I am drowning, I must yell, "Help." I don't want to say, "Will you please come to my assistance?" What a poor way that is to yell, "Help. I need you. Come into my heart. I ache for you." Our expressiveness has to come out of the inside. I can't adapt this style of mine as a mannerism. I can't say, "Well, this is really great. From now on I'm going to speak the language any way that I want." I've got to feel something. The more I feel something, the more that feeling will bring forth the words to communicate itself. The deeper I feel, the more my body and facial expressions will reflect that also. Sure I'll make a few mistakes in my communicating. But once I start using the language like it really is I can start improving.

You've walked down the street and seen people whose faces are etched permanently into sadness. If they laughed their whole faces would crack and fall on the sidewalk. That's what happens when you suppress your feelings so much that all you show is that pickle face. It gets etched into all the muscles in your face. If you really want to wear a pickle face, fine.

How does a pickle face get etched in? Simple. Your

mouth is going down at the corners much more than it is going at the corners. It is a simple probability. The percentage of the time that your mouth spends going down at the corners versus up will determine whether you have a pickle face or not. Now if you try to paste on your Brownie smile in the morning it doesn't work. You can be aware of needing to smile 2 per cent of the time or 5 per cent of the time, but you aren't going to be smiling very much of the time unless that smile starts deep inside you someplace and just bubbles out.

You respond to body language intuitively in the same way. I went up to Missoula to speak to the counselors. We were going to sit at a big solid table with the chairs around the outside. I looked at that setup and said, "No, I don't want to do that." So we pushed the table over to the side and took the chairs and sat them around in an open circle. Why? Because it removed the barrier of the table. But more important, I could see their whole bodies. All the different positions of my body tell something. Without tables in the way, my intuition can read each person's clothes and body movements.

How do we react to that? Intuitively. I can't tell you just exactly what combination of hand, leg and facial expressions say a certain thing. But I can look around the room and just let my computer tell me what's happening. Like the kids put it, I am getting good vibes or I am getting bad vibes from this person or that person. That is what they are talking about. They are reading the body language primarily, but partly the words and the tone of voice. So this is the advantage of the teaching in the open circles, or circling up the chairs. I haven't talked to an audience in rows but one time in the past year. That was over in Dillon where there were fixed chairs and they couldn't be moved. Now in that case, I sat up on top of the lab table at the front of the room, which gets some informality in there that I couldn't have gotten if I had been standing behind the table.

The thing I hate is rules for reading body language. It's not that simple. What I see about people that is so interesting to me is their dynamic nature. I'm trying to look at their total response. I have seen people who have sat quite still but their faces and eyes said to me they were hanging on every word. The deeper I get into something, the quieter my room is. When I'm really deep into something, you can hear a pin fall. In a church, when the minister gets boring you start to cough. But boy, when he is on something that is really deep, there isn't a sound.

"Wouldn't the problems we have with our body language and touching other people be cured if people could just be themselves?"

That sounds good, but I see the problem as the exact opposite. The problem is they are being themselves. They just don't like to admit to the self that they're being. I'm not trying to be natural any more than a ballet dancer is trying to be natural. What we're talking about isn't natural for us and never was. If we work on it long enough and well enough, it can start to seem natural. But that deep finding and being ourselves, as I see it, is the whole point of our life. We will all be searching for that until the day that we die. If the rest of the people in this world don't want to touch anybody else, fine. Let them not touch anybody else. But I'm going to touch anybody where I feel it's appropriate and when I feel like it. If I want to stand and talk to somebody and hold their hand or put my arm around them, I'll do it.

I don't think what we are right now is our real self. I think our present self that shows is all the walls and defenses we have built up through the years. The real self is usually buried so deep you won't see it but briefly and only in the most relaxed environment. I think our present self is a self that is like a little child caught in a war. It ran and hid in a deep hole too much. I think we are going to have to do some things mechanically like smile or reach out and touch people mechanically for a while before it gets more natural. To some extent I am always going to be mechanical. Say 10 per cent of my touching in a day is mechanical touching where I am stretching out the frontiers of my touching to be more expressive. There is 10 per cent of my language that is going to be forced and consequently is going to be inappropriate in some degree. I have said some words that have troubled some of my readers, I know that. But most of you are nice enough not to hold that against me.

Only by trying things can I find out if they fit me. Some of the stuff I try I find is comfortable and fits me so it stays and eventually becomes comfortable and natural. The stuff I try that doesn't seem to be me I put aside. I don't think I will ever change if we wait for some new way of talking or touching to be perfectly natural before we do it.

I'm moving away from my present self which I don't regard as me. That has been my rather maladaptive response to a bunch of pressures. I'm moving towards that self that I see deep within me. I will never get there. But I'm working on it. As I watch myself today I see how a rather maladaptive present self reacts to the world. I would guess that my real self is a quieter person. I don't like to have someone tell me what my real self should be. And I don't like it when someone tells me in a harsh way what I have to do to get to my real self. I want to find my own way, you know. "Mother, I can do it myself!"

"This is a continual process, then, and we just never

reach the end?" That's right. You never reach it—but you do get closer.

One of the teachers in my class was a woman my age who had been in a class of mine when she was taking her teacher's training. She said, "I know that when we were talking about coming to this class, I was telling another teacher that I didn't know whether I wanted to or not. The class I had from you five years ago was such an emotionally involved thing that I didn't know if I could go through it again. But I thought of your words so many times and they have helped me so much—'You either grow or die.' I have been hit in the face with several things since the last class and those words will come back to me: 'I'm either going to grow or I'm going to die.' So I've got to learn these things. Sometimes you are forced to learn them. So I thought another tour of the class would help me some more!"

I'm involved in the same process. I didn't teach that class or write this book to solve your problems, I'm doing it for me. I know I occasionally shout at you as if I want to lead you out of the darkness into the light. But if you pin me right down and you say, "Jess, what's your proposition?" I will retreat and settle on my essential proposition which I believe in so much. That is I am teaching and writing to help myself discover more about who and what I am. I am asking for your help and thanking you for the assistance you have already given me in that quest. If you want to say to me, "Jess, what about me and the way I am?" I will say, "Since you've done so many things along the way to help me get to where I want to go, I can do nothing but just thank you for being what you are." And if you want to tell me, "Jess, I want to change, I want to be different, I want to be better," then I would say what I would say to Sullivan. That is: "Okay, you can change some things if you want to but for God's sake don't change too much, because you might lose some of the very precious things that make you what you are." Rather than say, "Oh boy, you better get in gear and really change fast." If you really pinned me right to the wall on how you should change, I would go the opposite way and say, "Your charm is the way you are. If you want to change something that really pleases you, fine. I hope it's for the best, but please go careful so that you don't lose the you we know and love."

I used to think we started out in good shape and got screwed up. If we were in good shape at some time, then we would have something to return to. But I don't see that we ever really had these things. Sure children touch one another and they seem honest. But their so-called naturalness won't stand up to the troubles of any imperfect society.

It's just like dancing. Yes, kids have some natural rhythm and grace of movement. But no kid will turn into a ballet dancer naturally. It will take years of very unnatural movement.

As I mentioned in the first chapter, the American Indians of the Plains felt we were all born equal in one respect—our loneliness. Each of us had certain strong qualities. But our quest in life is to complete the circle of the medicine wheel and strengthen ourselves in the four great qualities of Wisdom, Introspection, Illumination and Innocence. In Innocence is touching. We can't make contact with the world without touching.

This is where I see we are in such deep trouble when we suffer from "Don't touch me." An awful lot of women have this and a great many men. I must respect the wishes of the person who doesn't want me to touch them. So I just find someone else to touch who wants me to touch them.

So touching is not just fun. It is not just sensual. It is not just communication. It is a crucial need we have and a means of contacting the world. Without touching we die, spiritually and physically.

My friend Vince tells of being counseled by former winos like himself just off skid row. He said, "Jess, they would sit on either side of me and hold onto my hands trying to reach me, to make me understand." That picture is one I'll never get out of my mind.

Sure some people in society will look at us funny if we do things like that. But let them. They don't understand that today is life or death for you and me. They think they are going to live forever. They think being "normal" is good. But that's their right. We have to do what we have to do to save our lives. That's our right.

We say we can't touch. What we mean is we won't. Our hand isn't tied down. We can lift our hand. We are strong enough. What we mean is we won't. We won't take the chance of making a mistake. We won't take the chance of a rebuff. And worst of all, if we are absolutely honest with ourselves, we won't let people get that close to us because we don't really want closeness. We say we want closeness but I'm convinced we don't really want it bad enough. If we did really want closeness we would have found some by now because it ain't that hard to find. It's like going through life saying you have been looking for gas stations and can't find any. There are still quite a few around.

So I now see touching as far more than optional. You and I can argue all we want that our families weren't touchers so we can't do it. It isn't inherited. And if this hung-up Norwegian can get pretty good at it in eleven years, then there is hope for everyone.

Yes, it is "normal" in America for friends meeting to touch each other only four times per hour. But what we're trying to get away from is what people call normal. Being normal is what nearly killed me with a heart attack. I want to get as far away from normal as I can.

Do you know what normal people are like? They are the people who go to doctors with half or two thirds of the pain in their heads. They are the people who need some drinks before they can have fun or dance. They are the people who are trying to find happiness in their cookie jar or refrigerator. They are the millions who contemplate suicide. They are the people who are lonely in the midst of their families. They are the people who in World War II urged patriotism on their sons and then cheated so much on the gas rationing that the government will probably never try a similar system again.

What it all adds up to is that being "normal" is the worst thing I can imagine. I'm trying to find what I am and be that. Whatever it is has to be worlds better than being normal.

Because of our human imperfections, we all come into a certain amount of neurosis. Some of us come into a lot of neurosis. But there is so much neurosis around and we have lived with neurosis so long, we think it's normal.

That's just fine for someone else, if they want it, but not for me any more. My last year seemed like it was ten years long, so many good things happened in it. Most of the good things started happening once I admitted how neurotic and crazy some of the things were I was doing. It wasn't until I saw I had a problem that I could do anything about it.

When I saw I was drowning in the ocean, I started

to holler for help. It took a while for me to realize that I wasn't hollering as loud as I could. So now I have taken off my restraints so I can really communicate my need to the people around me. One crucial part of that communication is touching. If you went through a day with me now, you would see me touching a lot. Not touching everyone. And not touching anyone the same way. But touching when it is appropriate and touching to the degree it is appropriate for me being what I am today. Often when I talk to people now I will hold their hand or have my hand on their shoulder or arm.

I told my class to start touching a lot more to find what their real level of touching was for them instead of the one they had inherited from the family they were raised in. It was like I had given them a license to steal. My students would touch each other very often when they met in their schools or on the streets. One teacher said she touched every person in the building in the course of the week. Another woman spoke of touching her own children. She said, "You know they don't think anything of it, but I love them so much more. I was really touching them and really thinking about it instead of just doing it mechanically."

A number of nurses have told me that they started touching people a lot and found it really calmed them down. They actually even needed less medication. The nurses touch them practically all the time they are in the room. They will have a hand on them someplace in some way. And they have gotten tremendous results from it—but always the biggest benefit comes to us.

All we have to do to find out who to touch and in what way is to pay attention and read the signals and gradually escalate the touching. You can tell the person who wants to be touched. You touch them and they will move

towards you. They will move into it. The people who
are really hungry for it will just literally cuddle under it.
Whereas the person that doesn't want to be touched will
squirm in a bad way and draw away. So more and more
I have found that just by looking at their faces and their
body positions I can tell whether it is appropriate to
touch them. And like I say, in the last six months I
haven't seen any sign that I have missed the boat. Sure,
once in a while you can misread some message and
touch somebody inappropriately.

And people have a way of telling you "Hey, that's
great. Keep on touching me, and touch me more."

What if you don't have any relationships where you
can do any touching? Then you better get to work on
your relationships.

One teacher had a problem with standing close. "You
told us to stand close to people. Well, today my principal
came up to me and I actually took two steps back,
because he got so close. After I did it, I thought, 'Oh,
I'm in Jess's class, I shouldn't have done that.'"

Supposedly in America you can't stand close to somebody else. But that's not true. In America you can, if you
have the guts. But, too, the thing that is so striking is
when you are with someone you really love you can't get
close enough. So it has nothing to do with our culture,
it has nothing to do with a lot of things. It has to do
with emotional closeness. Your inability to stand close to
some people tells you about your ability to handle emotional closeness with the particular person involved. And
this is why an assignment to touch people is so valuable.
It is like giving you a yard stick to use on all your
relationships. Because if you can't touch them, it makes
you think, "What kind of relationship have I got here?"
It doesn't mean you should be able to touch everybody

you have a good relationship with. But that is one way of looking at it.

We want our touching to come smoothly and easily, for it to be natural. Some of our touching can be this way. But if we are going to improve our ability in this crucial area of communication, we need to be willing to take our chances and risk some mistakes. We can't stretch our touching level without doing it mechanically for a while. Now it seems kind of strange. In the last paragraph of my book one of my students said, "It seems kind of strange to have to mechanically reach out and do something that should be so natural, but if I don't make myself do it, it will never happen." We have to go through that.

We can't limit our touching to the people who make it easy for us and expand our level of touching. We are going to have to reach out. We have to risk making some mistakes. You can't learn to ski without falling down.

Sure you should touch the easy ones as much as you can and more. Step it up there, but you can't get by on that alone.

"It is real hard for me to touch someone unless I feel real strongly about them," a young girl teacher said. "I may have no trouble with my husband and the people in my family. But to touch someone I don't know that well without feeling they are ready to touch me back, that's so hard for me."

That view of touching and opening ourselves up can hurt us badly. What you get from somebody else, you can give to your husband. What you get from your husband, you can give to somebody else. There is this kind of network, you see. And if you are too restricted you don't have the income coming into you from your other relationships to feed into your marriage. Actually you can strengthen your touching in your marriage by being able to touch outside of it. This is not just true of touching, but it is true of all expressions of affection. When your expressions of affection and communication are limited to too few people, you get way overdependent on them. I have had husbands and wives say about each other: "It is just like they have got their hooks into me." The overly dependent one communicates, "Don't go away from me, because you are the only person I can love." The more widely you can love in appropriate ways, the more loving your central relationships get. The more loving your central relationships get, the more widely you can love. So it is reciprocal, back and forth. This is why I think it is crucial for you to learn this.

Sure it is hard. But I am teaching you about just the hard things. This is the stuff I am working on, the hard stuff. It is like my old boss said: "If somebody asks you, can you swim a half mile, the best way to show them you can is you jump in and swim a mile." If we know we will have to swim a half mile and our life depends on it, then we better practice swimming a mile.

It communicates so much, doesn't it, touching? When we rob ourselves of it, as we have done so much in our country, we have cut ourselves off from a precious thing. On the radio there was a news story about two gals who conducted an experiment. Every time they met they touched each other and hugged each other and kissed each other. They did that for two months and they got terrible repercussions on their college campus. They got accused of being Lesbians and all kinds of stuff. It was an experiment they set up in a psychology class just to see what the consequences were. This shows you, again, we have entered into a mutual pact with each other throughout our whole society which says, "Don't you touch anybody, because if you do that shows that there is some kind of humanity between you and somebody else and I don't want to see that. And if you do that to me, I will call you a bad name."

We are getting just exactly the kind of society we want, which is a "don't touch me" society. The only way we can deal with this and not pay too fearful a consequence is to touch in settings where it is reasonably appropriate. We have to use some sense. If I'm a high school teacher, I'm not going to hug any girls, I will tell you that. No way. I will touch them on their shoulder, but I'm not going to put my arm around them. I am gutless, man, when it comes to taking chances that foolishly. I may be venturesome, but I'm not 100 per cent stupid.

We can get an awful lot of touching done in settings where we don't run too awful big a chance, where we don't pay too big a price if we're wrong. And particularly where there is mutuality.

I think what we call "primitive societies" are often much better at meeting the human needs. We call them primitive because they haven't got machinery and they aren't bookish intellectuals. But they have some things that make our machinery and bookishness look like poor bargains. We paid a high price for some of the material gains we made in our society. It is a higher price than I would personally have liked to have paid.

Many of my students see these natural direct qualities they are trying to recapture as being in their young students. I think what happens to a kid is he's got a lot of good instincts, but his techniques and methods are not strong enough to handle the onslaught that he gets. He isn't born strong enough for life. The hurts that he gets make him build a shell. While he does have some of these good, natural instincts, they aren't strong enough. His technique isn't strong enough to get him through except in the case of the individuals who have had a tremendous amount of love, like a Duke Ellington. In him that occasional rejection was so little and so occasional it mostly ran off his back because he knew that there were a lot of people who loved him just as he was. Whereas the kid who is brought up by a mother or dad saying "I despise you" hasn't got any strength at his center in who and what he is. So of course they start building walls to protect themselves fast.

What we are dealing with here is how do we get the walls torn down? Because not only do we not need them any more, they get in the way of what we really want to accomplish. And if we leave the walls up too long, they are going to kill us. They are going to bring about a worse hurt than what they were built to protect against.

I think the people who are talking about utopian-type societies are crazy. I don't see where they get their foolish hopes from. What do they see in history that gives them a basis for optimism about there being a utopia? I would rather deal with the people the way it seems to me they have always been and figure out how I can build my own utopia. I'm an anarchist. I obey all of society's written laws. But I refuse to obey all the unwritten laws. I would like to see every one of you finish this book as well-trained anarchists where eventually, because of what we talked about here, you don't do anything unless it is right for you. You follow the written laws—but then you follow your own thinking instead of the crowd. For example, I pay my income tax as honestly as I can. This way I can stay out of jail and have a clear conscience. This is obeying the written law. But I want my work to be as easy for me as possible and I go to friends who lift me up instead of people who pull me down. There is a fairly general feeling in this country (an unwritten law) that we must think of other people's interests and not our own. Another unwritten law is that we need to conform in our dress. I find there is more freedom possible than people realize. I don't mean dressing like a hippy. They all dress alike. They aren't free. They just follow a different law.

This freedom from unwritten laws frees you, not just to touch you so you can reap these rich rewards, but also to run your whole life for you instead of trying to please others.

I used to think that touching was just a good way of communicating but it's much more than that. There was, I can see now, a need in us to touch others. But that is a much deeper need than I ever imagined for us to be touched by others. We have lots of research now on how a lack of touching can actually kill little babies. And we know how much good touching helps improve physical and mental health at all ages. Our skin is the biggest organ in our body. Laid out flat it would be the size of a blanket. The more touching and holding that skin gets, the better it feels—and the better the body that skin covers feels. Ashley Montagu's book *Touching* and *Intimate Behavior* by Desmond Morris are two powerful books in this area.

The biggest point of touching people is that way you can be touched back. If enough people touch you and me then we won't shrivel up and die. Even more, if we get enough touching, we will start laughing and smiling more. That's a pretty good reason to me to be continually increasing my level of touching.

But if I've got the "don't touch me" syndrome, you can't get near enough to me to give me what I need. It's like a person whose house is burning down yet he is shooting at the fire truck to keep it away. I've seen men and women I couldn't touch with a stick. Many of them couldn't be touched by anyone else, either.

So we have to find a way to get some touching into our life. Then not only does the touching improve our communication, it helps open us up to ourselves and to the people around us so we have something different and something more to communicate. That's why touching is so important.

There is a special, unusually intense form of touching that goes the furthest to meet our needs for being touched. That's the kind of touching we call sex. I think it is easier to understand sex when we see it as a form of touching and of communication rather than as something isolated and apart.

Most people seem to me to be deprived of sex even if they have sex a lot. It is easier to understand deprivation if you look at something like drinking water. Water to drink is usually free and widely available. Most days we don't even think of how often we drink water or where we drink it. Only when we are especially thirsty or water is hard to get are we conscious of our thirst. But even then as soon as we have a few glasses of water our thirst goes away and we forget it. Our use of drinking water is a good example of how we are about something important to us when we aren't deprived of it or there's plenty of it. We don't pay water any special attention. Some of the people in this country are that way with food. They enjoy eating but, after they finish eating, they don't think much about food until the next meal.

Interestingly, it's both our fat people and our very poor people who think of food constantly. Neither can get enough food to satisfy them. The poor man can't afford enough food and the fat person can't eat enough to satisfy the deep craving they have.

I see sexual intercourse the same way. How satisfying sex is to us is more crucial than the frequency. I see people who have a lot of intercourse who are just as frustrated as those who don't have near enough. Because sex is such a deep and fundamental hunger in our life we need to find some way of meeting our needs well enough so we won't be so sex starved and sex frustrated that our minds are constantly on sex.

Sex is such a strong basic urge in any society that it has always been hard to handle. I don't see any society that has handled the problem perfectly. But I do see lots of signs that our society handles the problem very poorly. The starving man constantly thinks of food, the thirsty man constantly thinks of drinking fountains. Our mass communication shows how constantly we think of sex. And our mass communication isn't forcing this on us. We may not admit it, but our mass communication gives us what we want. If we want a clean, nonviolent newspaper we can take the *Christian Science Monitor*. Yet very few of us take that much trouble.

Now, I'm not so concerned about my society's obsession with sex as I am my own. My own obsession is what I have to live with twenty-four hours a day. That's why it is so important for me to get the best satisfaction for my sexual needs I can. I have access to the problem in many ways. As I improve my emotional relationship in my marriage, the physical satisfaction will improve. As I deepen and improve my sense of who and what I am through the mutuality of my relationships, there is more satisfaction in sex. And as my understanding of just what sex can provide for me and what it can't increases, my satisfaction is improved. So it is just like food in a way. It isn't the amount of food a person eats that determines how satisfying that food is to the person's basic needs.

Until I can get my sex needs satisfied at a reasonable level or learn to handle them in a reasonably good way, I can't see and experience the rest of life. Make a man hungry enough and all he thinks of is food. He can't think of anything else. Once you feed him and meet a few other very basic needs, his sexual needs will start controlling him until they are at least partially satisfied. So the man or woman who is sexually frustrated has no freedom.

When I see a person who is constantly telling sexual jokes, I figure that's a person who is very deprived of sexual satisfaction. And their constant talk of sex shows their tunnel vision. All they can see in life is sex. They can't see into emotional relationships because they just have physical ones. This is a mistake I have to avoid if I'm going to live. So I need to bring all the understanding I can to the sexual part of my life.

Also no problem exists in a vacuum. As I improve other areas of my life, the sexual side improves. As the sexual side improves, other areas of my life improve.

Someday I'm going to write a book called *Sex—If I Didn't Laugh, I'd Cry*. The reason I'm going to call it that is because there are more lies told in the name of sex than any other thing that I have ever seen in my whole life. One of the lady fiction writers said, "Nobody has ever spoken of those desolate things that happen in bed." She is so right. And to me the terrible crime against humanity is our awful fear of speaking the truth about sex. We have been taken in like the population in the story about the emperor's new clothes. The two sharpies came to town and got the emperor to give them all his gold and silver so they could weave beautiful cloth for a suit of clothes. But, of course, they were fooling the emperor. They kept the gold and silver and fitted him out in a suit made of imaginary cloth.

There's a whole bunch of people looking at sex just like they were at the emperor and he ain't got any clothes on. And everybody in the whole damn crowd knows that he ain't got no clothes on. Yet nobody has got the guts to say it. Not a person. Here are two friends standing side by side who say they love each other like brothers, but yet neither one of those people will admit to each other or even to themselves that the emperor hasn't got any clothes on. They know that their brother thinks that they think he has got clothes on. They know that their brother feels terrible because here he is wondering, "What the hell is wrong with me? Is my eyesight so bad or am I so screwed up that I think that this guy is running around naked? And everybody else is saying what beautiful clothes he has on. Boy, I must really be screwed up. I must really be weird."

Now that to me is a sign of the greatest hate and the most awful thing that you can do to a fellow human being. Yet we are doing it to everybody around us, almost without exception. Because we have got sex like that emperor. He should have clothes on. That is what we have been told. We have been told all about this splendid garment woven from all of these golden threads that this emperor has on. But then when we go to see the emperor's suit of clothes, we look and we say, "My God, he ain't got no clothes on." But yet everybody else is going, "Ooh! Ahh! Look at the emperor's beautiful suit. Look at the radiance. Look at the cut of those garments." And we think, "My God, we're insane." And there ain't a single damn soul who will give us any support. When we turn and ask for support from a friend they will shoot us down in flames. We say, "I wonder. Does that guy really have clothes on?" "Well, of course, you creep. What the hell's wrong with you?"

There is a policeman who I'm sure tells all his buddies what a great man he is in bed. And his buddies tell him back what great lovers they are. Yet the truth of the matter is, this policeman can no more than touch his wife and he goes off leaving her frustrated. Now there's nothing wrong with that. It's very common. There are ways to compensate for it and there are ways to improve it. But what's so terrible is the way we lie to each other and say we haven't got a problem. That makes each of our problems look to us like the most awful thing in the world.

Sex is like anything else in life. It's like going fishing. It's like riding horseback. It's like going to the movies. It varies. Some days when you go fishing, you get rained on. Sometimes you get arrested for having too many fish. Sometimes you have a lot of fun. Sometimes you have fun for a while and you don't have fun at a later time. It just varies all over creation. But you can't get anybody in this whole world to admit to the honest to God truth about sex. Every man and woman in this world, it seems like, is firmly dedicated to the proposition that sex for them is just fantastic, absolutely fantastic. And they just have never had any problems in this area like all of the other screwed-up people around them. Yet when I look at the marriages that I know, and I have had a chance to observe a lot of marriages real close, I see that there isn't one marriage in twenty where there is anywhere near that ideal kind of sexual relationship.

When a couple first gets married, the hormones are strong enough that for a year or two or maybe even three or four, they can coast along. For a while you can make love to practically anyone under almost any circumstances.

But it is amazing how that always eventually disappears and then you are face to face with reality. Then what you have built, if anything, shows up so clearly and usually the two of them haven't built any kind of emotional relationship. They find they are enemies and the two split.

In a good, well-established sexual relationship between the husband and wife, the two can't keep their hands off each other. They go by each other and they are constantly touching one another in a quiet way. There is a special way that they are together where they are relaxed and loose, not tight and strained. I see that in about one out of twenty marriages. Most of the rest of the nineteen, those two people can't get far enough apart from each other. Now they co-exist fairly well in that home. I don't say that only one out of twenty marriages is a good marriage, because sex is again just one leg of a ten-legged stool that keeps a marriage up. You can saw off the sexual leg of the stool in a marriage and in an awful lot of cases the marriage doesn't suffer that much. It can be a better marriage with that leg in stronger shape but it isn't that crucial. I've even seen cases where a homosexual has married a woman and they have had kids and kept that marriage going and it is a reasonably satisfactory marriage.

So, again, sex is neither as drastically big and as important a thing as it is made out to be, nor is it as great or as fantastic an experience for the people involved as it is made out to be.

We have had a lot of books on sex lately. I can't understand them. Ruben said that he was going to tell us everything that we ever wanted to know about sex. All he did was tell us about the mechanics and the statistics. He didn't tell us about the most crucial thing of all and

that is, yes, you can have sex without an emotional relationship for one to five years. But, by the time that the
power of sex wears off, if you haven't built up an emotional relationship to underscore sex you are in trouble.
You are in exactly the same predicament as the student of
mine who met his old nurse friend. He got a lot more
affection out of his hug from this nurse than he did from
intercourse with his girl friend. So if you don't build
an emotional relationship, sex turns to poison. Having
intercourse with somebody who hates you and you hate,
and somebody who won't open their heart to you and
you won't open your heart to them, that becomes the
most awful thing in the world. That's why sex dies. The
reason it dies is because the toughest thing in the whole
world is to build an emotional relationship. Any child can
have sex. Building an emotional relationship is work for
men and women. And I've seen how hard it is for me
to stop being so immature. I'm forty-eight and I'm still
working on coming to maturity.

Most guys and gals who are impotent in their marriages
for one reason or another are very successful sexually
outside those marriages. So true impotence with a good
sexual partner is rare. Unless you go without sex for
a long time into your later married years, up till some
time in your fifties or sixties, there is very little impotence, strictly speaking. Almost any guy or any gal
can make it with some other individual where there
isn't that poisonous heart between them, where there isn't
that continual infliction of hurt on the other person or
refusal of openness.

What does it mean to say we love someone yet deny
them the gift of ourselves? Look what happens when we
say, in effect, I will not give you my heart. When you
haven't given your heart, then giving your body even-

tually becomes at least distasteful and mechanical. And often it becomes so horrible that it is refused altogether. Yet here we sit with a situation among us that is, as I see, one of the most destructive things there is. And we are all sitting there lying to each other about it.

One noon at the University of Minnesota I didn't have anybody to have lunch with so I went in alone and sat down with a couple of guys. One says to the other, "Boy, did I have a great night of sex last night!" Well, I know what his wife looks like—all tense and drawn. That isn't how a woman who has had a lot of good sex looks like. She's nice and loose and relaxed. And I know how a guy acts who has had a lot of sex successfully, he doesn't say a thing—he just smiles.

It is just like Bill Oriet, who is one of our great elk hunters. But Bill Oriet doesn't ever talk about what a great elk hunter he is because he doesn't need to. So the guy talking of his great night of sex is probably a liar. Furthermore, he is a hurtful person, because he is theoretically a halfway friend of mine and he doesn't know what my sex life is like. Maybe it is horrible. That is just like somebody bragging to you about their money. That's an awful thing to do to people who might have poverty instead of prosperity.

The other guy at the table was a guy whose wife had been in a mental institution more than she had been out. He is supposed to be one of the closest friends the storyteller has. But I know that this guy has got to have some problems with his sexual life because of his wife's mental condition as well as her absence. To me that little incident typifies the way we handle each other.

I see guys and gals, men and women suffering year after year after year because nobody, absolutely nobody, will tell the truth. Now we talk about giving of ourselves, but that's one way I've seen in which so few people are able to give of themselves.

There was a study done on guys in their forties to see what the effect of sex was after a heart attack. What they did was they implanted a sensor near the heart to send an EKG signal to a distant monitor. The guy kept a diary of what he was doing at the different times of the day. They would monitor his activity in the morning, driving to work and however strenuous his work was. And he would have the times of his intercourse in his diary. What it showed was that in the typical male in his forties intercourse brought about a slightly elevated EKG for a brief period of time. That was intercourse for the man in his forties. Now you read the novels and it doesn't sound like that. But to try to get those forty-year-old types to tell the honest to God truth to their brothers and sisters is the hardest thing I have ever seen.

Of course, part of the problem is that one of the deepest needs we have is sexual. But part of the sexual need is in our heads, in the sense it comes from the illusions we have. We talk about the illusion of married love and of how the marriage should be in the first year, the Hollywood romance and the one and only and the pink cloud and all that crap. That is nothing compared to the illusion that is fostered about sex. And even as I say those words, I risk the danger of you saying, "Oh well, that's just Jess. He is so far over the hill he doesn't know what he is talking about." And you can all put me down. I'm sticking my neck out a mile.

But the truth can set you free. You see that while your sex life is pretty crummy, it's about like everybody else's. Those other people who are doing all that lying, they aren't the sexual athletes that they pretend to be. In fact, that they are doing so much lying and talking about how great sex is says that they have probably got some real serious problems. The minute you see that, it does a lot for you. It lets you take more advantage of what you do have. It lets you go in a realistic way to get a little bit more, do what you can. And then it helps you not be troubled so much by the rough spots.

In *Lady Chatterley's Lover*, their love was going along great at first as it always does between two strange sex partners. That is pretty exciting. Then all of a sudden it dropped off a little. And the old game keeper was reminded of porridge in the days when there were hard times. Near payday you have lots of meal to make the porridge with and it is nice and thick. When you get away from payday, the porridge gets pretty thin. And he was trying to calm down the lady, who doesn't know anything about any part of it. She is feeling bad. "Where did our love go?" And he is saying, "Honey, you've got to take the thin with the thick."

To me, that's reality. And there are only two or three books that I have ever read that come anywhere close to telling any kind of truth about sex *Lady Chatterley's Lover* has sex, in a sense, a little bit romanticized but there is some real warm-hearted loving in that book. And there is an understanding of the difference between warm-hearted loving and hard-hearted loving. That hard-hearted loving is the kind that goes on in most places that tries to masquerade as love.

We have a lot of surveys where you go around asking nineteen-year-old guys and gals what kind of marriages they want. They describe the marriage of the future. Well, that's just really beautiful. Sure they want open marriages with no possessiveness and jealousy. But I find my twenty-five-year-old students who have been married for a few years want to kill their husbands or wives for playing around.

A good example of this is a story that I saw about a group marriage in Sweden. Five guys married five gals. The point is you rotate as you choose around the circle. You sleep with whoever you want. Whoever goes to bed first has the first choice and you go on down the line. It starts out beautifully. You all sleep in a circle with your heads touching. Everybody is making love simultaneously or as the spirit moves them. It is a beautiful idea, very commonly thought of as the great solution to the sexual problem. The only thing was, it didn't work.

Why didn't it work? What happened? Well as near as I can see what happened in that group marriage was one of the gals or all of them finally said, "Hey you guys. No way. No more. You stay with me until you want to leave. If you want to leave, that's fine, but don't come back, because I can't stand these one-night stands, this musical-chairs routine." They went into their group marriage with all of the modern ideas, and what they came out with is close to monogamy.

So the thing I've seen is here again commitment is a fantastically crucial thing. Yes, you can have emotional relationships with other people but you can't have but one sexual commitment. You can have one at a time and we've got cases where people will have three or four or five happy marriages. But it seems like it almost has to be where one of the people, one of the partners, dies. Because I don't see it happening as often in divorces. I don't see divorced people having a successive group of happy marriages—have one happy marriage and then they divorce and they have another happy marriage. A divorced person either makes a happy marriage on their second try or else they seem to keep on making miserable marriages.

So here we've got this terrible conspiracy not of silence but of lies. I know how hard it is to build a deep emotional open relationship. And yet we think that it should be easy.

How many of us are foolish enough to look at a ballet dancer and say, "Oh gee, that's sure easy, isn't it? Look how light and fancy she floats around. I think I'll be a ballet dancer tomorrow. And I'll dance on the stage the following day!" But that's exactly what we do when we look at a deep emotional relationship and say, "Oh, I'll have one of those! I'll have one tomorrow afternoon." Or, "I have a lot of those right now!" When you say that you show no respect, absolutely none for the price in mistakes and suffering we have to pay to learn to build a deep emotional relationship.

I know why there isn't but one in twenty marriages where sex persists on into the fifteenth and twentieth years in the beautiful, powerful way that it can under ideal circumstances. And that's because it is so hard to build and maintain a deep, emotional relationship. There are so few places where it is taught, and there are so few people who are good at it who will teach us. And we are so poor at telling who has got one so we can go to them and listen to their words and respect them. Because of that we aren't ever going to see and we aren't ever going to experience what is there potentially for us to experience. By accepting reality as it is right now we can be way ahead of where we were yesterday. By seeing reality as it is, we can open our hearts to someone, instead of lying to them.

"You're saying that we aren't being honest with our brothers. That we aren't sharing these things and that we have problems. But are you saying that we should be sharing these things by saying this is the way that it is with us. Maybe it is good, maybe it is bad, but this is the way that it is?"

Yes.

"But it is such a personal thing. A private thing. And you say share it?"

It can be done. I've done it. Frequently.

"In a group like this?"

No. I'm not saying that.

"Okay, I was going to say that would be awful hard."

No. I don't ask that. I ask that you think on these ideas and talk to somebody, preferably more than just one person. I have tried to be as honest as I can with many people.

"Were they having marital problems?"

Different kinds of problems and people, you know, guys, gals.

"Well, did they think that they had happy marriages?"

No, most of them didn't. That was why they were willing to talk to me. Because they were hurting. Some cases were fairly happy. Some weren't. What was so sad was that I was the only one that they were able to talk to and they were around a lot of people.

"Well, but by virtue of your training and so forth they felt that they could, maybe more so than to others."

No, I've never made anything of my psychology training. The people who come to me are almost always my students who come to me because of the kind of training that I'm suggesting that you get and that's the kind of training that makes people feel that they can open their hearts to you. You get that kind of training by trying these things out and putting them up against life and seeing if they work, not by being a psychologist.

"I have a mutual friend and she has shared with me and yet I don't know if I have helped her very much."

Did you share back?

"Sure."

Okay. That's all you can ever do.

"Is this common what I'm talking about?"

No. I see that in people it is a lot easier sometimes to share or confess a problem that you have to a total stranger rather than somebody for whom you have a mutual respect. You know, if you get on a train or a bus with a stranger, they will tell you things they wouldn't tell someone they know.

Part of the reason for that is a bad one, as I see. What does it mean to call a man a friend and then refuse to open your heart to him in a crucial area of your life? I think part of the reason we can talk easier to strangers is we are unwilling to have that deep relationship. We don't want that deep a relationship so we will tell a stranger because there we aren't threatened. We will never see that person again and have a deeper relationship.

"I must have grown up very maladjusted because I still would rather be alone with that type of thing than to open myself up to someone I know. I mentioned this once before that once I find that real close friendship starting to develop, then I am the one that backs off because I don't want that kind of commitment because it means a commitment to that person."

That's right.

"Not just getting from them, but giving to them as well. That giving, you can talk about it all you want, but to get it so the giving really comes out of your heart is really difficult."

I think it's the hardest thing there is in the world. That's why it is so seldom that you see it. And that's

the answer to what I'm saying. Maybe you talked to one
other friend. But each of you have got a lot more people
around you than need you. Almost all of the people
who talked to me say they haven't got anybody who has
told them the truth so far, sometimes maybe it is just one
other person. But that isn't very much. It's better than
nothing. But the minute I open my heart to you and you
see what a weirdo I am, that's some comfort to you. You
say, "My God, if Jess is as screwed up as I am, there
must be a lot more out there like us. So one is a whole
lot better than none. But two is a lot better than one
because then you see, "Hey, Jess and Sam and I are all
weirdos."

"You know, I wonder if there is a difference between
men and women being able to talk about these things?"

I don't see any. I don't see that women are any more
honest than the men. Because I worked more with women
than men, I have talked to more women than men in this
area. But they are all in the same boat. Neither men nor
women have anybody talking honestly and openly to them.

"Well, I don't know but it just seems like when fellows
are young they've always got all of these contests and
are lying a lot."

And girls don't do that?

"No, they don't. I don't think."

Oh! Women don't?

"They don't go bragging around."

No. They don't brag around, but they lie. They lie
about their virginity.

"They say that they are a virgin when they aren't."

Yeah. And sometimes they will do the opposite. They
will lie that they aren't a virgin because in some circles
it isn't stylish any more to be a virgin. But in both cases
it's a lie and it's just as hurtful. So there is just as much

lying. It's just a different kind. Okay, they don't talk. But that's just refusal to talk. It isn't lying, but it is a conspiracy of silence. Whatever the point, they're no comfort to each other. I don't see that women are any more comfort to each other than men are.

I have my five friends. I have been able to talk about sexual matters and exchange comfort with many people. But what is increasingly important to me is that with my five friends I can say some of my feelings about problems in the sexual area and know that I will be understood. None of the five pretend to be saints. And why would I want to talk to a saint about my human problems?

We all need friends we can trust. I have had the good fortune by now to have had enough intimate friends I could trust so that I could tell my deepest thoughts, troubles, feelings and experiences. Everything I've ever done that's ever troubled me I've now been able to tell to at least one other person. Once I had told those things to another person and saw they didn't drop dead with shock and horror but just yawned, I was freed from the power of those old memories to haunt me. That's been just one of many values to me of having intimate friends I could trust. And never has any one of those friends ever betrayed a confidence.

What about the rest of society?

I can't solve the problem this society has with sex. All I can do something about is working on getting my own head out of the sand. Here's one more way in which my five friends and all the other people who love me are so important to me.

7

commitment
in the marriage

Ideally our marriage relationship is the central relationship in our lives. It is the mutual relationship that is so great we have made the deepest possible commitment to the relationship—a written commitment for life in front of an audience of our friends and relatives and usually in the presence of our God. In addition to the deep mutuality in which we will have the precious opportunity to discover ourselves, we expect we will find the source of our sexual satisfaction for life.

Now it's a tall order for two nineteen-year-olds to come up with a good decision on the deepest issues there are in life. I see that I was pretty lucky. I did the right thing for the wrong reasons. I married a beautiful, dark-haired girl of nineteen who was the most enjoyable person to be around I had ever found. But twenty-five years later, I found I married a woman who can be as strong as steel when she has to be, who knows me better than I will ever know myself, yet has compassion for what she sees, who is a fine mother and a grandmother and who, despite many shocks, disappointments and frustrations, is still willing to stay married to me.

When so much is involved, who could expect two nineteen-year-olds or even twenty-nine-year-olds to always make the right decision about the hardest choice in life. My friends in business tell me you can make a million dollars if you are right a little more than 50 per cent of the time. Even though our present divorce rate is high, it still suggests we aren't doing too badly at this crucial choice in our lives.

And certainly marriage isn't in the trouble many people claim it is because most people who get divorced can hardly wait to get married again. Most people haven't got any argument with marriage, it's just the person they were married to.

There are lots of articles and books being written today about marriage without a commitment where each person in the marriage does their own thing. I think that's a way of justifying a failure instead of a way of building a better marriage. I see the issue of commitment as central to mutual need therapy and to mutual relationships. I discussed the point of commitment earlier in a general way, but the place where it is most vital is our marriage.

When I have a deep and satisfying mutual relationship like those I have with any of my five friends, why would I ever put such a relationship aside? When I do put such a relationship aside, I show no appreciation for what it gives me that I need and I show no understanding of how long it will take to bring a new relationship to the point these five friends are. I see commitment as arising inevitably out of what understanding. When I have five such satisfying relationships as these, I can't help but go back to them consistently so in that I show my commitment to them.

And when I break this commitment I hurt the relationship. I show there is no more mutual need. If I stop going to see Vince, I tell him he isn't important in my life any more. Here's where my students want to argue and deceive themselves. "Oh, Jess, a person is still my friend even when I stop seeing them any more." That may be their definition of friendship but it isn't mine."

If these principles are true in my mutual relationships with my five friends, how much more so should they hold with my wife? The words that we used in our decision to get married and in the marriage ceremony speak of the deepest mutual need there is where two people need each other in such deep and special ways that they become as one person. If I meant what I said then I had better find a way to live up to my expressed hope.

Another justification for not tying ourselves down or making a commitment is that we are changing constantly. Often the implication is that "I'm changing so fast here I've changed into a butterfly and you're the same old nag you always were." I know that feeling but there is no basis for it. I didn't change into a butterfly. I just thought I did. And if my wife could accept the mess that she accepted when we got married, she can sure accept any mess that I change into.

The commitment that is made in a marriage to the mutuality that only a marriage can provide is to me very, very deep and vital. I think that we all need to examine that. I know I have gone through periods of my married life where I cannot say that I was committed to that marriage. The most obvious period was the first fifteen years of our married life when my work came first and my marriage second. I would move my family at a moment's notice for an extra $500 a year. That is just plain stupid. I moved to Chicago over my wife's objection to take a job at an advertising agency. I was completely wrong in forcing a wrong and hurtful choice on her and I really screwed things up.

We hear a lot of talk about commitment in marriage, but I don't really see much of it in practice. I don't often see this deep and fundamental commitment to our marriage as the source of the crucial mutual relationships in our life.

I ran into a gal in the hallway recently. I asked her, "How are you doing?" She was a former student of mine from I don't know how far back. She said, "Ah! Not so good." I said, "What's wrong?" She said, "We are separated." I said, "How long have you been married?" And she said, "Two years."

"Why don't you tell me some of those good things that you told me about him two years ago when you married him?" She said, "I can't think of any." I said, "Why didn't you work harder?" and she said, "Well, a year ago I thought that I should come to see you but I never did." She is a gal who was in my class and all I remember is her face. She sat in that class as a twenty-year-old and didn't say a thing. She didn't contribute to it at all. She sat there taking a free ride on what all the other people in class were saying. I didn't even know her name. All I remember is I had seen her face.

She sat there and let that marriage go and didn't do a thing to stop it. She is hitchhiking in life and until she starts realizing she had better start making some commitments, she is in deep trouble. And she is going to stay in this deep trouble.

A lot of my students want to come in and criticize the person they marry. Again I say, "You married that person for a reason. Remember it. Think about it. Give that person a chance to do some changing in their own life. If you feel that you have done some changing in your life, how much have you done to stay in touch with your husband or wife to share what kind of moving you have done in terms of growing and thinking different with that other person?"

Another thing that of course we don't do in a marriage is give the other person the right to be human. Typically we have got them on some kind of pedestal and they have to meet some exalted set of needs that no single human being could ever meet. You could take Raquel Welch, some fantastically intellectual person, some deep, sensitive person, some very motherly person, some go-go dancer, wrap them all up and put them in one body, and that still wouldn't come close to satisfying the illusion or the dream that some guys have of a wife. For you women, well you can take your favorite movie star and put him in there, and put some deep, fine talker in there, and a musician, and a guy who is good at fixing everything around the house, and a guy who likes to do dishes and cook, and somebody who is a hell of a provider and makes a lot of money, and somebody else who is a fantastic saver, and roll them all together and put some of God in there and he still wouldn't live up to what you think a husband should be.

What we need to do for our husbands and wives is to take them off the pedestals we have put them on and have some compassion for them. We need to see that they are just dumb human beings like us. We need to look at ourselves for what we are, and see that we are lucky to have someone who has some good qualities.

Now I grant you that some of us get a little more lucky than others and get a lot better start in our marriages. But, also, a bigger part of it is work and being open to life and calling spades, spades. And not sitting on a pile of horse manure and calling it roses.

Again, this goes back to seeing ourselves in a relationship. To me a marriage is one of the most fantastically productive and the most satisfying things, and a source of deep mutuality. But it is also a living hell, in the sense that periodically I have to see my own shortcomings in that relationship. And that is just like being in a great big vise and having all of your bones crushed. You hurt so bad and you want to run so far and so fast, but there is nothing you can do. You just have to stay and face the music. You want to run away and never come back but you have to stay there and take it. That is all that you can do. But that comes out of commitment.

In my early years of marriage, the only thing that would sustain me sometimes was just the notion, because I'm a Catholic, this marriage has got to go, it has got to work. I can't have another one without offense to the religion that I profess. It must have been true many more times in my wife's case, I'm sure. No matter what your religion, if any, that commitment is just as crucial. Now if it is broken, then a new commitment has to be made.

I've seen a lot of times where people benefit from their mistakes and really see the necessity for work. But they feel that their present marriage has deteriorated too much, gone too far beyond the point of saving. I certainly respect that decision. Most of the married people I work with, though, really want divorce counseling. They come to me and say, "Jess, tell me why I should divorce this person." Or, "I want to divorce this person. Tell me how right I am." I won't do that for them. I try to make them see how they are contributing to the trouble. Since I have never taken any pay for the counseling I do, I can take an unpopular approach. Those who choose to stick around and work with me will often work two or three years on a marriage. Usually they can patch it up, and sometimes get it pretty good. In some cases it just goes down the tube, but then they really know that they have worked as hard as they can to make the marriage go.

When we talk about mutual need, you've got to have that central relationship marriage provides. It is your primary source of getting your needs satisfied. That's the relationship we are in most of the time.

For most of us, the issue is: Okay, we've got a marriage. We've got a degree of commitment to it. How can we deepen that sense of commitment to it and make it the far more productive marriage that we ideally would like? Here is where it is so important that we are opening our hearts, being human beings, seeing the other person with compassion as a human being, imperfect, like us. We need to put away our childish dreams. We're not going to get a composite of everything in our marriage. Our husband or wife has the right to be just as imperfect as we are. Each party brings some strengths to the marriage, each party brings some weakness to the marriage. That's humanity.

Very often, when I look at the particular set of strengths and weaknesses in a marriage, I find them very illustrative of what it is that each of us really want. Some women will complain to me, "The only reason my husband wanted to marry me was so he could have a mother.

I can see that now." That may be true, but also there must be an awful desire for her to be a mother, instead of a wife, or she never would have bought the deal for twenty years. Now that is the part of it that we don't like to think about. "Oh, not a good cleanie like me. I wouldn't ever do anything low like that. Everybody knows what a great person I am. It's that dink that I'm married to. He is the one who is the problem."

I'm not convinced because I have seen that person's life after their divorce. In one case I'm thinking about, I see a good many of the very failings she is blaming her husband for, continuing into her life in her other relationships. In the wives of the alcoholics we see this same failing so often. She cries to everyone about the way her husband beats her. But I've seen that when her husband gets sober, often she will divorce him and marry another alcoholic who beats her. I saw one woman do that three times. I've seen husbands do similar things. So I think that one of the hardest things to recognize is the fact that in our marriages we usually are getting just exactly what we really want and what we really deserve. If we say we want to get something different, then we had better start really wanting something different and we better start really deserving something different or we aren't going to get it. And it is going to take awhile. We've got to have some patience.

Again, I see how often, with the other person, we are sensationally impatient. We want them to change immediately. But when it comes to you or me changing, we want lots of time. You may want me to change my language, for instance. I may be a terrible example to those of you who feel you speak this beautiful language of ours flawlessly. You want me to reform my language. Well I would argue that it might take me ten to twenty years to do so, if I was interested in doing it. Whereas, when I think about how fast I want you to change I want it done in a week or so.

Also, we'll get into a marriage relationship and we will make some serious mistakes, for example, my over-commitment to work. For fifteen years I sent my wife the message: "You're not important. My work is more important." All of a sudden I decide, "Hey, you're more important than work." How soon is she going to get the message? How long should I wait for her to be convinced that I really mean that? Well I suspect I had better wait awhile. Again, so many people come in to me and say, "Well, I changed around in my marriage, and I gave the other person a week or two and they didn't really believe that I changed around." You may laugh at that but I have heard things like that. I'm sure you have, too. In fact, I've heard it even worse than that. "I told her yesterday that I was reforming and that wasn't enough for her. She was yelling at me, 'You're just like you always were.' What is wrong with that woman? I have only been a drunk for twenty years."

I see a lot of marriages that are being used as ornaments. The whole thing is managed. I have seen situations where the husband says to the wife, "You play around all you want, but don't get caught, and just keep it under cover. I'm not interested in trying to be a husband to you but I need a wife who can present a good appearance and entertain the company." It isn't all just the husband's fault either. Lots of those wives married them because the woman needed the ego patch of marrying a moneymaker or a doctor. Then once they've made the deal they don't like it.

Now there is a lot of that kind of thing going on where you have got a marriage just because everybody is married and you have to have one, or you want to keep things un-ruffled and looking pretty. The marriage is just for show. It's just like a lot of people who say that they aren't going to church for show. It's always the other people who are going for show. Well, it is the same thing in a marriage.

So, it is amazing to me how many problems there are in an institution that is as important as that to us. I was teaching a class for teachers over in Livingston, Montana. I was telling them that they were teaching because they needed teaching. One of my students said I was wrong. "I'm teaching so that my daughter can have pretty clothes and we can have motorcycles for the boys and things like that." One day her daughter got mad at her because she hadn't ironed any clothes. The teacher got mad back at her daughter and said, "What's wrong with you? Don't you appreciate anything that I do for you? I'm teaching just for you. I'm doing this hard job just for you. Then you complain because I haven't ironed a blouse."

The mother got to school and started thinking about what I had told her, that you teach because you need to teach. She started to realize, "If I asked my husband and my daughter, would they rather I stay home and we would get along on less money, they would say, 'Yes, you stay home and we will be happy to get along on less money.'" She finally realized that she was teaching for her own needs.

Of course, once you do that it helps to give you a lot different perspective. The next time that the daughter bitches about a blouse not being ironed, the mother can say, "Honey, I'm sorry about that. I appreciate all of the consideration that you have given me with all of the time I'm not home when you get home and you would like to have me there. I know what it meant to me when

I came home and my mother was always there, waiting for me. That was really something, and I appreciate you putting up with my not being there." See how differently you can approach a problem when you start getting things straightened out?

When I bring up the idea of commitment in the sexual side of marriage, one of the first things people do is throw up the percentages of people who are unfaithful in their marriages. They use these percentages as proof that commitment in marriage doesn't work. To me that's looking at the hole instead of the donut.

Of course people aren't perfect and they do make mistakes. Some people who believe in sexual commitment to their spouses do something that goes against the commitment. Others may go through a period of time when they aren't committed sexually to their spouses but come to see that as a mistake. And there are those who play around without any sense of commitment.

You can look at the sexual affairs in marriage another way. Yes, here is a high percentage of people who have made mistakes, maybe half or more. But almost all of those mistakes were small numbers and of short duration. Show me the percentage of husbands and wives who consistently play around sexually over a long period of time. Those are the ones who don't believe in sexual commitment. The rest of the people in marriage do believe in commitment. They are just human enough to make mistakes or have their thinking get screwed up for a period of time.

What proof do I have that sexual commitment is vital to a relationship? Mostly just my experience. I see what happens in the marriages where there is no sexual commitment. I wouldn't want to be in one of those marriages or be one of those people. And I've seen what a sense of sexual commitment can do to strengthen marriages and get out of them the best there is to be gained for both people in the marriage.

A lot of my students and other people I see have tried to tell me how great the life of a swinging single or married is. But I'm not impressed by what they can show me in their own lives.

A woman from Buffalo, New York, wrote me about my first book. She was offended by my statement in it that intercourse was for marriage. She thought I made the statement too flatly. I should have qualified it by saying "I think." She was right in that.

She went on to say she was divorced and having intercourse with lots of men and it was working just fine for her. There were no problems. I was happy for her. But I have heard that same story from many of my students. I told them the same thing. I was happy for them. But most of them came back later and told me a new story. They had decided to stop having intercourse or they were going to make a commitment, or they were going to try. When I would ask them what happened to their previous beliefs, they found they couldn't live with them.

Because I live in Montana, many people figure I don't really know what's going on in the world. That's not quite true. The people I work with come from all over the United States. I'm not right in the midst of Berkeley or the communes, but I have some contact with them.

A student from Antioch was drifting through with his old lady. He visited my classes. A few days later I got a call from a very scared gal. She asked if she could see me. I said she could. She walked from town. When she got to my office she was trembling all over. I asked her what was wrong. She had been using intercourse as a tranquilizer and it wouldn't work for her any more. At first it quieted her down fine. But now, she would be climbing the walls fifteen minutes later. We talked about her life and she decided to go back home and make peace with her parents. The last I heard from her she was home and making a new start for herself.

But I could just see all the guys she had been with telling themselves how great this free and easy sex was. And all the time they had been pretty blind to the little bird they were with and what she really felt.

I have seen the worst sexual chaos there could be. One of my students was a gal who was in a couple of fraternity gang bangs where the boys were lined up outside the door. What was so amazing to me was that she gained something from the experience, part horror at herself and maybe some part satisfaction of something. She progressed to one-night stands where if a guy didn't ask her to go to bed with him on the first date she thought he was queer. By her junior year she was going steady with a great guy but didn't feel worthy of him so she tried to drive him off. But then she stopped that, married him and they now have a happier marriage than most of my students their ages.

I have seen sexual commitment come out of chaos like that. But when there is a denial and withholding from commitment I've seen some terrible things happen. One story that shows what I've seen is in Terkel's book *Working*. The prostitute in there had to steel herself against any feelings in intercourse with her customers. Pretty soon she found she couldn't have any feelings with anyone in intercourse and turned to drugs.

So in the area of sexual commitment I'm guided by what I've seen and what I've experienced. Much of what is written in the "new school" today goes against what

I have seen. But that's fine. I'll stick with what I've got. It's working great for me and my friends.

I believe that the best marriage comes out of a commitment to a deep mutual relationship and a commitment to the sexual relationship. There will be plenty of difficulties and plenty of mistakes. But I find that once I can get a principle to guide me that I know works, then the battle is half won. But not until I see this clearly can I get my priorities straightened out. I can't have my family as my second priority (with my higher power first) until I am willing to commit everything I have to the family relationships. And since my wife is my central family relationship, it really makes my priorities: 1. my higher power, 2. my wife, 3. my family, 4. my five friends, 5. my community and 6. my work.

I can't take my work from the top spot where it was for fifteen years and put it in the bottom spot until I have decided to settle for reality in my relationships. I have to be willing to take what I have and can get instead of guaranteeing failure by seeking a fantasy in marriage and family.

So I'm going to give to my marriage and my family the same commitment they have been giving to me for so long. My wife and children could, in all fairness, say, "It's about time." But they are nice enough not to say that.

What do I get back? I get the greatest gift there is: another human being who has freely given herself to me. And I get one of the most beautiful mirrors to myself I can ever conceive of so I can much more clearly find out who and what I am. The more commitment I give, the more I get back. And the commitment is necessary to the deepest kind of self-disclosure and self-knowledge. Why would I continue more deeply into such a frightening process with a person who, at any moment, plans to leave and go on to some other relationship?

My marriage is my central mutual relationship. I speak so often of how Vince and Jerry and other people have given me so much and made it possible for me to see myself. But roll all they have given me together and it isn't but a part of what my wife has given me. Much of what she has given me has been indirect. As she started working on her problems in life and talked of them to me without holding back, I was eventually able to see the problems I had and to some small degree to talk to her of them. In other cases, she would see some problem I was having and when she could see I was halfway ready, she would let me have the benefit of her wisdom. She usually had the truth and the truth sometimes hurts—but it helps me get in harmony with life and that helps more than it hurts.

But that's another advantage of the deep commitment of the marriage relationship. It is about the only place where we can find a person who will tell us the truth in a truly loving way. And where we know they will stick around and help us patch things up.

Do my other commitments interfere with my commitment to my wife? Usually they don't and they shouldn't. When we have a clear sense of the priorities in our relationships, then our commitments usually don't clash, they dovetail together. And the good things I get from my five friends and my other relationships feed back into the family and help me be a better husband.

There have been times when commitments have conflicted. Looking back, I can see that it was because I had my priorities mixed up and didn't know it. If my work comes before anything else, then those commitments will conflict with my commitments to my wife and children, who I claim come first.

I see that if there is a conflict in commitments or relationships, it is a sign something is wrong with the relationship because mutual need relationships are freely entered into for the good of the two individuals involved. Their only goal for the other person is whatever contributes to that other person's well-being.

There is no question that conflicts will come up. But when they do I find it is a good sign something is wrong because in this system, as I've experienced it, there isn't any deep and permanent conflict. How can there be any conflict when the other person in the relationship is always completely free to do anything they want or need to do to fulfill their spiritual quests. It isn't easy—but there shouldn't be any conflict with the other person.

There is talk today about the renewable marriage license. That isn't a new idea. We've always had that. When you don't renew, it's called divorce. My wife and I have chosen to renew our license twenty-five years. I think that's quite an accomplishment for her to stick with me that long, because I was sure a born bachelor. I think all this talk of naturalness in relationships is very misleading. As near as I can see, what's natural for us is trouble and pain and loneliness. Living in relationships is necessary to our survival, but it sure isn't natural.

There isn't any one of us born a ballet dancer, you learn that. There isn't any one of us born a good liver of life. You learn that. And you can't inherit it from your parents. You can inherit a good start, just like you can inherit a good start for being a ballet dancer. But you don't inherit being a ballet dancer, and I sure didn't inherit being a husband. What I am as a husband is the result of lots of hard lessons. But it's nice to share the learning with such a lovely lady. In my dedication I mentioned the Arab proverb that a woman isn't your wife, she's your fate. That's true. And I've got a lovely fate.

8

you raise carrots
but you don't
raise kids

My wife contends that I was a natural-born bachelor—
maybe even a natural-born monk. When I see how hard
it is for me to face some of the constant problems I have
living with my wife and children, I'm inclined to think
there is a lot of truth in what she says.

But I know I'm even more poorly suited for a solitary
life than the married life. I crammed into my first twenty-
three years practically everything anyone could want
to do. I had plenty of fun and hell-raising as I grew up.
I went to army college and to the Army in a year and a
half. I graduated from college with trips out west skiing,
mountain climbing and fishing. I took a long canoe trip
into Canada. I worked many jobs to pay for all my
activities. I had many friends and the deep love of a few
good young women.

In August of 1947 just before I was twenty-one, I

was visiting Berkeley after a summer working in the mountains. I was looking for my high school love who had ditched me while I was in the Army.

As it got towards dark and the lonesome time of day, I looked out across the bay at the lights of the Golden Gate Bridge. I thought, "Here is one of the most beautiful sights I have ever seen. But I'm alone and don't enjoy seeing this by myself. I'm going home."

I went back to the hotel and checked out that evening and started hitchhiking home. I wasn't in a rush to get married. I was still scared of it. But that was the time I turned my back on the single life.

The point of my story is that I had all the opportunities in the world to stay single and enjoy it. But I chose not to stay that way. I chose to be a family man. If this was my choice and if I believe my family is the most crucial way to satisfy my need for relationships, then why don't I act like it?

All I can say to myself in my defense is that what I'm trying to do is for me one of the two hardest things I've ever tried. One of the hardest is to find God as I understand Him, and make a continuing, conscious contact and give up playing God myself. The other terribly hard thing is to be a husband and a father.

In neither of these two problems can I blame anyone else. I can't blame the troubles I have had trying to find a higher power on the people who taught me about religion. Everyone who taught me religion was as kind and loving as they could be. I was never punished. But because of this awful conspiracy of silence we maintain with the people around us on talking about spiritual matters, I see so many people who think they are all alone in their spiritual quest. They think they are so alone that it takes them quite a while to admit to their own problems and fears because they think they are so weird and different for having them.

I see a number of driving forces in us. We can do something out of a sense of compulsion, driven by something inside that we don't understand or feel comfortable with. We can do something out of a sense of fear where we are driven by the fear of a punishment. We can do something out of a sense of dedication where we drive ourselves because as near as we can see this is something that is right for us and that we should do.

Dedication is about the best I can say about most of the things I do in the family. I do them because I believe in them for me and I'm dedicated to them.

But there is a higher driving force—the highest of them all. That is when we do something out of love. This force is so powerful yet there is the feeling of no power at all. It is like the perfect golf swing—there is no feeling of strain or effort, just smoothly focused speed in the club head that lifts the ball straight and true. You can feel that near perfect shot in your whole body and you know how good it is the minute your club head makes contact with the ball.

When I do something in my family because I really enjoy it, then my duty has become my pleasure. And it is a pleasure for all the people around me.

When it comes to my children I have to continually fight my tendency to try to raise them—to make them go the way I want them to go so they will make me look good. And I expect more maturity from them than I had when I was their age or even more maturity than I have now at forty-eight.

When I talk to other parents what is so unreal is their horror at some of the things kids are doing today. The only way they can be so horrified is to have forgotten what they did when they were kids. I ran around with every kid my age in Bricelyn, Minnesota. And I knew most of the other kids two and three years older and younger than me. They were all cut from the exact same cloth. The degree of hell that they would raise would be a little bit different, but it just wasn't that much different. Yet, I'm sure that today some of those kids' parents in Bricelyn are holding up a level for their kids that they were never able to measure up to themselves.

Recently one of my kids got in some trouble. I was telling him of some similar trouble I was in when I was about his age. Jackie couldn't restrain herself. She said, "Yes, I know you did those things, but I don't want to turn out like you!" And that's the problem. When we raise kids we know just exactly how we want them to turn out.

I want people to see my kids and marvel at their manners, their poise and their talent. I wasn't that way, but that's the point. I don't want my kids to start out like me. I don't want them to make the mistakes I made or that anyone else made and I want them to turn out better than me. And I want this exact same thing for all five of them.

There's no freedom for them in that. And no real learning either. How can you learn ballet or life without making mistakes?

When you ask me why I don't want my kids to make mistakes, I'll claim it's because I don't want to see them get hurt. But that's not really why I don't want them to make mistakes. I'm worried about my ego. I don't want people thinking less of me because of what my kids do. I don't want to have to fish my kids out of the police station. I want them on the stage at school winning awards. I want my children to be ornaments for me just like a new Cadillac sitting in the driveway is an ornament.

One of my students claimed that when she was faced with the issue of a kid getting a haircut, or whether they are going to make the honor roll or not, what she was really worried about was that kid. The more I thought about it, the more I thought she was crazy. We like to say what we are worried about is that kid, but I don't think so. I think we are more worried about our own egos. We're using our kids as extensions and instruments of our own egos, to build us up.

If we've got kids that are straight as a string and on the honor roll all of the time, and never give any adult any back talk and don't steal anything, and they are always respectful 100 per cent, and things like that, they are an adornment to us, just like a big diamond ring. They help show us off and we can walk downtown real comfortable knowing that our kid is always just exactly where he is supposed to be and doing just exactly what he is supposed to be doing. Nobody's got kids like that but that's the pressure we're putting on them to be. Well, what kid can ever live up to that kind of thing? And why should any kid be an ornament for us? They aren't a necklace or a piece of jewelry. If we want ornaments, buy 'em. But again, our tendency is to make our kids into things that will build us up. Any time they threaten to tear us down in any way in the eyes of our neighbors, boy, we really climb right up their frame. We let them know, by God, we ain't taking any of that crap. They are going to get their hair cut short like everybody else so their ears are showing. They're going to do that. Sure we justify it in the name of our concern about them.

Self-justification is the most dangerous thing there is because it blinds us to truth and reality. Sure it is awful to face that I am so mean to my kids because of my fears about what my neighbors will think. I can see this very clearly if I imagine my family was on a desert island. Would the long hair or not studying hard bother me there? No, it wouldn't. Well, that's the answer. If I say that my priorities are my higher power first and my family second, I had better act that way in my family. When I let my fear of what my neighbors might think control me, I'm putting his views of me in first place. And I shatter my commitment to my family.

If my family is my most crucial way of getting my needs met for mutuality, then I break down right in my most important relationships. Commitment means just that—commitment. And it means all the commitment I can muster up—until I can manage a deeper commitment.

"Well, should we as parents teach our kids the values that we have?"

No, we shouldn't try to teach values the way we want to by talking about what we think our values are. I think the only way you can teach them those values is to live them. I think that the saddest thing in the world is when we talk one value and live another. If you want to ask me am I a Christian, I will say, "No. I'm working on it." If a kid wants to ask me, "What do you think about honesty, Dad?" I will say, "Well, just look at the way I run my life, son, and you will know real fast how I really feel about honesty." I could defend honesty as a logical virtue, but what he is going to be most impressed by is what he sees. And I would far rather rest my case on that than run the risk of telling him these things.

I think the danger is we have a set of values that are hopes, for us. We're trying to live up to them, but failing. We want our kids to realize those hopes. Well I'm not realizing them, why should I ask my kids to. I've got a lot more muscle than they have in that area. So I think that we doom our kids to failure by a very unrealistic set of goals for them. We want them to do the things that we can't and didn't do. And the parent who wants to tell me that he can do the things he asks of his kids, just let me follow him around for a day.

We have all of these people who claim they are so law-abiding. There are a lot of you, I'm sure, who don't know how to make a legal turn off of one four-lane street into another four-lane street. If I was a cop, I could camp on your tail and I could arrest you, I bet, within fifteen minutes for something. You say, "Oh, I don't mean that. That's not really illegal." You want to redefine, all of a sudden, legality.

I don't steal any more. I used to. Well, I steal a little, but I don't steal like I used to. How come I cut down on the amount of stealing I did? Simple. I just found out that it didn't work. It made me feel bad. And I got so nervous that it canceled out any gain. And then there are some other things that entered into it more recently. Okay, say I'm going to tell my son, "Don't steal." I argue that is a value I have learned. Well, how did I learn it? I learned it by making mistakes and I got some of it from my father and grandfather, not by what they said, but by their example—what they did. I'm still learning from my father's example and he has been dead twenty years.

I think we are awfully overwhelmed by what we want our kids to represent. We overlook their strengths too much because we have our eyes so strong on their weaknesses.

I talked to you about the idea of valuing a person just as they are. That is the most precious thing that we can do for a human being. If valuing is as good as I say it is, it seems to me that I should do that first for my wife and the next most obvious people are my five kids. If my mind is full of a program for their self-improvement, I'm not valuing them as they are. And they feel it.

My old friend Vince believes you should sponsor a kid as you sponsor an alcoholic. When a guy gets drunk on one of my friends in AA who are sponsoring him, they don't go and yell at him and holler at him and slap him around. They wait until he sleeps off his hangover. They don't come butting in on him when he is feeling bad. They come around the next day and say, "Hey, how are you feeling?" And he says, "Gee, I'm sorry that I let you down and got drunk on you like that." They tell him, "Don't think anything of it. Hell, I've slipped, too."

This is what Vince means when he says, "You don't raise kids, you raise carrots. You sponsor kids." And that drives people up the wall when I even tell them about it. They say, "Oh my God!" But as near as I can see, my mother and dad did a lot of that with me. And I sure appreciate it. I don't say that I'm a good advertisement for the idea, but I sure appreciate it. They spent a lot of time asking me, "What do you think you're going to do next?" I would say, "Well I think that I'm going to do this." And they would say, "Fine. We were just curious as to what you had in mind." I made all my own decisions so my mistakes were all mine, too. There was no one I could blame them on.

"You talk about letting kids assume some responsibility, which I agree with, learn by their own actions, which I agree with, but how, for example, do you teach your kid not to ride a tricycle out in the street when they are only three years old? You can't avoid your responsibility for him. Obviously, you aren't going to let him get killed or get hurt."

That's right. It's like trying to teach somebody to float, you have your hand under them for a while and you take that hand away gradually. As fast as you can. But you don't go so fast that they drown on you. What I think we do is we use this principle to justify pounding hell out of that kid. Like so many parents who have left thousands of temptations in the kid's way and they go around slapping the kid's hands. Gotta teach him. Gotta teach him. The simplest way is to put temptation out of sight.

I don't say you necessarily let a kid reach out and touch a hot stove. But a kid is going to make mistakes. He is going to get hurt some. And the job of a parent is like teaching a person to float. You've got the hand under them real heavy at first, you may even have both hands under them practically holding them out of the water. Then you gradually move your hands away.

Let me tell you a story that has some bearing on this. My friend Vince was in the news store with one of his kids, Charlie. This is Vince's second family. He lost his first family to alcohol. So he is really taking care of the second one. Little Charlie is next to the youngest of five kids. Vince always had his kids ride in his plumbing truck with him until they were old enough to go to school. So they were in the news store together so Vince could buy some Copenhagen tobacco. Charlie says, "Can I have some candy, Dad?" "Yeah, go ahead and help yourself." Charlie came back with some candy in a sack and Vince asked him, "Are you sure you've got enough to last you all day?" And the little guy ran back and got some more candy. He came back and again Vince said, "Are you sure you've got enough? It's a long day." So Charlie went back and took a little more candy. Charlie's important to Vince.

We think that is indulging that kid and that's terrible. But our parents did that for us and it didn't screw us up, especially when it wasn't done in a sick way. It's just an open-handed gift. But I see a lot of times when we will use the idea, "Well, I've got to teach my kids. I've got to protect them from this or that, and I've got to guard them from this and that," and we use that way past where we should. Sure it is impossible to argue with the principle of not letting a three-year-old kid out on a street on their tricycle. There are some things we have to say "No" to. But you can say "Oh, no" to only so many things. So you had better set some priorities and say no to the things that are really important to you as you see it. And then that is it. And there has to be a lot of places where we aren't saying no. If you say no to everything then you're in trouble. And I think a lot of times that's what we fall into. The person who raises the point you have to protect the three-year-old doesn't fool me. The question is too obvious to need an answer. What is probably really bothering her is she wants to keep her eighteen-year-old son from going steady. She wants to protect him from girls.

A lot of people get mad at me when I talk this way. "Well that Jess, he says anything goes." I'm not saying that at all. But I am saying we are stepping in, in a lot of places with our kids where we shouldn't. I can show you kids coming out of our high school here in Bozeman who are beautiful illustrations of over-control. They are so packed into a Brownie box by the time they come to the university, they are just little mechanical men. They are just studying machines, Brownie point makers. It is going to take a lot of hard knocks to teach them anything about life. I have watched some of them go through four years of university trying to live with their fellow students and not learn a thing.

"At some times, don't some children not have enough discipline?"

Yes. You can go off either end. I don't see the kids in the bottom end very much. I see some of them but not so many because most of them don't make it to the university. I *can* see, though, that at least a third to a half of those kids on the high honor roll are really in trouble.

I was reading a biography of Einstein this morning. He took violin lessons from about eight until fourteen. His instructors were very mechanical. It was pretty much play the scales and stuff, no fun. He got ahold of some early records of Mozart's sonatas for the violin. He started studying them all by himself and he really started coming along with his love for the violin. This story in his biography was just another example to me of how we learn so much faster out of love than out of duty.

I was asked to speak at the National Honor Society initiation at Bozeman Senior High. I tried to tell the honor society that some part of their grades came from love of subject and some part of them came from a sense of fear and competitiveness. I told them how I made the honor society partly because I liked some subjects and partly to get better grades on tests than my friends. Hopefully they would work towards increasing the part of their grades that came out of studying out of a love of something and enjoyment of it, and decrease the part that came out of a sense of fear or sense of competitiveness and destroying the other person.

After my speech, the mother of one of the officers of the honor society came up and said, "Dr. Lair, you don't believe that anybody would ever study anything because they liked it, do you?" What can you say to a woman like that? The mother of an honor society officer? That kid has gone to school with a hot spear prodding him in the back all of his school life.

Most everything I have learned, I have studied because I liked it. Two thirds of my psychology courses I liked, or half of them at least. Sure there is stuff you don't like. I like psychology in general and I liked a good share of the courses I took. That is why I took the Ph.D. in psychology. I have done a lot of studying. I know more things about more out of the way subjects just because I love to study things. I have made a deep study of the ballistics of the 7-mm. magnum. It doesn't make any sense to know all I know about the ballistics of the 7-mm. magnum. It's dumb. But once I get interested and start studying, I'll soon have six books on the subject, and be reading like the dickens. I'll have a pile of notebooks full of notes. There's no grade, no nothing prodding me, just love.

When I talk like this about self-direction and doing things out of love, many of my students, young or old, get angry at me. They say, "That Jess, he is really screwed up." Again we can look at Einstein. Do you realize that the same year that Einstein was coming up with some of his crucial equations there were three other men who were publishing articles that contained most of the basic equations for the theory of relativity? The three of them were just a gnat's eyebrow away from it. In fact, they say you can derive the theory of relativity out of any of those other articles with just the equations that they put down. But I think the one thing that distinguished Einstein from those other three cats was they didn't have the guts to step away from tradition like

Einstein did. I think those others would defy tradition up to a point and then they would get frightened. What I think happened was Einstein had been raised in the same orientation towards the past as the other three men. But Einstein had the courage to go past the accepted boundaries. I will grant you this point, you can raise some very mediocre lawyers, doctors and scientists by this red-hot spear-at-the-back treatment. You can get exceptionally dutiful, high-achieving kids, but they have got an automatic ceiling in their training because their fear stops them from going so far or deep into things because that would be irreverent and disrespectful.

Some of these overtrained kids end up cussing us. "Why in the hell didn't ma and pa let me know that there were some other careers than the kind you go to college for?" I heard a dad get the shaft from his son for that back in Minnesota. I thought, "Hey, man, you are paying." He had these kids who were really straight. They had short haircuts and did everything right. For a parent with all my problems, it just makes you sick to your stomach watching kids like that. They have a sense of duty. They are on scholarships. But one of his sons who was in a profession said to him one day, "You know, I wish that I hadn't had so much pressure to go to college. I wish I was a tool and die maker."

I think he is a little frightened by the profession he is in. And he doesn't feel up to it. And yet he doesn't see himself as being free to change. If he really wants to be a tool and die maker, simple. Learn tool and die making at night while he is doing the job that he has got, and five years from now he will be a tool and die maker.

So, you can get anything that you want from your kids. The only thing is you've got to be willing to pay the particular price for whatever it is you want. And the price tag I'm talking about is if you are trying to treat your children and other people like individuals and trying to give them a degree of freedom, you've got to pay the awful price that freedom exacts. Which is, the mistakes are out in the open. All the mistakes are out in the open and you've got to face them straight on.

There isn't anything that doesn't have a price. You can stamp out kids just like cookie cutters, all you've got to use is enough fear and enough pressure and you can have anything that you want, and you pay the price in a different way. But not only do you pay the price for the kids but you pay a price for yourself. You separate yourself from them. Here are all these old people sitting around saying, "Why won't my kids come to see me?" Well, like I said earlier, why should they? Why would they want to? You see this in families. The minute those kids get married they go as far away as they can. I know all kinds of families where the kids have got jobs in all different corners of the United States and its possessions. Isn't it strange it happens that way? In my grandpa's family most of his seven kids never went more than sixty miles away. It wasn't in a dependent way but in a good way. They wanted to have work so they could stay close by home. I don't think that's an accident either. We still see families who stay together today. That's supposed to be impossible because of mobility and specialized careers. But in northeast Minneapolis where the Poles live, you see kids coming back to the neighborhood. They might come back as doctors or lawyers, even. But so many of them come back. If you want to be close to your family, you don't decide to be an oil engineer and go to North Africa. I think much of the mobility we see today isn't a basic cause of problems as much as it is an effect. A good way to avoid closeness is to run and keep on running. If your family rates a higher priority than work, then you find work that lets you be close to family. If work is most important in your life, then you go anywhere your work takes you. You may say, "Oh, I love my dear old dad and mother. I haven't seen them for ten years, but I sure love them." I don't understand that.

Each spring the trout are in the creek. Each fall the elk are up the Gallatin. Each winter the powder is on the Bridgers. Each day the sun is on the hills. Those of us who want to will be here together enjoying those things.

You can put distance between you and your parents for two reasons. You can go to some far place as a part of your own spiritual quest. Or you can put distance between you and your family because you can't stand to be around them. The person who leaves his family because he can't stand them will be a prisoner of that family. He has unfulfilled hopes and expectations from that family that tie him to them emotionally no matter how far he goes. He is just as tied to them as the one who hangs around forever who is also looking for something he didn't get.

The only way you can ever really leave your family emotionally is walk away from them seeing they gave you what they could. What they didn't give you, they didn't have to give. The son or daughter who leaves a family this way is free to move away or stay around depending on what's right for them.

It is hard for me being on the other end of this decision. I've watched three of my five children struggle with leaving home with more or less success. And it is sad to see some needs on their parts I couldn't fulfill. And the only thing they can do is see that it wasn't malicious-

ness on my part, just incompetence. By the time I had
learned even a few of the things I learned as a parent,
it was too late. Lord Rochester said, "Before I got married I had six theories about bringing up children; now
I have six children, and no theories."

Even worse, I'm still no good at some things that
are very important. I'm terrible at listening to my kids
when they are trying to talk out some problem. Once
in a while I can do it, but most of the time I can't. Fortunately, Jackie is good at this. She yells at me to listen
more, but unless there's a very special problem, I can
see I'm not good at it. She says to do it anyway. I try,
but it is easy for them to tell my heart isn't in it.

These are my failings as a parent. I see a few things
I can do and I'm thankful for them. But I would sure
hate to see my kids hanging around me until they were
fifty hoping that someday I would finally see the light
and start listening to them. I see the light now, but so
far the gift of listening to them well hasn't been given
me. And I know that thinking positively hasn't worked
very well for me. So I'll just have to bear down harder
on what I can do and hope for compassion on the part
of my kids. So far they have given me far more of that
than I ever hoped for.

I think the biggest problem I had as a father is realizing
how different each of my children are and learning to
respond to each of them as an individual.

My oldest son went with me from his earliest years
hunting and fishing. When he got to be fifteen he made
close friends and was with them. So I figured, "Okay,
it's now my second son's time to go hunting and fishing
with me." But he didn't care much for hunting and
fishing. But my youngest son did. My thought was, "I
can't take you, youngest son, because it's your middle

brother's turn." Except he didn't need or want his turn.

I finally got that straightened out in my head. Then I realized something even worse. My middle son enjoyed cars and would like to work on them. But I didn't like working on cars. I realized what I had been doing. I had been saying to my sons, "Come on and share my interests with me. If you do that, we will be able to do things together." That's a very limited deal.

I'm now seeing much more clearly how different each of my five children are from Jackie and me and from each other. And I've pretty well reconciled myself to the fact I'm not interested in a lot of things they are interested in and I'm not going to be able to pretend much interest I don't have. So we do together what we are interested in together. On the other things we find what companions we can.

My relationship with my wife was mutual. I chose her and she chose me. But my children just came. Another hard thing to face was that I couldn't change the amount of mutuality there is between me and each of my children. All I could do was accept the differing amounts of mutuality and do with it what I could. This hasn't been easy either. My ego says I'm a groovy parent. I'll have groovy relationships with all my kids. Except it doesn't work that way.

Once I woke up to the reality that I had five separate different relationships things got better fast. Now I can enjoy the wonderful qualities each of the five have and not try to force something artificial. In the process, I've gained what mutuality that is there so I've got five relationships that are valuable to me. They give me lots of good feeling about life and myself. And they hold up a clear mirror so I can see myself better and move along more smoothly on my spiritual quest.

But all this time, the hardest thing to do is let them make their own mistakes. I'm constantly screaming at myself, "What kind of lousy father are you? Don't you care about your children? Why don't you do what you are supposed to do to raise them up the way they should be raised and set their feet upon the paths they should be set upon?"

The only thing that helps me is so far I can't see that anyone did that to me so I'm trying to do the same for my children and not try so hard to raise them, but to do some sponsoring of them.

9

building a tribal community for ourselves

What I'm going to talk to you about now is mutual need in the community. In the next chapter I will talk to you about work. These two topics are closely interrelated and I see great confusion on both of them in myself and others. We feel we suffer in these two areas from a fault of our society. But as near as I can see every society has always been screwed up. Back in the biblical times you see this in the different troubles that the people went through in the Old Testament. They would go through upsets in their society due to the advent of new outside or inside forces. Maybe their crops gave out. Or they cut down all the trees and ran out of wood. Or the soil went bad after all those years of farming right there around that Mediterranean crescent.

So I think that upsets in society have always been

with us. But it is an immaterial point in a way because we didn't live then. We live now. And there is no question but that there are plenty of upsets in our society today. So the question is, what am I going to do about it? I've got two alternatives: I can sit around and bitch at society and think we should have a new one. Or I can build my own society the best way I can. And that's what I'm in the process of doing.

The funny thing I see is family, community and work are all tied together much more closely than I ever suspected. And really a major problem with our present society is that the three are unfastened, and we've got to find a way to fasten them back together. So, in a way, it is going to be hard for me to talk to you about these three things separately because we will overlap and there are some concepts that I need from work to talk about community and vice versa, but we will just have to deal with that as well as we can. Because ideally, in a way, if all those relationships are totally sustaining—family, community and work—they are all pleasant and they blur one into the other and you cannot really tell which one you are in. But if we think of work as unpleasant, and the community as strangers and our family as just our family, much of what should supply our needs isn't there.

I think the central problem in our family is we have tried to make it bear way too heavy a burden of mutuality in the sense of fulfilling our mutual needs. There is no way it can do that. There is no way a group of kids, much as I love them, and much as we love each other, can ever be to me all of the different things that I need as a human being. There is no way my wife can. The more I turn back to that family and the more load I put

on them—"Hey, you guys have to give me everything"—
the more I really frustrate them. And the less they are
able to give me.

In a way, the best example I have seen of what I'm
talking about is the romanticized version of what we see
as primitive tribal life. I told the Zulu story as I saw it
in my first book. In that kind of society there are many
people to help raise the kids.

I grew up in a small town in southern Minnesota
where we had some of the same benefits as a tribal community. I was mothered some by my aunts and uncles.
I was mothered and fathered some by three or four
other adults in the community so the burden that in a
big city would fall just on my parents was spread to
many others. Furthermore, no matter where I was in
Bricelyn, Minnesota, I was around people who knew who
I was. This had a tremendous effect in the sense of keeping me from feeling so alone and it helped keep me from
doing things as crazy as I would have done if I felt no
one knew me. You know, when you are anonymous
then you can do anything crazy.

I recently saw a study that showed school vandalism was highest in communities where there was the most
anonymity. The closer knit the community was, the less
vandalism. This is typical. I'm not going to throw rocks
at the school if I figure Mrs. Peterson is looking out her
window watching me. And if the janitor is Ralph Black,
who is my friend and he is going to have to clean up
the mess. And maybe some of the windows are in the
room Coach Anderson uses, who has been a good teacher
to me. And Ed Lund, who runs the school board, is a
pretty nice man. But if that school building is the place
mean old Miss Henry teaches and nobody knows who

I am, I'm going to throw a rock right through the window.

Good as the little town of Bricelyn was, it wasn't perfect. And even Zululand that I talked about in my first book wasn't perfect. I was romanticizing there. I thought then that some place in some time there must have been a Camelot where everything was beautiful. The stories I told about early Indian culture in the first chapter suggests something very different to me now. Things were never perfect. When we dream of a perfect place we hurt ourselves by looking for something that isn't there. But even worse we miss what things life can give us today. And while that's no perfect dream, it's better than nothing.

I see in these two contrasting views I have held about society a good answer to many of the problems we face today. I used to believe that we could solve any problem in our country or the world if we just approached it in the right spirit and threw enough money at it. I don't believe that any more.

When I see how hard it is to change even the simplest things in myself, I begin to see the near possibility of solving all the world's problems. We can and should take the sting out of some of those problems. We should feed the hungry and help cure the sick. But there is no way we can take all the suffering out of the world.

Even if by some tremendous effort we were able to evenly distribute food, medical care and housing, we would still have the greatest problem of all left, the grave emotional problems so many of us have.

The Indian stories show me life from an opposite viewpoint. Rather than try to change everything in life we should try to change what we can and try to learn to fit in with anything we can't change.

When I see things this way, I'm not wringing my hands about the terrible lack of community we have, I'm quietly going to work building the best community for myself I can. This way I get some help in satisfying the emotional needs of my family.

The family works at its very best when it is nestled in a community which will perform many of the functions that the family is now asked to perform. Now these aren't necessarily replacement functions. In a way they can be looked on as supplemental functions. But it takes a tremendous load off Ma and Pa to know that the kids have got five to ten mothers and five to ten fathers. Two or three might be people who play a very substantial part in the child or young person's life.

One of the things I'm trying to do here in this town is I'm trying to build an emotional community where first of all there are people who can serve some of my needs, but secondly people who can help me with some of my fathering and my wife with some of her mothering duties. A neighbor of mine commented on the tremendous obligation that he and his wife felt for what I had done for their daughter. I recognized that I had been able to listen to her and value her when few others did, but I said, "Hey, you are doing some things for my sons. And you are doing some things for me, and that's the way it is." And I said, "There are lots of times there are things we can do for somebody else's kids that we can't do for our own, and this is where this back and forth thing comes in."

So it helps me directly in this community to have other people who can satisfy my need for mutuality and then they can also help in this mothering and fathering process. Now the sociologists talk about this, I guess, as the extended family. This is easy to talk about but very hard to do. Until you can put some names on the people who are doing some mothering and fathering for your children the extended family is just an idea in a sociology book.

Our friend Sharon, who lives neighbors to us up the canyon, was telling us how much we did for her. And then a little bit later we were saying Mike would like to come up and play at their house and she said, "Oh, I hate to even suggest that. I love to have him around, but I just am hesitant to interrupt and impose into your family." We said, "Hey, that is exactly opposite of the way we would hope you'd feel. What we mean is we want you to be part of our family in that way. Because Mike gets some very special things from you, that only you can give." And she hadn't thought of it in that way. In that case, she and her husband are people who are very close to my wife and me, so they are friends of ours as well as doing some mothering and fathering.

Old Ralph Black, our school janitor, was kind of a dad to me; he started me off hunting and some other things that my dad just didn't have time for or didn't like to do. He didn't like to go hunting with kids but that was fine because Ralph Black did.

These relationships don't always involve both the husband and the wife together. The idea of mutuality says you don't try to force mutuality when it isn't there. My wife has her friends, I have my friends, and my wife and I have our friends. I'm not going to stop having somebody as a friend just because the wives don't groove on each other. It's simple. We will just set up our own deals. It is the same for her. If some husband of a friend of hers and I don't hit it off too well that's no problem.

I have an obligation to try to be as compatible as I can, but nevertheless, that shouldn't be a bar to her to have the friends she wants. We are fortunate that in many cases they are friends to both of us.

Until I came here I had almost no sense of community even though I was raised in a very tight community in a very tight family. I had some sense of family, but I had very little sense of community. I am just now getting some. "Well, that's kind of late," you say. It is. But it sure beats never. And I'm building for my retirement right now in the sense that the more integrated I am into this community the more people there will be who are interested in me twenty years from now.

Even though I had a community I didn't realize what I had gotten from it and what I was losing by not having a community. When I would move my family at a moment's notice I never let a community have a chance to form for me. In Bricelyn I had one because my grandparents settled there and because of my dad's good work and my mother's good work.

Now I've got to switch over and get one because of my good work. Here is this twenty-year gap of me just doing nothing about community and ignoring my needs. But like I say, that is too bad and better late than never. Maybe you don't need to make all these mistakes.

If somebody had talked to me along these lines, at the time I was twenty-five, I wonder if I would have paid much attention to them. I don't know. I do know you don't hear much of this kind of stuff around. So many people are in the process of just throwing up their hands and saying, "There is no community." The heck there isn't.

We romanticize so when we look back. But things

weren't so good in those good old days. The great pioneer who started our town, John Bozeman, deserted his wife and two small girls back in Virginia. Many other men who settled this area left their families behind and spent years away from them. The letters they sent home are full of self-justifications and reasons for not bringing their families out. The truth most likely was those men were happy to be away from their wives or they wouldn't have let five to ten years go by before they saw each other.

Here in the West there is a great glorification of the strong-minded independent men who won the West. There is some truth in that being a good quality. But there needs to be a balance in everything. Too much of anything can kill you. And too much independence and strong-mindedness leads me to the position that I am completely self-sufficient. I am a rock. I am an island. But I don't want to live that way. I've seen what people who live that way come to. I think that's why our state almost leads the nation in its suicide and divorce rates.

I don't think those good old pioneer days were all that good. And I don't think these bad new times are all that bad. I've just been in this town eight years. And I didn't have anybody here before me to pave the way. But I'm already finding a real sense of community. Much of what we have came because I finally saw the need for commitment in my relationships.

What I am so struck by, about half of the people in Bozeman are really part of this community. Each of them are members of a whole set of interlocking circles. A whole bunch of different people's communities. And it is pretty well permanent and fixed. But the other half of the people in this town feel no sense of community. This is just a pretty place to live. It is just like a tent camp down at Jackson Hole. You don't know who is going to be in that tent on either side of you the next morning. So there is a half of the town that is just like a bunch of nomads floating through and another half of the town is people who have really made a commitment, not necessarily to the town, but to some of the people in the town. So half of the people in Bozeman say there isn't such a thing as community left any more. Yet right in the same town, there is half of Bozeman that is experiencing a good community. The funny thing is it's always been this way.

I have made a commitment to Vince. I've made a commitment to Jerry, I've made a commitment to Dave. If I say, "Jerry, I think I will move to Chicago, they're offering me a promotion to professor," I'm sure Jerry would very rightfully wonder why I would be willing to give up so much for so little.

I can see the fact I had a community when I was young gave me some strength, tremendous strength that I needed through the years. I didn't realize where some of that strength was coming from until I started looking back.

One of my students wanted to defend and justify my moving around the country as a valuable experience. Only in a small way was it valuable. Mostly it was a mistake. But I needed that mistake. I got something out of it. But it was just a mistake in the same way going out and getting drunk on wine for twenty years is a mistake.

I broke up my relationships in Minneapolis where we lived for quite a while and went to Chicago. About the only friends we really made there were the Oquists, then we moved away from them after we just got acquainted.

So one of the primary messages I was giving to people in all those transactions was, "Drop dead for all I care."

I read a story in *Fortune* recently on executive mobility. That's a system top corporation executives use to select and produce people as single-mindedly devoted to their corporation as they are. You move people so often that the only thing left in their life is work, money and power.

One businessman was about to be moved for the tenth time. His two kids were fifteen and seventeen. They had changed schools eight to ten times. The kids refused to change schools again. The dad tried to tell them about the extra money and power that would come with the new job but they weren't interested.

But see how narrow that businessman was. In business he would never try to make a sale where he had nothing to offer and everything was against him. He would know he'd be laughed right out of the office. But here he was at home telling his two kids that he would give them some money as a replacement for the pain of breaking off their relationships.

His other mistake was in even talking with them about the move. When I was doing those things, I just told my family we were moving. I didn't give them a chance to object, because it was my work that was involved. And work was the source of money and power, which were my gods. I used to think it was only in Babylon that the people had put up strange gods before them. I wondered why they would be so foolish as to worship a golden calf. And all the time I was worshiping a corporation. Whatever controls us is what is our god. When money controlled me, that was my god. I try not to worship money any more and use it to buy groceries instead.

A student commented, "One of the people I feel closest to in this community is Harry. We have been very close friends for about eight years. And he made a comment one day that if he were to get an offer from one of the other universities that he would go and then forget the people who are here. When someone you feel close to says something like this, it really makes you stop and think."

This is what I mean. I might have some relationships like that but I don't want to have them all like that. That's the kind of relationships I used to have. When I left nobody missed me enough to write me a letter. That helped give me a heart attack and led to an empty life. I've found now there's something more to life and this is it.

"You can build a community, can't you, if you move often. I mean five or six months. You can still build a community, don't you think?"

You can make yourself believe you can, but you see how little it is when you see how few of those people you write to and really keep in touch with. The test that I see of a deep relationship is, when you meet them, there isn't any of that strain. You pick up where you left off. And it is easy and smooth between you. And I find that smoothness only in a few of those relationships I broke off in those different communities I left so fast. In fact Jim Larkin, Bits Osterbauer and maybe a half dozen other people back in Minneapolis are all I can do that with. But that's not very many for all those years.

You see, what we think of as cordiality and friendship isn't what we are talking about here. I can move and within three weeks have people to be having coffee with and saying "Hello" to and things like that. And there can be a fair degree of warmth and cordiality there, but to say that that is a good relationship to me is a terrible thing. Look what Dave Sullivan and I have got between us now after seven years together. There is no way we can rebuild that thing in less than seven years. Or build something like that. You can't re-create instantly those experiences between you, where you open your hearts to each other, where you go through things together.

Mutual need therapy is about the *deep* relationships that lift you up. Sometimes I go to lunch on campus with someone I'm just cordial with. And I can tell the difference. I can go to lunch with one of the guys that I say "Hello" to quite a bit and I come back and I don't feel anything. When I go out to lunch with Jerry or Bob Hickman I feel different afterwards. It's the difference between two things that look very much the same when you first think about them. We hear a lot about cordiality and warmth and ain't that great. But in my experience now, that is a way of keeping people at arm's length without being aware of it. It is a way of creating an illusion, a fantasy. Those relationships don't nurture our souls. They don't let us see within ourselves. We don't reveal ourselves to those people. If I move every six months, I will never find out who I am.

"These people you have mutual need with, are they the only people in your community, or are they the main ones?"

They are the main people in my community. Many people make that mistake and I have done lots to foster it when I say things like "You are either in my club or you ain't." I don't mean it that way. But I do discriminate between the main people and the others and I find it very helpful. If I'm going to lunch with somebody who isn't going to lift me up I say, "Well, I'm not going to get lifted up at lunch today, probably." I'm not closing myself to the possibility that that relationship can deepen. But I am trying to see the reality of that relationship at the moment.

The thing about these communities I've got is that they are like a bunch of circles. There are different people in different circles. There's my university community, with Jerry Sullivan, Lowell Hickman and Dick Horswill and some of the other people who are in that community. There is my neighborhood community, with Sullivan, Dick Wike and some others who live around me. And there is the Main Street circle, and the church and the school. It is a series of circles and they interlock to some degree and some of those people are in some of the same circles. And then each of those people have got their own circles, too.

A lot of people get the impression that I am talking about a closed system. They say, "Hey, you aren't reaching out." I am, too. When I presented these ideas originally, I was reaching out to the twenty-five people in my evening class, forty people in the noon ed psych class and twelve people in the graduate behavior modification class, plus most of the other people who go through my life. I'm not going to force myself on anyone, but I do try to reach out my hand with love and friendliness to all the people I meet. If they choose not to take what I offer, which is myself, that's fine. Some people I see frequently communicate to me, "Don't touch me." I must respect that, too. Others have communicated to me, "I don't want to be really close to you, I just want to pretend we are close." Those people I can't oblige. I don't want to play that game any more. They can play it with someone else. I know that game can kill me.

The whole thing is a community. One of the reasons I came to Montana is that it was a small enough state so no matter where my students are they are still in my community. I haven't lost touch with them.

"Don't women hang onto their friends much longer than men?"

As a general rule, yes. They are so much more personal. Guys have the same opportunities but they are too dumb to recognize it. That's why the guys die so much faster. They use the business world to run away from themselves. They use that structure. I refuse to buy this baloney about how the structures change men. We've got fantastic sense of the structures available in certain situations and we just justify our actions. The structures exist for our benefit rather than vice versa. We created them through our choices.

Someone wants to argue, "Well, the corporation is the way it is and it won't change." But that's simple. I don't need to work for the corporation. I'm not asking to live any way I want on my terms. The corporation exists as it is because lots of men want to live that way.

The men who stop having money and power as their gods leave the corporation or they settle for the best jobs they can get without moving any more. And it is not all of the corporation life that is characterized by mobility. Mobility is a fact of life mostly for the guy who wants to get to the top in a hurry. I knew a great many people in the big corporations in the Twin Cities: Cargill, Honeywell, 3M, Control Data, General Mills, Pillsbury. Most of the people I knew moved once or twice or not at all. But we need to justify our crazy conduct by arguing that everybody's doing it. We won't accept that excuse from our children: Everyone's wearing long hair and smoking pot. We laugh at that. And then we turn right around and justify our own actions by saying everyone in corporations moves all the time. No. Only those who are rushing to be president. And yet the president usually turns out to be someone who plugged away at the home office for a long time.

So it is a whole group of our choices that shaped the structure of the corporation. The minute all the people in the corporation refused to be moved like checkers on a board the corporation would change. But we don't need to wait for that. All we need to do is find structures in society that favor the things we favor and use them to help us instead of deciding the minute we change our minds and decide to live differently, then IBM must change its mind and life differently. That's childish and immature to ask the world to bend to our will. My job is to accept most of the world just as it is because I can't and shouldn't try to change it. All I can change is the few things I put my hand to today. But that's enough for me. And it's enough to make the last few days very lovely.

Our school systems are much criticized today. Actually they are beautiful instruments to serve just what most people want, which is to keep the kids quiet and out of the way for eight hours a day. The majority of the people want the schools just exactly the way they are. You try to change them and you will find out how much that is so.

When I spoke to the Montana Mental Health Association there was a minister from Livingston at the head table. I said, "Our churches are just exactly the way we want them. We complain about how cruddy they are."

I said, "Pastor, if I were to tell you next Sunday you go into your church and preach the sermon you want to preach to those people, I will subsidize you the rest of your life if they try to throw you out, wouldn't you be different?" Or to put it a better way, I said, "If your parishioners came to you as a whole body and said, 'Pastor, we've been holding you down all this time and we finally realized that we want you to start preaching to us the sermons that you really want to preach.' " I said, "Wouldn't that free you to say what you've always wanted to say?" He was sitting right there beside me at the head table where I was speaking. He just grinned. Nobody had ever made him an offer like that before. But boy, he had a ready-made "Yeah, that would really be great."

So our institutions serve us rather than molding us. Now, this again goes right back to this question of will we take responsibility for our choices or won't we? We can sit around and cry and blame the institutions or we can do what we can. It isn't ever too late. I have seen people sixty-five and seventy who come into AA saying "Thank God I have this much time," instead of cursing the forty-five years of drunkenness.

And again, we cry, "What can poor little old me do against the fantastic combined forces of society?" I could care less about what society is going to do. Well sure I care a little bit, but 99 per cent of my energies are devoted to having a nice society for me. I was driving by a teacher-friend's playground the other day when I saw her out there and I stopped to talk to her. Okay, she is in my society. She is a very pleasant lady. Now, if she doesn't want to be in my society, she can get out by treating me mean and kicking me when I come around.

In most every community that I have been in you could build a community within that community—except for a few. In Edina, Minnesota, one of the wealthiest suburbs in the United States, I think it would be nearly impossible to build a community. It was a bunch of people who would eat their own young, they were so competitive and grabbing for money. There were a few nice people, but most of them are like I was, intent on the buck and their social standing. While there are some people in Edina who sense and believe in the kind of ideas I do, they are so scattered and there is so little real community structure there, it would seem to me ridiculous to try to make the effort. So if I would have had the ideas I now have when I was living in Edina, I would have moved, because it would have been too tough to do it there. There is no center for the community. And money is too much in the way and too much on everybody's minds. Part of this is my problem with money and people who have it.

I think what I might have done is gone farther up in northeast Minneapolis and live with the Polish people if they would have me. Those guys are still buying their houses with cash. They walk into the bank with a cardboard box full of bills and they start counting them out onto the desk, the whole $30,000. Some of the money smells of socks and mattresses and other hiding places. Now that's the kind of people who understand community. Any metropolitan area I have ever seen has got places in it, many of them, where you can build a community for yourself.

Also, the closer relationship your community and your work have to each other, the better. If I am a traveling salesman in Bozeman, that is the worst possible kind of an occupation. Then I've got to do extra things to integrate myself with the community, because I don't have the effect of my work. Now, my work being over at the university is about the next worst thing to being a traveling salesman, because I have so little contact with the community. So that in a way I am really living away from the mainstream of the community and it would be somewhat better if my work were directly with the community.

When I first came here I thought because I had been a businessman so long I could be a part of the business community and not get into this town-gown controversy— the problem you find in small towns with big universities. I had been a businessman for fifteen years and a professor for only five, so I joined the Lions Club and some of those other things. But because of that doctor title, and because I worked up there on the hill, there was no way I could get out of that bag that they had me in.

Here some guy comes into the Lions club meeting who runs the filling station and he has his filling station clothes on and he knows I am from the university and he feels crummy. That makes him start feeling mad. There were plenty of mad people. I heard comments about guys like me with their noses in the government trough as if I have never done anything to make a living. If I wanted to make money and pay a lot more taxes I could do a lot better financially than what I was doing. I have met more payrolls than a lot of these guys here. And I know a lot more about what kind of contribution I am making in relation to the money I am getting than they do.

I was educating their kids in a sensible way, and yet they wanted to put me down for being a leech or parasite on society. Okay, I couldn't take that very well, so I got out of that group.

I have been in the process since then of finding the businessmen I wanted to live with and have as part of my community. It was partly my fault because I was pushing. I was saying, "Hey, we are going to have a relationship on my time schedule." Anytime you start pushing human relationships you are in trouble. It is like forcing flowers.

A lot of new people make another mistake. They join so many things they can't be active in any of them. I have seen some of those guys, and that is a real mistake. And this is something I saw I needed to avoid. So I picked one organization I believed in, the Gallatin Sportsmen. I was on the board of directors and I was going to be president except I got sick and I could see I wasn't suited for the presidency, but I was active in a number of ways. I was able to be active by keeping down the number of things I was in. We had some guys who were trying to do twenty-six different things, and it was just a disaster. It was very unpleasant for them, much more so than for us, because we always had back-up people to do a job.

Okay, I have made a commitment to this community. I have made a commitment to a number of people in the community, and I am in the process of slowly establishing myself here, because this is crucial to me. The people in this community are the people who are going to help raise my children. They are the people who are going to lift me up when I need lifting up. They are the people who are going to help me discover who I am.

You know, one of the funny things I like about a community is it keeps me honest. I got a telephone call recently from a gal in Los Angeles. She said, "Jess, there is a college down in Dallas that's just dying to have you come down there. They want your hot little body. The students down there are using your book as a Bible. Would you be willing to go down there and speak to them?" I said, "No, I don't want to do that kind of stuff." She said, "Well, keep your mind open."

Okay. That's really great. I have been to a few of those campuses before. Here are all these people coming out to see the famous person. Well, it is very easy to buy that picture of yourself, except for one small difficulty. That is, my students and my communities keep me honest. As I would be standing in this huge auditorium speaking I would know all the time that back home I'm running a class where a third of my students can't stand me. That's reality. Almost anybody can draw a crowd one time around. You don't ever have to come back to see if you can draw a crowd the second time. What they are doing is buying just a name that is on a book a lot of people are reading. It is very easy to think that means a lot. It actually means very, very little. But I have seen a lot of people get sucked in and start believing their own publicity. Then you are really in trouble. Again, this is why it is nice to have a community.

Speaking about community, Vince and Wally were saying that there were some awful nice people on skid row. Vince said, "Hell, if I had my choice, I would rather live with those skid row people than here in Bozeman. Them were nice people. They were awful nice people. A good class of people when they were sober. And they were entertaining and sympathetic." He and Wally had both spent a lot of time on skid rows all across the country.

The interesting thing about a community, of course, is the tremendous variety in interests it provides for. Our little country club performs a very important function for a certain part of our community. We have a little symphony that does most everything a big symphony can do for the people in a community. To me, what is crucial about the community is there should be a diversity of human needs served. I don't want everybody to be like me. To me that is the power of my individuality. If everybody was like me wouldn't that be awful? And boring? Okay, so there's diversity, you see.

So we have this tremendous variety of people. It is our diversity that holds the world together. And if there is a lesson to me in life that I would like to learn, it is indirectly reflected in the book *Siddhartha* by Herman Hesse where he has Siddhartha seeking peace. Siddhartha ended up ferrying people back and forth across the river on this ferry. He got to the point where he could view with some tolerance the diversity of people he ferried across: the businessman who was all preoccupied with money, the woman who was all preoccupied with social status, the prostitute with her affairs and the ignorant man with his prejudices. But the sadness was, you see, he was still conscious of them as apart from him. He saw himself as pursuing godliness and as a man of higher philosophy. Yet he saw himself as being apart from the other people.

To my mind, the ideal person in the community is not seeing himself apart from other people. He is seeing himself as simply a member of the community, most particularly, a member of his subcommunities. But he is not looking down or up at the other people in the community—just across. And you see, Siddhartha was looking down on these people he was taking across the river and in that sense his search for peace may not have gone as far as it could. I think that's very crucial. Now I tend to be too judgmental. I sit awful light in the saddle and I'm not real comfortable with what I'm doing and what others are doing.

More and more I would hope that I could be increasingly comfortable and increasingly oblivious to what people do and what their preoccupations are and what is their diversity. Because you see I need that diversity. It is fantastically precious because it is only that diversity that defines me. If we are all cookies stamped out by a cookie cutter, if we are all robots with interchangeable parts, then everything I value is gone. So while there is a part of me that wants everybody to be like me, there is a sane part of me that realizes that would be the most awful thing in the world.

"It seems like people and myself don't have time to get involved with other people," one of my students said. "Maybe we use lack of time as an excuse. Because I know a lot of people that I would like to get to know better. But I know they don't have a lot more time than I do." Sure we're too busy. But as I told that student, I think we're too busy because we need our busyness to run away from each other and keep from facing ourselves. When we're ready to step down off the merry-go-round we can have lots of quiet.

I saw in a newspaper column the other night a comment that the more associations and committees a woman belongs to the more unhappy the marriage. Vice versa. The more associations and committees a man belongs to the unhappier the marriage. Now I see those activities can be a means of running away from ourselves. One of my few associations is a group that I meet with every Wednesday night. And that is a group that is a part of my community.

Someone asks, "Who is going to run the Boy Scouts? Who is going to run the Little League? Who is going to run the rest of the stuff?" The answer I have to say is, "Not me, man." If that is important to you, run it. If it isn't important to you and somebody doesn't run it, okay, my kids aren't going to be in it.

"I don't have a deep relationship with anybody outside of my family," said one of my students. "Sometimes I feel like I would like to, but I just never did. When I was thinking about it, I realized that's why you gave us the assignment to look at our relationships. But I keep thinking, 'I will do it later when I have the time.' And I can pick quite a few people out I would like to have a deep relationship with, but I don't do it."

"She has a community in our school," another teacher said, "she just doesn't know it."

But this is the difference between cordiality, which I am sure she has, and that deeper thing where you can say to that intimate friend, "Hey, look at the awful thing I did." That's the deep one that heals your soul and lifts you up and transforms you into a different person. Now there are a lot of large size children in this world. I'm not going to name any names. But one of them is writing this book. I would just as soon that large size child grow up some more in certain areas. To do that, I need more than cordiality. And again, cordiality can be a means of both protecting ourselves from close relationships as well as a means of hiding ourselves from our lack of depth in relationships. You can't have swarms of close friends.

To have a close friend means that you are there when needed even though you do not know ahead of time that you are going to be needed. When we get in trouble, the world usually closes in on us so much we can't even see our need for help. But when we have close friends, our inability to call for help doesn't hurt us because one of our friends will be by soon anyway. But this can't happen if I try to have a hundred friends. That's why I have five friends. That doesn't sound like many to lots of people, but even with just five friends I see how hard a time I have at being a good friend to them.

"I know some people who want to spend as much time as they can away from home so they don't have to be around the family. They would rather be out and do as many things as they can and still hold onto the family."

The first mutuality that we've got to face is in our family. Now, if running away from the family a lot is the best a person can do, okay, that is the best they can do. And I have seen situations where the person will finally face the music and develop some mutuality outside the family which could then help feed back into the family.

As I have said, I think our basic problem is loneliness. I see that loneliness coming out of our self-centeredness. We have ourself at the center and ask the world to revolve around us. "Man all wrapped up in himself makes one small unhappy bundle," said one of my students. We need to get out of the center and to see that we need one another. And, of course, the point is most specifically we need those where there is mutuality. It is like the body analogy where the kidney needs the bladder most of all, or it is going to burst. The kidney needs the ankle and the foot, but not so much. So while we are all part of one body the specific things that we need the most are the things that are in that sense of the body analogy right around us, where there is mutuality.

One of the points brought up was, "Jess, don't these circles in the community that are so separate eventually become one?" And I said no, I didn't think so because of the tremendous diversity in us. And it is the diversity, you see, that makes individuality meaningful. There is a great circle of humanity, a great circle of all life, which includes inanimate objects like the rock. In that sense we are all part of one circle, but I don't expect to come to this sense of oneness. I have too much trouble with the diversity I see around me.

The funny thing that I see is the more we see each of these little circles and the more specifically we work on them, the more we can become part of the bigger circle at least in a partial sense. And the more love that we give in these mutual relationships, the more we free those other people in those relationships to be also part of the larger circle. And this goes right back to the biblical idea of "Love thy neighbor as thyself." What we are talking about is how to love thyself more. As we get stronger at loving ourselves, then we can reach out to the other person.

If you despise yourself, there is no way you can love anybody else. Absolutely no way. You can lie about it and that is the most common response. But there is absolutely no way. And like we said here, again in the religious context, there is no way you can love God if you despise the most principle of his creations, which is yourself. Until I can see that I am really kind of a cute little fellow, and a kind of a loveable little guy, there isn't any way I can reach out to somebody else with any kind of love and friendliness. The minute I say, "Boy, when God made me, he sure used the wrong recipe," there is no way that haughty so and so can do anything for anybody. As one of my students said, "God made me and God don't make junk." Even that is much easier to give lip service to than it is to practice.

"Can't you be a little dissatisfied with some things about yourself?"

Yes, maybe some things. But hopefully, you are working on changing some of them. But again, a lot of people are saying, "Oh woe is me, I hate this and that part of me." And I say, "Well, what are you doing this afternoon to change it?" "Well, nothing. Who can expect anything out of me?"

A guy said, "Hey, Jess, you're talking about a tribal society but we can't have a tribal society. Our country is too big for that any more." I said, "No, it is the opposite to that." Because our population is so large is no reason for not doing these things I'm talking about. If anything it gives us more reason to do them. We need to be realistic about who we can really have mutual relationships with and about our real abilities as they are. The more real relationships we have, the nicer we can be to our neighbor who isn't in our circle and the more we can come close to his ideal of loving everybody. The more real love we get in our life, the more we can love ourselves and the more we can manage a better love for our neighbor. Otherwise we pretend a phony love that comes out of self-hate, not love.

So, in a way, this is building a tribal society. But out of the tribalness comes a vaster sense of our interrelationships with all creatures as well as with all things. Because so much of the destructiveness we see comes out of the tremendous ego scenes: making money and conspicuous consumption. I've still got way too much ego, but I have progressed enough so my ego isn't tied up with my automobile or my house as badly as it once was.

Each of our new relationships is like love: It is like a butterfly sitting on your open hand. You don't try to hold the butterfly. You let him sit there. You enjoy his presence. But if the butterfly flies away, okay. Put some honey in your hand and hold it out again. There will be others.

Some of my students didn't like the risks I was suggesting. I have bad news for that point of view and it is this: The minute I adopt a no-risk philosophy, I stop reaching out so I don't get hurt. That way I automatically guarantee my immediate death. And I have incurred the biggest hurt of all. The minute I say I won't risk anything any more, I ensure and guarantee my own death. You only have two alternatives and they both are very risky. You either say, "I'm never going to risk loving again," or you say, "Okay, I'm going to risk loving as soon as I heal up a little."

Sure we have to pay attention in life. I won't go around loving the cockleburs of this world. I love the easy ones. I'm looking for the easy ones, and I will love them, and that way I have so much better chances. How do you tell who is a cocklebur for you? I see a lot of clues.

A young guy about twenty-five I was skiing with had some trouble with his first marriage and got divorced. He said, "Jess, I want a woman with a good heart. Somebody to really talk to." So then we are riding on the ski tow and he says, "Wow, look at that dish!" You stupid jerk. What are you looking for, baby? Are you looking for a good heart like you said? Or are you looking for something else? You don't find a good heart by looking for a pretty face. You find a good heart by looking for a good heart. If it has a pretty face, that is okay.

One of my students got really upset with me. She said, "Jess, you're telling us all these good things and I want them. But you aren't telling me how to get from here to there."

This is a question I get very commonly. I know I don't explain in careful detail just how you can do what I'm talking about. But I'm explaining in the very best way I can. I can't break this process down into simple steps. When I do that you lose the truth. All I can say to such a question is to go back over what I've said and think about it. Look for the implications of the stories I've told. Try to see what principles I've found it necessary for me to follow. Then figure out what would be some good things for you to try.

Most of the people who write me about my books get the point of them in just the first few chapters. Others finish the first two books and say, "Jess, tell me what to do." I can't do that. Only you can tell you what to do. The biggest deficiency I see in the psychology books available to you is that they are too logical. So they miss the truth. They are too intellectual. You can't analyze feelings that much. As the Chinese Tao say, you can't divide the ten thousand things. They are one. Anytime I try to speak of one thing at a time, I take the chance of destroying everything. Our chaos, confusion and loneliness is an entity that needs to be faced for what it is: confusion. If we try to escape the confusion and organize it completely, we take away truth, too.

So the only simple rule I can give you is practice.

It is just like riding a bicycle. You tell your child that

if he starts falling to one side, turn the wheel to that side and keep going. You give him the basic principle and then he practices. He falls down and gets hurt but he doesn't let that mistake and that hurt stop him. He gets up and keeps on practicing. Because if he doesn't he has to sit home and he can't go where the other kids are going on their bicycles.

I've been practicing for twelve years now building a community for myself. I've looked at my mistakes as honestly as I can. And much as my daily lessons sometimes hurt, I'm going to keep on practicing. It is very clear to me each day what the beautiful benefits are. I'm living a life I didn't even know existed five years ago. But if you want to look at the consequences of poor living, look at people who retire. Most of them don't have anybody who really cares about them, including their own children. Their only happiness was tied up in their work and their clubs. When that's taken away from them they die in a few years.

They wouldn't honestly look at their lives while there was time to do something. And now they're paying the price. The only person who will listen to their complaint is "Dear Abby." So they tell her what lousy, ungrateful kids they have. That may be fine for them, but I don't want to go that way. So I'll keep on working, practicing, making mistakes, but slowly building a community for me.

10

loving our work

The most common escape from life isn't drugs, alcohol, sex or soap operas—it's work. Until we can stop escaping into our work, there is no way we can see life as it is for us and live it. Not only do we use work as an escape, we get our egos all wrapped up in our work. For many of us this is so common that our first question of a person we meet at a party so often is "What do you do?" And we mean "What is your job?" We define ourselves and our worth by how high or low our jobs are.

We have to get our work in proper perspective before we can have our energies free to develop mutual relationships. Not only that, I've seen that when we work for the right reasons, our work goes better too because we have things in better balance.

I mentioned earlier that one of the greatest football

coaches who ever lived got such good work from his players by putting football third in importance in his players' lives. The priorities Vince Lombardi had and that he urged for his players were: 1. God, 2. family and 3. the Green Bay Packers. By putting football third he produced great winning records by men who also had outstanding achievements in their later lives off the field.

So just as you can't do a good job of developing mutual need relationships if you are constantly hiding in alcohol or pills, neither can you see life clearly if you are hiding out in your work.

Our health has also suffered because of our work. We have made many health advances in the last seventy years. I have wondered if a new disease will come along we haven't a cure for. What I see is that's already happened for men and it's happening for women. The disease is "hurry sickness." It mostly comes out of our work where we are trying to go faster and faster and it's killing us.

When I had my first heart attack I was told to slow down. But I could see it took so much struggle for me to slow down that I wasn't gaining very much. So I saw my personality had to be changed if I was to go slower. About five years later I saw the first reports on Type A behavior[1] which confirmed what I had guessed about myself. For twelve years now I've been working on finding ways to change my personality. Originally I just wanted to live longer. I now see these ideas are even more valuable because they make each day more enjoyable as well as let me live longer. My writing is simply a reporting of my struggle to find a better way of life. That's why the title of this book is *I Ain't Well—But I Sure Am Better*.

[1] *Type A Behavior and Your Heart*, Meyer Friedman, M.D., and Ray H. Rosenman, M.D. Fawcett Paperbacks, 1975.

Things are going good for me now compared to before.
But I can see so many things that may yet come to me.
As I saw originally one of my most crucial problems was
the way I buried myself in my work, so that's why seeing
work clearly is so important to me.

Freud thought there were two things a mature human
being should be able to do: to love and to work. But I
think most of our work can be done out of love. So then
there is just one thing a mature human being has to do
and that is to love. When you see it that way it eliminates
the idea of work as the curse of man.

That sounds simple, but it has taken me many years
to be able to understand that simple statement. I chose
the advertising business so I could make a lot of money
and impress others. I decided I was going to be an advertising agency account executive because I presented a
good appearance and was a good talker. I was guided
strictly by my egotism and self-centeredness. All I was
looking at was what I wanted.

I believed in the power of positive thinking. I believed
that all I needed to do to have success was to think
success. I just needed to have a clear enough picture
of what I wanted to do and I could do it. I pushed those
ideas as far as a human being could push them.

Fortunately for me, after a few years in advertising
I ran into two books that had an exactly opposite idea.
David Seabury's book, *How to Get Things Done*, said we
should find the things we were good at, that we loved.
That was the way to get things done. I had trouble
believing that what he said was possible. It didn't sound
practical.

But I also ran across another book that put the same
idea in a practical sounding way. It was William J.

Reilly's book, *How to Make Your Living in Four Hours a Day—Without Feeling Guilty About It*. Because I was afraid of my work, it was hard to make myself work. Reilly's book appealed to me because it promised I wouldn't have to work so much. Reilly's basic point was that you separate your job into two parts: the activities you enjoy and the activities you dislike. What you dislike or find hard, you call work. His book helped me see that what I disliked I wasted energy on by putting off. So I found I had much more energy by taking the hardest jobs and doing them first.

But Reilly's book made me look at advertising for the parts of my job I liked and there wasn't much of my job I liked. I was always afraid of advertising. The last five years in advertising I had my own business. I would get up each morning with the fear in my stomach that today all my accounts would leave me. It was a completely irrational fear because for five years very few of my main accounts left me. And when I sold my business all but one of those accounts stayed with the new agency. I had as good a training as an advertising man could have so I knew my recommendations were sound. But I had this irrational fear about the things I was doing.

A year before I had my heart attack I started trying to switch into something else. I was going back to the university and get a master's in physics—a subject I had loved so much in college. But my plan was to keep running the advertising business on the side and there was no way I could do the two things.

At the same time I was frantically laying plans how to make enough money in advertising so I could invest it and retire in fifteen years. But that meant working harder at something I was frightened of. And as an escape from the craziness of what I was doing I was spending lots of money on things I didn't need in an attempt to take my mind off my misery.

It took a heart attack to make me stop and look at my life. One hour after my heart attack, it was plain to me as anything that all I had been doing in my work, as well as lots of other things in my life, was wrong and I wanted to find something else.

For the first time in my life I turned to the people around me with an open mind and asked for their counsel. They thought I should get out of business, too. It wasn't that there was anything wrong with business. They were in business and doing fine. But they could see I wasn't suited for it. My wife and my friends thought a good thing to try would be to go back to the university and prepare to be a teacher.

I considered high school teaching. It would take as long to prepare myself in high school teaching as it would to get a master's and teach advertising. So I never went back to the advertising business. I sold it on the phone.

When I went back to school the fear went away. I was good at going to school. I decided I didn't want to teach advertising because I didn't believe in it. I enjoyed psychology courses so I took a Ph.D. in psychology with the idea of going to Montana and teaching at a university.

I started teaching while I was completing my degree and had no fear of it. Each year I did such good work, I was promoted to a better job. Finally, after ten years of thinking and working on Reilly's and Seabury's ideas, I was doing work that was right for me, and what was so strange, the fear was pretty well gone, too. Even as a very new and inexperienced teacher, I had a reasonable confidence in what I was doing. Because I wasn't afraid of teaching or my students, I didn't hesitate to ask them to evaluate me. They quickly led me to vastly improve my teaching until after just three years they started telling me to leave my system alone and not make many more changes. It was fine the way it was.

I continually moved into new areas of teaching and then into writing. And the confidence I never had in advertising, I do have in teaching and writing. I have been willing to open myself up in a classroom in a way my colleagues tell me isn't done very often. I have been willing to take positions in my writing that are counter to the mainstream of writing in the self-help psychology field. And I have taken these positions without the support of any of the current theoretical positions.

Although I use some ideas from Eric Berne, Carl Rogers and Fritz Perls, I don't believe in their systems. I won't trust my life to those systems. Most people think my training must have been in humanistic or clinical psychology. Actually, my training was mostly in learning theory and experimental psychology yet it doesn't frighten me at all to take a clear and definite position in an area where I have had little formal training. My experience is all from my own study, but even more important from life and a careful study of what works and doesn't work for the people around me.

My point is that even though I was very good at advertising, I was afraid of it. Once I got into something I liked and that was right for me, my fear went away.

Now I'm in the beautiful position of just doing work I love and believe in. It took twenty years for me. But it was worth it.

Does that mean it will take twenty years for you? Not

necessarily. I had one of the world's biggest egos. It took a heart attack to break through that ego. I see lots of young people who are already pretty well along to making peace with what they like to do. Duke Ellington started right out in music doing what he loved. We don't all need the fame of a Duke Ellington. I see people here in Bozeman who are completely happy with what they are doing and no one but a few will ever know of their greatness. But that's fine with them. They aren't trying to do something important. They know it's enough to just be what they are—that's important.

These are the experiences I've had that have helped me see work in a totally new light. There isn't any such thing to me as work any more. There are just activities in my life. Some of those activities are directly hooked to money to live on and others aren't so directly hooked to money. But all my activities are things I love now and they all fit smoothly together into my day.

How do my activities affect mutual need therapy? When we are frightened we have tunnel vision or are almost blind. And our fear drives out love. In the advertising business, I was so confused and frightened I couldn't begin to see my needs for the people around me. With my fear gone, now I can see the need for the people I have mentioned so far. And I have the joy of work that has dignity. When we are afraid of our work, it makes us less than we are.

Some people say, "Sure, Jess. If I had your life, it would be easy to feel like you do." That's not the point. What I'm talking about has nothing to do with income or prestige. I can name waitresses, cooks, telephone linemen and garbage collectors in Bozeman who love their work and bring it dignity. I can name you doctors, law-

yers and university presidents who have no feeling or love
for their work and do great harm to the people around
them. What I'm talking about has nothing to do with job
hierarchies. What I'm talking about is what is in our
hearts. How well are we paying attention to the precious
clues life gives us to guide us to work that's right for
us? How much are we ignoring those clues and instead
following our egos like little children saying, "I want my
own way! I want life on my terms. I don't want to think
that there are some things that aren't right for me. I want
complete freedom to be anything I want to be. I don't
want to be limited in any way. I want to decide what I
want to be—and be it."

That's ego and self-will run wild. There is no acceptance of ourselves as unique individuals in that position.
There is no sense of a spiritual quest where we go
willingly and freely in search of what we are, accepting
what we are good at, but also accepting what we aren't
good at. This is why I see that we need to look at the
activities we call work in a new way to find the activities
we are good at and can enjoy. My experience has shown
me that the idea that work is a curse doesn't need to
apply any more. Maybe there was a time when work
was a curse. But there are too many exceptions to that
idea for me to accept it as a principle any more.

Some people ask, "Well, Jess, if people just did the
jobs that they wanted to do, who would empty the garbage?" The answer is, "Simple. Sonny Suhr would empty
the garbage. He loves to do it." At least he's got me
convinced he does. You've got to have some feeling for
emptying garbage when you put signs on your truck
like, "Your garbage is our bread and butter." Or, "Our
business is picking up after you."

We get our egos all mixed up with our jobs. For much of my working life I was what I did. It has taken me until now to see that my work is just a way to put food on the table. Some few people are able to see work without ego very early in life. My friend Bill Oriet came to Bozeman from Great Falls about twenty years ago. He was a lineman with Mountain Bell. He saw he wanted to live in Bozeman. So he told his company, "Don't you ever promote me or ever transfer me. I'm going to climb those poles as long as I'm able.". All these years Bill has stuck to his statement. I'm sure it hasn't been easy for him. But his life speaks of the rich rewards he reaped for not getting his ego mixed up with his work. And Bill did this when he was only twenty-five years old. In my mind, he's a great man.

I asked my students to write me a paper analyzing their work. Those papers showed me signs my students were letting their work dominate them and overwhelm them and occupy more than its eight hours rather than less. To me that is an especially bad sign.

I learned in business that taking things home was a delusion. The minute I would run into something hard to do I learned to do it right then. I didn't kid myself into thinking I was going to take it home and do it; I would go home without a briefcase. I wasn't quite as fashionable as the rest of the guys, but I had my work done. When you go home at five o'clock without a briefcase, you can plunk down into an easy chair. You aren't driven to read anything just as a way of escaping from something, you read only what you really want to read. Or, after an hour's rest from your work, you can get up and go outside and hit some golf balls or just go out and take a walk around the block or go to a show because you have earned your evening of freedom.

What I see so often is how we try to avoid feeling good. Reilly had an interesting last part to his title *How to Make Your Living in Four Hours a Day—Without Feeling Guilty About It.* I saw that I did feel guilty about not working a full eight hours. But now I think there is more to it than just guilt.

I found a funny thing happened when I told my students how to have a happier life through mutual need therapy. When I told them to spend more time with the people they liked and less with those they didn't like, my students balked at this. They claimed if they didn't spend time with the people they didn't like, no one would. Eventually, I could get them to see they couldn't do much good for anyone by spending time with them when they didn't like them. But they still resisted the idea of spending more time with the few people they really liked. At first I thought the feeling was like Reilly said we would have when we worked less. We felt guilty about feeling good. After a long time of thinking about it, I now think the feeling comes from a different problem. I think the problem is our fear, not our guilt. I think our deepest fear is self-knowledge. Hating our work helps us avoid self-knowledge through our constant misery and complaining. Living in confused relationships where we can't tell our friends from the others helps us avoid self-knowledge. Busyness, confusion, chaos, sick games, all serve us by distracting us from our search for ourselves, our spiritual quest.

When I offer you the chance to spend time just with people who are good for you and work that you like, most of the confusion would be taken out of your life. In the deadly quiet of no self-inflicted confusion, you and I are face to face with ourselves as we really are. I don't think there is anything more awful that I've ever faced than the clear sense of what I am and some of the sick games I play to meet some of my sick needs. Why wouldn't I run away from the mirror a close relationship holds up to me?

This, I now feel, is why my students hang on so tight to work they claim is too much for them. Work in this country is our most common escape from life. There is no way you or I will put down our unpleasant work until we are ready to face life. Only when we are ready to see ourselves as we really are, can we give up our escapes. And only then can we start getting some of the good things this life has to offer. And here we can't take a short cut. We can't go immediately from burying our heads in our work to the joy of full living. We have to first live with ourselves as we really are. We can't skip the bottom rungs of the ladder. We have to start living where we are. And we have to keep on living where we are until we know what we really are and where we came from. Only when we have that knowledge deep and solid in us can we progress up the ladder.

The same part of us that wants to escape self-knowledge wants to run away as soon as possible from self-knowledge we are given. We are like the little kid hiding under the covers from the boogeyman. We peek out from under the covers at life, then jerk the covers over our heads again. But we can't live that way. We can't take one quick look at our real selves and then fly up and become some kind of butterfly. That's a stage of living we can't force. We need to spend our time as a caterpillar crawling before we get changed into a butterfly on nature's time schedule, not on ours.

That's why I think so many of us don't want to get rid of what we see is the curse of work. The reason that we don't want to is we are using our work to run away from our families. And we are using our work to run away from our communities. We are using our work as a hideout. We aren't going to want to give it up, any more than we are going to want to give up these clothes that we wear right now. We need them, thank you. We're not about to give them up. Work serves as such a beautiful escape. But our work isn't an escape if it's fun. Work is an escape only if it is on top of us and we can bitch and moan and groan and feel miserable and yet occupy ourselves with our grief all day long. We've got some hidden but very real burdens of grief, some heavy burdens of alienation and separation from our families and our friends and our communities. So it takes something that is really preoccupying to escape from our grief. Something that is fun isn't preoccupying, because you can pick it up or put it down as you choose.

So we've got to have the work and it has got to be a taskmaster. It's got to be something where we can say, "Oh boy, I have to work two or three hours a day overtime just to barely keep ahead of that job." Or, "I have to work so hard to do the kind of job that I, God, feel should be done. I have to be there every night, in addition to my daytime activity, or things just won't go right. Nobody else sees the need like I do, to get these things done." And we really heap it on ourselves when we are in that kind of a mood. But the sadness is that because we are confusing work with hours and drudgery, not very much happens, not very much gets done.

"What fun is there in life if I don't bitch and moan?" Well I have news for you, there is smiling and laughing and saying, "Hey, isn't this a great day, isn't it great that we are together? And isn't it great that God gave me work that I love. There are a lot of good things. And maybe the way we are together at the particular time isn't so great, but we will change it."

There is a lot of resistance to the things I'm going to tell you now about getting rid of work. That's because so often we have our priorities screwed up. It isn't God, our family and the Green Bay Packers. It's the Green Bay Packers, our family and God. "Oh! Not me! Not a great little Christian like me!" Well, so often my friend, I can prove it to you. All you do is you give me a few minutes of questioning you about your different activities, your priorities, how you feel about different things, what you are doing. And I can prove it to you in most of your lives, you've got your priorities just exactly upside down. You've got your work, the Green Bay Packers, first instead of last.

"My work. My beautiful, noble work," you say. You would think that you are Michelangelo, or Leonardo da Vinci, you think that your work is that important. I've got news for you, Michelangelo didn't look at his work that way. An even better example because he lived in our time was Picasso. I don't know how many of you have studied the life of Picasso, but Picasso's life was just exactly what I am working for in my own life. You couldn't tell Picasso's work from his play. One minute he would be playing with a painting. The next minute he would be playing with his kids. The next minute he would be playing with his wife. And the next minute he would be playing with some visitor like Gary Cooper, who had brought him some six-guns and a cowboy hat. And then he would be drinking wine and then playing with his paintings. It was all just love, love of his wife, love of his family, love of his friends, love of his work. He just floated back and forth between his activities without any thought to there being a division or a gap.

A nice thing I've seen in my own life is that I've gotten to the position where my life is a lot closer to Picasso's than to that old life I had of work first, second and third. I'm awful happy and thankful that I've got the kind of life that I now have and I can see each day it gets better.

How do you get started when much of your work is a chore? I found one good idea from what an old sales manager, my first boss, Carl Nelson taught me. When he had a real tough selling job where he had to call a hundred merchants to get them to pay a buck apiece for their name on a page congratulating the basketball team he used this system: He would call two or three of the easiest ones first to get his morale up. Then he would call the five toughest ones, the ones he would be most inclined to put off. He would get them out of the way whether he got their money or not while he was still fresh and in a good mood. Then he would go ahead and call all the rest of the names just as fast as he could so he could finish the job rather than putting it down and losing his momentum.

We should use exactly the same principles in our work. We do our work as quickly in the morning as we possibly can, just as fast as we can. Maybe there is a report we usually do at three o'clock in the afternoon when we are more tired so it takes us an hour. Instead, "Hey, I'm going to grab that the first thing today. Maybe Tuesday morning I will have the information that I need to do it. I'll do it in ten minutes and save the extra time and the burden of thinking about it."

I've got a rule that when a job comes to me I try to do it immediately if I can. The other day at lunch Jerry Sullivan said, "Hey, Jess, I need three questions for a comprehensive examination. Can I have them this afternoon?" I said, "You sure can, Jerry." I sat down and wrote them out right there. It took me about three minutes. So I handed them to him. The job was done. I could have gone back to my office and wasted an hour or two on that job. Because I do things like that, I've got very little commitment any more to my office.

Another thing I've done is I've turned down all kinds of jobs of an administrative nature. I'm not good at that kind of a job so I just turn them down.

There is another trap which I see many people around me getting into. I would judge from the way they act that they are being paid somewhere from $30,000 to $50,000 a year, because they are trying to do the work of four or five people. They must think they are supermen. What I do is I look at my paycheck. If they are going to pay me $10,000 a year, then I'm going to do $15,000 worth of work for them just as fast as I can. But I'm not going to try to do $50,000 worth. That's stupid. Especially if I sit around complaining that they won't pay me three men's wages.

Now if you are the last of the great philanthropists who just want to keep this whole economy going because of your magnificent dedication, bully for you. If you want to do the work of three people, blessings upon you. I just don't want to be very close to you, because you are going to get plumb cranky. I think you are real stupid though, because you tell me you are overworked. I say, "Why are you overworked?" and you say, "Because I am trying to do the work of three people. And that's why I can't be at home with my family." And I say, "Would you please tell me why you work so hard?" "Well, somebody has gotta do it." Or, "I have high standards for the work I do in my job instead of being like you, you low crumb."

Many of my students, young people as well as adults, think I'm a little immoral because there is a sin in this country which is even worse than jumping in bed with your neighbor's wife and that is having a bad attitude towards work. This is a work-oriented society. If you aren't working and aren't miserable you are a sinner. I have said we have a one-commandment society: "Thou shall not jump in bed with thy neighbor's wife." But we've really got a two-commandment society. The second one is: "Thou shalt work thyself to death."

This is something that most of my students really don't want to hear and something that goes a lot against the grain because you and I are dedicated to upward mobility which means keep your nose clean and work hard and pretty soon you will be one social level higher than you were before. That is very important to people like me who grew up on the wrong side of the tracks. I felt looked down on. I wore hand-me-down clothes and stuff. So I've got to have upward mobility. I've got to get out of my low class because it really bothered me being there.

So the more we work at finding parts of our occupation we like, the more there ain't any work left. Some people want to argue with me. They hate their jobs yet they insist they can't get different jobs. Someone will moan, "Oh, what could I do?" I've got news for you there, nothing. You are miserable where you are. You love being miserable. You are going to stay miserable. And I'm not going to try to take your misery away from you.

Some of you say, "Hey, Jess, I'm willing to try anything because what you say sounds so good to me. Do you think I can make it?" And I say, "Yes you can, brother." How many jobs you are going to have to try I don't know, but you are going to make it. Because you want to. How long is it going to take you? I don't know. It was over twenty years ago that I read Reilly's and Seabury's books. Was it worth it? Sure was. I have an unbelievable amount of freedom in my days now, far more than I would have even believed possible five years ago.

While I now have great freedom, I've never been busier. I'm trying to hatch a new book, which never lets me have any rest. The minute my mind pops out of sleep I start thinking about some problem. It is on me all of the time, but I enjoy it. To me that is a fascination for the same reason that Einstein was constantly working on physics problems. In the hospital when he went to die, as soon as he got well enough he asked for some paper. They show in his biography photographs of the last equations he wrote on the day before he died. At seventy-six he was still writing physics equations. Not because he was driven to that work, but because he loved it. And it was his love for the work that made him the great physicist that he was.

Andrew Wyeth said, "It is my belief my art can go only so far as my love goes. The more I can love the deeper can be my art." Now that isn't very pleasant news for some of us because there isn't any more love in us for our work than what you could put in a teaspoon.

But, if that's the case, then here's where mutual need therapy comes in again. Let's get around some people who've got some love to give. Soon we've got a little more than a teaspoonful. And we've got a little more capacity to love. And we've got more capacity to love in our work. And we can be part of progress for the people around us instead of part of the pain for the people around us. We deny this pain we inflict on others by saying, "Oh! I'm such a sensitive, dedicated teacher." Meanwhile, our students are just screaming. The minute that class is over everyone of them flees like getting out of the penitentiary.

Reilly made his living in college by selling advertising in dance programs and other things like that. He made his living in just a few hours a day. When he got out of college, he had money saved up even though this was during the depression. The minute he started thinking about it he said, "Why should I ever work full time?" So he started making deals with bosses: "I'll do these things for you for so much money." He would do those things and more in considerably less than eight hours.

Right from the start Reilly found bosses who were willing to look at quality and quantity of work, even in engineering, rather than hours. He tells all kinds of case histories of the guys who were able to say to their bosses, "Hey, you know I can work better on some of these projects if I take them home and work on them." Some of the time the guy is home he is sleeping or reading magazines, but he gets some freedom from the office. He gets his work shifted over to a production basis rather than an hour basis.

When I was writing my Ph.D. dissertation I rewarded myself on the basis of my production instead of my time.

If I would do five pages of writing, I would buy myself
an ice-cream cone. And I would give myself the rest of
the evening off. So I put the emphasis on production of
work rather than number of hours. I didn't say I would
go over to the office there in the evening for three hours
and write from seven to ten. Because the minute I do
that, I start puttering around. I said, "I will go over
there and write until I get five pages written. The faster
I can get five pages done, the faster I can get back home,
and get my ice-cream cone."

But how do you get good ideas like that? Only if you
are looking for them. Only if you want them. If you are
using your work as a hideout, you don't want ideas like
that around.

Now the funny thing, too, is once you look at the
part of the job that is fun separately from the part of
the job that is work, you are a different person on the
part of the job that you see as fun. All of a sudden you
start seeing immediate favorable results from that. You
start getting more things back and you start up a very fine
positive circle. All of a sudden you are able to do things
that you couldn't do before. Maybe you were a teacher
who said, "Hey, the part I like best is teaching reading.
And the part I like best is reading the kids stories. And
the part I like best is playing with those kids at recess.
And the part I like best is talking to them about how
they feel about things."

Okay, once you have identified those things, when you
are doing them you are really with it. And you are free.
You are free to work on those things you really enjoy.
By compressing the time that you spend on work, you
have more time that you really enjoy so you can come
to work with a different attitude. Then you get more

back from people. So you have more to give. Within a year or two all kinds of things in you are going to be uncovered that you didn't know about. It could very likely be that some of you might be writers in your own particular field. And you never saw yourself as doing this. But once you start really paying attention, once you start really following your nose, you will find things nobody else ever found, because you are digging deeper. You aren't so superficial.

This is where my first book came from. I didn't know this stuff I write about was anything special. But I had been working on Reilly's ideas and following my nose and trying to find what I believed in for about fifteen years. When I went to speak to nurses about how to communicate, I said, "I don't want to talk to you about sentence lengths. I want to talk to you about the crucial 90 per cent of your communication, which is you can't communicate with anyone unless you have a good heart towards them. But you can't have a good heart towards someone else unless you get a good heart towards yourself."

Now following along the idea of going deeper into yourself, all of a sudden I saw this statement by Bill W., one of the founders of AA, in a magazine where he said there is no real communication between two people until they recognize their mutual need for each other. For years I had been saying in my classes "I need you" and "Some of you will choose to need me back." When I saw Bill W.'s statement it popped a little bulb. So now, all of a sudden, I'm coming back at psychology in a different way. Before I was concerned with a self-psychology but this is a relationship psychology. It isn't new. Nothing is totally new. But it is new for me.

Am I going to stay here the rest of my life? I don't know. Like Einstein said, "Ideas come from God and you don't know if you are going to have any more good ones or not." I will always have ideas because all they are are new combinations of old elements, novel but appropriate to the situation. So I can always have ideas because I know how to have ideas. How good they will be, that's in the hands of God. I don't care. I'm going to keep working on the things that I enjoy and keep working on finding out more. Not because I am some great, dedicated, public servant trying to develop a better psychology for you, but because I am trying to develop a better psychology for me.

The better psychology I can find for me, in my experience, the better psychology I find for an awful lot of other people. Because the deeper I go into myself and the more personal I get, the more universal I get. The more superficial I am, the less universal I am.

Once I started speaking fairly deeply out of my heart, then I started getting letters saying, "Hey, Jess, thank God I finally found somebody else in this whole United States that feels like me." Think of that! It took some dumb Norwegian schoolteacher in Montana to say something that some guy in a mental hospital down in Texas who is just fumbling and frightened with life needed to hear. In the letter I got from him recently he said, "You're just as weird as I am." But he didn't know that most everybody in Texas or anyplace else in the United States feels the same way he and I do.

So that is a ridiculous thing. But the fact I get so many letters like that tells you a lot about the state of our human relationships. The people around each of us feel so weird and alone. But if we were opening our hearts to people, nobody would feel weird and alone, because my heart is the same as yours, really, in the deepest parts.

This is the work that following my nose has led me to. Once you follow this line of finding the part of your work that's fun and the part of your work you can love, then, and only then, can all kinds of very positive things develop for you. Now, we need work that is satisfying. We need work where we can see its importance like in the old days of the spear-maker or the arrowhead-maker in an Indian tribe. He knew he was important, because he was cracking out sharp arrowheads that the tribe needed for hunting, for warfare and for ceremonial purposes. How are we going to have work that has dignity and value, if we are doing it as a hideout, as a refuge from ourselves? No way. We poison that work in the worst possible way. There isn't a chance it can be something with any substance to it. How can it be when we retreat to our work as a hideout and a refuge from the people who need us and who we need. It is only when we look at work from the standpoint of what part of this work do I like, what part of it do I enjoy, where does love fit into it, that we can have work that has dignity and satisfaction for us.

I don't see that there is any particular work that has more inherent dignity than any other. All work we love is a ceremony and has dignity. I have seen nurses who are dedicated, beautiful people who love their nursing. But most nurses who walked into my room were dead in the heart. I have seen doctors who are great healers, but so many doctors are blinded to the best practice of medicine by running an assembly line where everybody waits for them and they don't wait for anybody. And so it goes all through the occupations: garbage collectors, auto mechanics and what have you.

You tell me about an auto mechanic who loves his work and I will take my car to him right away. Because I know he will do a good job. Whatever he charges me, and I'm sure that it will be a fairly substantial amount, it will be worth it because I won't need to take it back and back. But look how rare these people are who love their work. And no occupation has got a corner on it. There's no occupation I have ever seen where there wasn't a majority of the people in the occupation who didn't show by their actions their lack of love for the work. And it is the minority who love their work. So the dignity of the work has nothing to do with whether the occupation is ranked high or low. Dignity of the work comes from inside the person doing the work.

There's the idea floating around today about fulfillment in your jobs, particularly in the women's lib movement. They are saying, "We don't have jobs that are as fulfilling as guys do." But guys are saying their jobs aren't fulfilling either. I don't see why gals think that guys' jobs are so groovy. I know it is partly because we have put work ahead of women and so we can't blame the gals for thinking our jobs must really be great if we prefer them to women. I agree gals should have the right to have any job they want. But I feel that the worst in that is this: I think that for both men and women there is no such thing as fulfillment in our work. If you are looking for that you are looking for something that is misleading and harmful. Work is a process, it is not an end in itself. Work is a part of the process that is life. If you don't find that process enjoyable, I don't see that there's anything else.

It is just like a man who is dedicated to catching a

lot of fish. If he doesn't get a lot of fish, he is miserable. I contend that he isn't a real fisherman. A fisherman is somebody who likes to fish. He has just about as good a day if he doesn't catch any fish as if he catches a hundred. He likes the process and the process is important. The goals and results, and fulfillment, are simply inevitable outcomes and side issues of the process. In a sense the outcomes are meaningless.

Einstein produced three or four fundamental sets of equations that gave us the general theory of relativity, the special theory of relativity and a couple of other basic theories. But they were not the point of his work. What Einstein was involved with was physics and equations. He was in love with the process.

Einstein also loved the beauty and order he saw in the world. "How would the God I know have given order and harmony to these events?" That question was a key one he used to guide him to the beautiful simplifications and unifications he accomplished. As near as I can see two things accounted for Einstein's discoveries: his independent spirit that kept him from stopping at the boundaries of accepted and conventional knowledge, and his love and belief in an order and lawfulness and beauty in the universe that went far beyond our feeble attempts to grasp it.

Many people do not understand that the latter half of Einstein's life was spent fighting quantum physics. And he came up with no major contributions in the last half of his life to compare with those in the first half. Most of his theories came by the time he was thirty-five. Quantum physics came in about fifteen years after he developed his ideas. So there was about thirty years that he spent struggling to find a way to overcome quantum mechanics.

He didn't like the indeterminancy of the Heisenberg principle. He fought that because he felt God would never have created a world as indetermined as the probability theory of matter implied. Einstein spent the last, major part of his life, when we thought he was such a great success, fighting something and failing. Even at his death he knew he had failed to find the hole that he felt there must be in the quantum theory. Because it didn't seem to fit his ideas. He believed in the God he saw in this beautiful universe. His guiding principle, the beauty and simplicity that lead him to his early theories, he saw being contradicted by quantum mechanics. He tried to demonstrate mathematically the weakness in quantum mechanics and failed. But he didn't put his life down as a failure because he spent the last half of his life failing. No. The last half of life was the same as the first. It was spent working on physics. It was a process he loved.

It is like my enjoyment of horseback riding. I like horseback riding so the places that I go to, or go by, in horseback riding are simply a set of side issues. I don't go horseback riding so that I can get to a place. And then get home. You see many people on vacations. They get in their cars and drive straight as an arrow to someplace, two thousand miles an hour, screaming at everybody in the car along the way. "No, you can't get out to go to the bathroom!" And they get there and then it is like they are pointing deliberately at the day ten days later when they are going to return. Then they get in their cars and zip back. As soon as they get home, they start thinking about the next vacation a year later. Nothing is ever now for those people. It is always tomorrow. Like one of my students said, "Jess, each day when I get up in the morning and look in the mirror, it is always tomorrow."

It is the process that counts. It is the five-minute-at-a-time business of living or, let's put it, business of loving that counts. Whether we are loving a woman or a man or our work or our family, or our friends, or what, it is immaterial and it all blends together just like Picasso's life.

We often think we need challenge. We think we have got to be out constantly climbing a higher mountain. I just read where somebody climbed the sixth highest mountain and they were the third party to climb it. What failures! Why climb a mountain that has already been climbed three times before? But when you look at life that way, once you have climbed Everest everybody else in mountain climbing might as well put away their equipment, unless they can find a harder way to climb Everest. Then, when all of the hard ways have been climbed, you might as well put your equipment away.

But when you look at life as the climbing then it's just as much fun to climb the last hill as it is to go to a trip to Everest. It's the same kind of process. And you haven't been spending your life as preparation for just one magnificent moment. That way what happens is a car runs over you just before you get to your magnificent moment and your whole life just went down the tube. So that's what is so ridiculous about this idea of challenge.

Jackie Gleason was asked about challenge on the Mike Douglas show. Gleason said, "I don't believe in challenge." And Mike Douglas said, "What do you mean, you don't believe in challenge? Here you have done some

of the great things in comedy on television like 'The
Honeymooners.' " And Gleason said, "Those weren't
challenges for me. They were the next logical step in my
development." And that's the point of life. Once we
start working for love and out of joy we are doing some
things that come easy. We are doing some things that
we could never have conceived of ourselves doing a year
or two years or ten years earlier. But it will happen only
if you want it to. As long as you are using work as a hideout you will never want to see the joy that can be in work.
As long as you are using your misery as your way of running away from the world you aren't ever going to be
willing to give up that precious misery.

Now, you see this is what I meant when I said earlier
that family, community and work all interrelate. If we
are working out of love then the people we are working
with feel some of this and become part of our community. And then the work we do out of love benefits the
community, the setting in which the work is done. People
come to me and say, "Hey, Jess, that is a great thing
that you are doing for my son." And I say, "Well thank
you. And because you are such a good friend to them,
it is a great thing you are doing for my son and my
daughter."

So these things interrelate. And it makes your work
and your fellow workers part of your community when
you are working out of love. When you are working out
of misery, no way is there a basis for mutuality in that
community. If I were you, the first thing I would do is
separate your job into enjoyment and work. The second
thing I would do is try to figure out what is the minimum
number of hours that I can spend and still earn my pay.
Turn it around and look at it that way instead of how

much work can I take home in a briefcase how many nights in a row. How can I speed up and do things at work so I never have to take things home at night? How can I participate only in those extracurricular parts of my job that are absolutely important or things I would like to do.

There are a lot of people who, if they were women, would be prostitutes because any time you ask them anything they always say yes. They haven't got the guts to say no. They are too egotistical. You ask them will you do this. They say yes because they know that nobody else in the whole world will do it and the job has got to be done. So they've got a job every night of the week, and they are moaning. Someone is going to run our life for us. Most of us are leaving that up to the demands of the people around us instead of taking a hand ourselves. We are responsible. We have to say no to the things that aren't right for us and our families.

I'm not saying these things are easy, I'm saying these ideas are simple. There are some simple basic principles here. All you need to do is find ways to implement them.

I get more objections to these ideas of work than to anything I talk about. Some students insist you can't do this. Work can't be handled this way. Yet in the same class will be lots of students young and old who will be agreeing that it can be done. I see that it goes back to, do you want to, and that takes you back to the threat of self-knowledge I mentioned earlier in the chapter. If you're ready for self-knowledge these ideas will make sense and you'll want to do them. Sure what I am talking about is hard enough to do. But thousands are doing it every day. I know. I get letters from lots of them every week.

11

a new beginning:
loving the
easy ones

Recently I have come to see life much differently than
when I wrote my first book. What I saw then was we
had to be satisfied on this earth with a very difficult life
at best. But I see now that's not true. Some of the abundant living and serenity that Vince has experienced I
can experience. He is a human being. He didn't spring
into life at age seventy, serene and content. He has been
growing and changing continually. Just ten years ago, at
sixty, Vince was still a little prejudiced against churches
and psychiatrists. Now, at seventy, he is pretty well free
of those two prejudices. He's changing and moving towards something all the time. He's so far down the road
now that very few people will ever approach what he's
got. But just a part of what he's got is so much more
than most any of us have, which is abundant living. It is
within our reach. All we need to do is, like taking an

apple from a tree, reach out and take it. It is ours as a gift, if we will but take it. We don't need to spend our lives in guilt, fear and doubt waiting for the hereafter. There's something on this side. There is a life before death.

But to live it we need to have these spiritual awakenings I have spoken of to you. We need to see there is a higher power and to realize that we can't completely control and run our own lives. If there's anything that's stupid it is our frantic attempts to hang onto our old ways. Those are the ways of living that nearly kill us. Yet we are hanging onto them like they are something precious, like they are heirloom china.

It's as if you've got a can of garbage. And I come and say, "Hey, let me empty your garbage for you." And you are clutching it to your bosom. "Oh my God, not my garbage. Don't take that away from me. I love my garbage." I say, "Hey, here's a splendid abundant life for you, all you need to do is let loose of your garbage. Here's a splendid, abundant, serene life waiting for you just like an apple on a tree, waiting for you to pick it— and keep working on it the rest of your life. That's available for you. All you have to do is give up your garbage, your old ways." "I don't want to give up my garbage. It's been so good to me." "What has it done for you?" "Nearly killed me three times." "Give up your garbage." "I can't give up my garbage, it's the only security I know." "What's it given you?" "Heartbreak. Disillusionment. I know it's the wrongest bunch of ideas in the world." "Give 'em up." "I don't want to give up my garbage. It's the only security I know."

These are the feelings I have and I'm sure you have about giving up those old ways. We find it almost impossible to give up those old ways. Yet if you hadn't been willing and even anxious to find a new way you wouldn't have come this far with me in this book. So you've gone a long ways towards taking down the walls that separate you from life.

Like I said to you in a previous chapter, the ideas in this book are my map to the gold mine. So now you have my map. It is the most reliable map I know. It was given to me by a bunch of people and by my higher power, and from my spiritual awakening twelve years ago when I realized, "Hey, from now on I ain't ever again going to do anything I don't believe in. As much as I can I'm going to give up attempting to control my life and go in search of what I truly believe in." And the reason that works is if there is a spirit and I believe there is, he is in each of us. So when I ask myself, "What should I do deep down?" guess who answers? That deep down me and his friend. There is no way you can ask that question without invoking your higher power and getting him into the act.

So all it is is giving up control, getting out of the driver's seat. And getting into an automobile and sitting down in the passenger's side. It takes off under its own steam. You don't see anybody over there in the driver's seat. And you want to scream, "Where are we going? Don't go so fast. Are you sure that you have enough gas? Let me drive for a while? How long are we going to stay on the road? I think I'm going to want to go potty and how am I going to tell you? My husband never will stop for me on things like that." Okay, but this is us, you see.

When I had that heart attack, I said in effect, "Hey, look where I got us to by me, my self-will, being in the driver's seat! With me keeping control." So okay, get out of the driver's seat. Get in the passenger's seat. Now that's the hardest thing in the world to do. It's simple to say, but the hardest thing in the world to do is to sit there as much as you can in the passenger's side. I'm regularly reaching over and grabbing the steering wheel, or putting my foot on the brake or doing some dumb thing to screw things up. But I know where I belong, and I know what I'm trying to do as much as I can during each day. I'm trying to spend as much time in the passenger's seat as I can.

But to me, even that figure of speech of sitting in the passenger's seat is a spooky thing. I'm filled with doubt and questions. "Where are we going to go?" "Well, we'll find out. Let's enjoy the scenery. Enjoy the trip. Turn the radio on, turn the tape deck on. Turn it off. Do a little reading. Check the map to see where it is that we are now. I see we took a turn here. I wonder where that's going to lead to. I see we just passed through a town, a beautiful town, all kinds of pretty things. I see we're going to stop here for the evening and meet some nice people and then go on." All the time just sitting in the passenger's side. And you find out where your particular car is going to go. While you don't ever completely find out, you can say, "Hey, we must be going south. It's getting warmer and the days are different. Look here, we're at the ocean. We're on a boat. It looks like we must be going to Africa because we're going more south than east. I wonder what we're going to do there."

What this voyage is, typically, is not a voyage to a distant land, but it's a voyage into ourselves. Deeper and deeper. In physical travel most often we will stay right where we are, because when you are happy you stay home. But when you are miserable you travel a lot.

And you stir up clouds of dust.

The thing I find is when you give up control, you don't need any of the hideouts. What are the hideouts? All of the great things in America: money, power, glory, fame, big house, big car, 100,000 acres of land, four thousand cows, eighty-six thoroughbred horses, purebred dogs, jewels, clothes, titles, big deal at your job, pedigreed friends, high society, name in the papers, eating too much, drinking too much, all those things are just ego scenes, to hide from the fact of what we are. An old cowboy used to come to town, plunk down his money on the bar and say, "Let's get drunk and be somebody." He didn't see he already was somebody—the most important somebody in the world—himself.

Do I mean by getting out of the driver's seat that we take a completely passive role in life? No. I see plenty of people who make that mistake. What I mean by that is we don't run life. We don't make the sun come up or make it rain. And we aren't in charge of how other people will act. We aren't in the center of the earth doing the driving. So as soon as we get out of the center, out of the driver's seat, we are freed from trying to do the impossible. And we are free to change what we really can change which is some of the things we do today. When I first saw that, an egomaniac like me felt that wasn't enough latitude. I wanted to do more. But now I see I've got plenty to do to keep me busy.

Also, I used to think that what I had was freedom and that by giving up control I would be limited in my freedom and variety. I now see that before I had no freedom at all. It was an illusion of freedom. I was driven by forces beyond my control. Every decision I made was ruled by the question of how would this make me look in others' eyes? I wasn't free to decide as I am now. "How do I feel about this for me?" As I have become more free of those forces that drove me like a slave, there is very little trouble in my life. I can see from this that most of the troubles I had I created myself. So what kind of freedom did I have when I couldn't do anything I wanted to do and was causing most of my own trouble?

There is only one answer and that is surrender, sitting in the passenger's seat and taking what comes. Now the sadness is that when we do that some of the days are stormy and the lightning is striking all around and it is very, very frightening seeing what we are. When I have to watch some of the things that I put my hand to it makes me want to vomit. That's why self-discovery is so damned unpopular. Because we've got our illusions and our delusions of what we are and we don't want them shattered, thank you. Me? That kind of person? Oh not lovely Miss Purity! Or Mr. Purity! I'm the white knight on the white horse. You mean there's some of all of the bad of everybody in the world in me? Yes. And that's no fun to see when that turns up on the wheel.

But that's what self-discovery means. It means accepting the recipe that was given us at birth and through later circumstances and taking that as a God-given recipe. We must accept it for what it is and quit arguing.

We all feel "If I would have written the recipe for me, I would have written it a lot different." Which of your imperfections would you really have freely chosen? Well, of course, none. I would be perfect. It would be you and God. But that's very lonely. And it ain't much fun. And it ain't very interesting. Because if we're all perfect, we're like a bunch of little wind-up toys, just following some mechanical path which is cut into the board those mechanical toys go around on. They all come up at the end in a certain place. Then you pull them back and wind them up again and start them all over. That's not heaven, that's hell!

To me the freedom we have to succeed and fail is the most beautiful thing there is in the world. To me our human imperfections and the variety they give to life is wonderful. Being what we call imperfect is really perfect.

I don't believe the person who talks about a hell on earth. It is possible to create our own hell on earth, but we've got to do something to create it, and that is to live in our delusions. And we can create a hell on earth, yes. But there is nothing wrong with these people around us. There is nothing wrong with that girl who jerked back from my touch in the Student Union building. That's humanity. That's the diversity. That's the imperfections. That's the puzzle. That's the mystery. That's what makes the mystery interesting. You wonder how it's going to come out. That's what makes it fun to get up in the morning. If you knew what was going to happen all day, it would be a bore. If I knew what was going to happen in the next month, I would probably kill myself. I've heard people say that and I think that's true. The very mystery and uncertainty we curse and fear is the thing that gives beauty and power to life.

Surrender to life and ourselves as we are is the crux of the whole thing. Then the question is: How do we surrender? How do we let our higher power take over, how do we have a spiritual awakening? How do we turn our life and our will over to the care of God as we understand Him? We can't change what we are. So we surrender to it. We can change what we do. How? What

I'm suggesting to you is that we do that through seeing our need for mutuality. We do that by being intelligent enough to realize that some of our friends have got something very, very important for us. And yet many others, who we think of as our friends, are not good for us. So each day we change one of the most crucial things we can change, which is some of the people we will see that day. We should stay away from the people who aren't good for us as much as we can and we should go frequently to those other people who lift us up. Because if somebody lifts us up we most always lift them up, too. It's like a teeter-totter where we lift each other up. This is what mutuality means.

When we go to people who lift us up, they give us the most precious thing that there is, which is a deeper self-knowledge. And that's the only way we can grow in awareness, you see. So we don't leave these encounters to chance, to accident. "I wonder when Sullivan is going to ask me to have lunch with him? I hope he gets around to it in the next two or three weeks." No way. I've already set aside some times when Jerry and I can have lunch. And then there are some other people who will come into my life because they choose to do so. Great.

I'm going through a bad time with a couple of the boys at home. I'm trying to get things patched up and smoothed out and get my own self in line because I'm creating a lot of the trouble. When I get my part of the problem removed, I know from experience that most of the rest of the problem will drop away or be easy to handle.

I'll get into trouble I don't see now. But fine, I'll go to somebody that lifts me up. I'm not telling you what you should do. I keep saying the word "you," but who am I talking to? I'm talking to me. Thanks to you I've improved my therapy system here. I've had a chance to think it out more clearly as I've put it down in black and white. As I've become more aware of my ideas, it has helped me add some more mutuality into my life that wasn't there before. As I searched for ways to clarify these ideas so I could present them to you, I was able to see them better myself.

One of the interesting benefits I find is that when I am happy I learn to live on the money I've got. When I am miserable there isn't enough money in the world to make me happy and there is no way outward circumstances can suit me. Every time it rains, it's a personal affront.

I see that I'm becoming much more aware than I have been before of some of these things that play a part in my life. I can tell when I've been away too long from people who lift me up. Last weekend we were camping so I missed the open AA meeting where anyone can come. This next weekend I'll probably be camping and I'll miss that one. The following weekend we'll probably be gone on vacation. So that's three meetings missed. But, okay, I can check in with Vince. So Friday or Monday I'll make sure I have a chance to see Vince.

I'm very conscious of the necessity to do what I'm talking about. Now, whether you are or not, that's up to you. If you like the kind of rewards that I'm talking about, abundant living, serenity, being in harmony with life, having lots of people around whose faces light up when they see you—then this might be something worthwhile for you to try.

Now, if you like discord in your life, if you love to hide in your work, if you're addicted to getting a lot of money so you can buy a lot of Cadillacs, if your idea is unless I can be president of my company I'm nothing, if those are your goals, I hope that you'll be as happy as I someday hope to be. And I'll try not to hassle you with my eyes.

Serenity is when I go my way, and just let the other person go his way. I'm not even aware of what way he's going. He's just a person. Whether that person is destined to play a very direct role in my life or not isn't an issue. Because all of us are one, everybody in this whole world, not just the people, but the plants, the animals and the rocks, and the trees, everything is just one, I feel. I don't see the world as cursed and despised and low. I see it as all one—and lovely.

I see the only question before me is the simplest question of all. The apple is hanging from the tree. Will I take that gift that has my name on it? Will I take that gift for my own, or not? That's the only thing in this whole world I have any control over, and that's surrendering to life and getting into that car and sitting in the passenger's seat, and staying there and keeping my hands off the steering wheel.

I think that if we work at that, each of us in the best way we can find for the rest of our lives that is our spiritual quest. That's all life is about. All I am responsible for is what I do with what I have been given. I can't use what I don't have. I'm not accountable for what someone else was given. I think we must dedicate ourselves to our spiritual quest. I think that by each morning saying, "Where am I going to find the people who can help me in this quest of mine?" the people will be given to us. Now you may not have an AA group like the alcoholics, but there are other opportunities or sources for you. Many of them do not necessarily exist right now, but you can create them. And particularly, the thing that I know you can create are the mutualities that are lying ready in your life, simply waiting for you. There are people standing all around you and me waiting for us to open our eyes to them and their love for us. And we are blind to what they offer us. Or, we even know what they have for us and don't go to it.

Many of my students tell me when they leave my classes, "Jess, I love you so much. And I'll see you again in about three thousand years." What does that say? It says that they don't know what they are talking about. They don't understand love much. I love you so much, but I won't ever spend twelve cents to write you a letter. I love you so much, but I won't ever call you at school. I love you so much, but I won't go out of my way ten miles or ten minutes to ever see you again. I know they are doing the best they can. But in their "I love you's," they are lying to themselves. They don't understand the commitment and giving in love.

This takes us into the idea of giving. The Indian medallion I have on my walls isn't a pleasing medallion, because I bought it. It wasn't given to me. And I'm going to give it away. I came out West and I wanted a cowboy buckle. So how did I get one? I went and bought one. But two students of mine saw my need and now I have two cowboy buckles, one of them was won at the University of Montana rodeo at Missoula in 1969. And another one is from someplace else. One of them came from Al Wagner and the other from C. R. Flemming. Those were the two guys who saw my need and filled it. So I gave away the cowboy buckle I bought for myself. So now that's a sweet buckle for someone, too, because it was a gift.

I thought of the finery that the Indian wears. I realized that of these things the Indian men were wearing every one was a gift. And I'm sure that many of the women's buckskins and beadwork and other things were gifts from a mother or sister. Because if you made something, you'd give it to someone else.

And we don't understand that. I'm the worst offender of all. I'm the greediest, most selfish person of all. I've got a lot to learn about giving, and it is hard for me, but I'm practicing giving in the hope someday it will be easier and more natural. I just bought a bunch of beadwork to give away. One of the belts was for John Barnett, a guy who has done a lot of things for me. So I gave that to him. I bought four or five of those little necklaces, which have a little ceramic thing on a buckskin string. They only cost a buck apiece. I gave those away to students of mine. Those things I gave away were very sweet because they meant much more to me than the three or four things I kept for myself.

I guess it's like the cowboy buckle that I bought when I came out here. It had to serve my needs until one that was given me came along. But again, the needs of so many people around us are so obvious. Yet, we don't think of giving them something. I've given away a number of copies of *The Prophet*, a book that has really touched me a lot. And there are other things that you see are needed so you give them. And in all this, I'm the one who benefits so much from the giving so what I'm doing is really very selfish in a sense.

My dad was trying to teach me this, but he never succeeded in his own lifetime. When he would go calling on people, during the depression, he'd buy a half gallon of ice cream to take along. There were four of us in our family and there might be three to six in the other family. You could maybe get by with a quart if you skimped. But he knew they would want to serve him something and they would want to be generous givers. So he would bring them a half gallon of ice cream. How many people come to your house visiting who bring a half gallon of ice cream with them? It only took me twenty-five years to realize what he was doing. I'm really brilliant, I'll tell you. Also, my dad often had a pint of blackberry brandy in the glove compartment of his car. He wasn't any drunk. He knew he'd be meeting his friends and they'd need a drink, just a snort. And my grandpa liked blackberry brandy, but he was too tight to buy brandy for himself. So my dad would pull into the place and he would have a drink of blackberry brandy with my grandpa. That was the kind of person he was. When he was buying something for you, he went that extra step. If he was buying a shotgun for you, he didn't buy a Sears Roebuck shotgun, he bought a Winchester. He went that extra step.

My dad died twenty years ago. We couldn't communicate with each other very well with words, yet, I'm still learning from him. How? From his example. I tell my friends that I'm teaching my children self-discipline—by example. Jerry is the only one who laughs at that because he's quick enough to see right away how funny that statement is. The only way I can teach generosity is by being generous. If I'm generous, I don't need to talk about it. If I'm not generous, look how awful it is to preach to my kids about how they should be generous.

I've found how hard it is to apply some of the things my dad did. When I'm buying a set of skis and Joe wants

VR-17's, my tendency is to try to find something for twenty or thirty dollars less. I can get Sears skis. Sure they are just as good, but this is a gift. So I say, "Hey, Jess, let's go that extra little distance." It's hard sometimes because so much I want to just hang on and do it my way, and then really screw things up. Yet everything we have is given us and the faster we can give it away again the better. Sure it doesn't hurt to put something by once in a while for a rainy day but not to be a miser where the most important figure in the world is how many dollars you have in your savings account. The minute you start looking at money that way, the roots of the money tree just shrivel up and die. You start this gimme, gimme, gimme, and how much have I got? And you get your eyesight all narrowed down. And nothing more comes to you for some reason, or very little. And you get all tied up in your bank account. There ain't much faith in that.

The Indian family who gave us a horse has given us the biggest gift our family has ever received. Yet their income is smaller than most our friends'. Recently another friend gave me another horse. Then a friend offered free stud service to his horse. So now this spring we have three gift horses. How rich can you get?

My students have given me so many gifts. Most of them they made. I've put them up around my office. I saw eventually that I was going to have to move out to make room for all my stuff. But then I saw a simple answer to it. That was to give them away to somebody. After those posters have been up in my office for a while then somebody else will like to see them and have them.

When Gandhi died he had two pairs of sandals, a couple

of bowls, a clock, a book and a fountain pen, his worldly possessions were sitting there in a little pile. If we really mean what we have felt here and said here, there is nothing important in this world except another person's heart. Absolutely nothing. And to the extent that we hang onto those other things, we are saying, "Hey, I want my possessions. I want the garbage, I want my old ways. I want money, power, glory, the security of my old screwed-up ways, instead of any kind of surrender, instead of any turning my will over to the care of God as I understand Him."

Speaking of Ghandi and his lack of possessions brings up the value of reading. I find reading can be useful because it is such a quick way to see how lots of other people live. I've heard people complain there are too many self-help books. I don't think so. I don't think there are near enough—especially good ones. I have five books on skiing, ten on hunting and twenty on fishing. But those are just hobbies. When it comes to living, which is the central question in life, what's wrong with one hundred to three hundred books?

I'm amazed at how little reading most people do. Jackie and I have spent lots of time reading very carefully and very selectively. Jerry Sullivan just finished my first book. He's had it at the head of his bed and he reads it every once in a while. And he takes it slowly and carefully. He just finished it here the other day. He said, "Jess, I've never seen a bibliography like yours. I've never read a bibliography before, but yours was so interesting where you were making the different comments about those books."

The reason I took so much care with the "Books I Use" section of *I Ain't Much . . .* was because of the big part that reading played in my life. Ben Franklin is a good example. Most everybody thinks of Ben Franklin as an old dried-up fogy. Well, he wasn't an old dried-up fogy. People think of him as a Puritan and a person totally dedicated to work. That's wrong, too. Ben Franklin went down to the dock with his wheelbarrow at five in the morning. But he left his wheel ungreased on purpose so it would make a lot of noise. Businessmen would hear the noise and say, "Boy, there's that Ben Franklin. That young Ben is sure a worker, isn't he? Up in the morning like that. I better give my business to such a hard-working young man." That noisy wheelbarrow was Ben's advertising campaign.

What was Ben really like? Well from twelve to two was his time to read and study. He would have a sandwich and study for two hours. But first he would go around and close all of his shutters and lock his doors so that nobody in town would come into his place and find him reading, because in those days a man who read was considered a time waster and a wool gatherer by small-minded merchants. Franklin worked quite hard to build his printing business. Why? To make money? No. So he could retire. By the time he was thirty-three years old, he had built it up to the point where he could sell a half interest in it to another man who would run it. By living on little money Ben Franklin then lived off the half interest in it. He devoted his life to the things that he wanted to do, not so he could serve the public but because he liked public life. Franklin's life is a good example of a fine balance between reading and action. He wasn't all reading and he wasn't all action. He found a balance.

I see many people who have some trouble with their

guilt in making their living in four hours a day. Yet in Franklin's case we see one of the earliest and greatest early Americans doing just that. Franklin was not of the nobility like Jefferson or Washington. He earned the same freedom the nobility had through the independent income his printing business gave him. He built up that business as quickly as he could, and then he quit working at anything he didn't want to do.

Sure, that was a Puritan society. And all them little Puritans could put their life to waste grubbing away for dollars. But old Ben didn't let society run him. He saw how people were and didn't try to change them. He just quietly ran his own life very differently from the Puritans. He was in Paris having a ball rather late in life. He did a lot of things that he enjoyed. He was held up to the Americans as a great patriot. And he was a great patriot. But it was because he liked it, not out of some firm sense of duty, where you grit your teeth and do something even if it kills you, and it probably will. Do that and a lot of people around you will also die just from the fallout.

I've read a lot of biographies. I have two biographies of Lincoln, one by Sandburg and one by Ludwig. I didn't enjoy the Sandburg one especially, but I learned something. Lincoln had been in Congress for a while and he saw the importance of the slavery issue. He saw there was a terrible inconsistency between our expressed ideals and our actions. He gave up his turn to go back to Congress so he could go home and think about this. He spent three or four quiet years there in Springfield practicing law and thinking about the slavery issue. When his time came he had done his homework. He knew where he stood and why.

A lot of people paint a picture of the Lincoln who failed a number of times for the state legislature and for the national legislature and failed in a number of other ways. But that is a misleading and distorted picture of Lincoln. Yes, he had some of those failures, but that's emphasizing the failures. The point is Lincoln was a man who had a clear and a deep sense of what he wanted to do and how he wanted to do it. That was very interesting to me. Also, I saw how he was able to function in the face of his own terrible depressions and his wife being so seriously troubled emotionally. Yet he didn't blame her for his lack of serenity. He had his own serenity and she couldn't take it away. Even the death of his son couldn't take his serenity away. It deeply disturbed it, but it didn't take it away.

I found there was a big problem with the "Books I Used" part of *I Ain't Much.* . . . Those books didn't speak to other people the same way they spoke to me. So you find the books that speak to you. I look at a great many books each year. I read about the book or just read a couple paragraphs to see if it's what I'm looking for. I find now that I'm not reading near as much as I used to. Most of my learning now comes from people, what they say and the expressions on their faces.

I think I'm beginning to understand, finally, what education means. My education is my getting the knowledge I need so I can make wise decisions. Is that the same education that you need? No, obviously not. So each person's education is not an ornament. It's not so that I can quote the Indian poet Tagore.

A woman I know read my quote from him in my first book and said, "Oh that Jess is so erudite." She missed the point. I'll quote Tagore. But I have quoted my local wino plumber, Vince, much more than Tagore. I'm not trying to quote Tagore to put anybody down. I was just trying to make the same point that we're making here. Who was it who forged my chains so carefully? It was I who forged those chains so carefully. Then how do I get rid of them? Simple. Take the hammer and chisel, cut them loose and then throw the damn things away. And walk free by having the courage to walk free.

The point is I needed that piece of knowledge as part of my education so that I could make a wise decision. In this case, get rid of that garbage, those old ways. See that I was the one who enslaved myself. It wasn't society. Society is like a cafeteria. We've picked out of society the things that we needed. I picked out of society the ego scenes I needed to impress people and make them think I was big. If society was so powerful, how come it couldn't force Ben Franklin into line?

Why should I blame society for my choices at the cafeteria? Well, it's a handy scapegoat. You say, "Well, I've never blamed society for making me act like I do." Maybe. Maybe not. But in any case, I absolve you. You are hereby free from all societal pressures. From now on don't you do a single thing unless you want to. And let's see you get out of your little Brownie boxes. See how quickly you make it out of there. I don't think it will take you long to see, "Hey, I'm in this box because I need it, aren't I? I've got these clothes on because I don't dare wear any less." That's right.

Now, you've got responsibility where it belongs. You and I have the responsibility for these dumb things we're doing. But that's a sign of great hope. If society lays it on me, only society can take it off. If I laid it on myself, guess who can take it off? I can. So see what hope there is in that. It's a simple thing when you look at it that way. There's a great hope, like I say, in seeing society isn't the culprit. You and I are.

And what's society? Simple. The combined total of our choices is what society is. The minute you and I decide to shuck off the garbage, society is immediately changed. The minute we make that decision and act on it, it's a new society, because one or two of its members are different. And when a whole lot of people do it, it will be a very different society.

You can see this very easily when you look at Ben Franklin's life. He had plenty of unorthodox ideas. He wrote a paper on "The Advantages of Having an Older Mistress." His point was that an older mistress was more grateful so gave you less trouble. How did he get away with such things back in the 1700s? Simple. He went his own way very quietly and didn't thumb his nose at society by publishing his paper when it was written. He respected society's ways as being fine for anyone who liked them. He was trying to find his own way.

His society was against his reading like I said earlier. So he simply locked his door when he was reading so no one would catch him. But we aren't usually that intelligent. When we get religion on something, we want the whole world to know about it—right now—so they can change, too. We went along for years making the same mistake but the minute we changed, we wanted the world to change. We don't see that just because something was a mistake for us so long is no sign it was a mistake for someone else. There's nobody so obnoxious as a reformed sinner.

We also don't see that someone may be doing the same thing we're doing and we're too blind to see it. I saw that in my own family. My grandfather was a very holy and pious man. He was a deacon in the Baptist Church and had a library of religious books. He sang hymns to himself during the day. But he was usually a terribly depressed and gloomy man. He was miserly, dictatorial and stingy with his wife. But I loved him because he was my grandpa and he loved me. Grandma wasn't the holy acting one. She just had a warm and giving heart. She was so glad to see you she just bounced. When she died, my grandpa and my aunt were wondering if grandma would go to heaven. My dad was listening and finally couldn't restrain himself any longer. "Hell," he said, "if ma ain't in heaven, there ain't none."

But we are so quick to judge other people and decide if they're going to heaven or not, if they're Christian or not, if they're patriotic or not. That judgment is what gives us problems with society.

I have found society will leave me alone to make my own choices. All I have to do is leave the people around me alone so they can be free to make their own choices. So I don't have to pay any big price in that way for my freedom. All I give society is what I owed to it in the first place which is leave it alone. Most martyrs I've seen just loved being martyrs and the center of attention. I think it is much easier in a way to be a martyr than to quietly go about our own spiritual quests.

Another mistake we make in judging society is we reserve all the good qualities for ourselves and a few friends, and let society have all the bad qualities. We don't think society is near as spiritual and dedicated to high purpose as we are. Oh we might admit that a few Republicans, or Democrats or Lutherans or Catholics feel as we do, but it's a tiny minority. All the rest of the world is going to hell in a hand basket.

I don't think that's fair. If I want to believe something good about myself, I think I have to be willing to allow other people to believe the same. I think *Jonathan Livingston Seagull* was so popular with millions because it expressed a hope everyone has which is to rise above where they are now to some higher form of living—to make a spiritual quest.

I don't see anything wrong with society. What you do about society is your business. I hope, I care. But I'm not going to sit around chewing my fingernails, waiting until some of you people decide to do something about what I might think is your miserable state. All I'm responsible for is what I do with what I've been given, so I had better get on with my own work and hope for the best for each of you.

I know the more I go on about my own work, the more I attend to my own business, the more I keep my long beak out of your business, the more I keep my great judgmental self away from you, the more you are encouraged to do likewise. The more I open my heart, to myself and to you, the more you're inclined to reciprocate. But whether you choose to or not to has to be your choice and love doesn't mean anything unless it is freely given.

Some people, when they talk about religion, talk about imitating Christ. I can't handle that idea, yet. It may be a great idea for you or for somebody else. I'm trying to imitate Vince, because I can understand where he is and where he is going. I'm not putting him as a God, I'm not saying he is perfection. But he helps me. And I'm interested in things that work in my life. Now if that stops working in my life, then I'll stop doing it. How long will

I do that? I don't know. I'll keep doing it until it stops seeming like a good thing to do. What I'm judging by constantly in my own life are the fruits of these different things. I hold my ideas up against life and see if they work. If they work. I keep them. If they don't work on life, if they don't bear fruit, I put them down. That isn't saying there's something wrong with them. But it is saying that they don't work for me right now. And what I need are things that work.

If there was a key idea in my first book, it was acceptance. The key idea in our second book was surrender. If there is a key idea in this book, it is that after we surrender, we need to look for the things that are ours to change. As Vince said, "I used to believe, Jess, that in the acceptance lies the solution. I used to teach that all the time. I have come to see that there are things we can change." What I'm trying to work on are the very obvious things I see around me that I can change. Now I need the serenity to accept the things that I can't change and I understand that. There are a lot of things about my life and my family I can't change. I need the serenity to accept those things. But I also need the courage to change the things I can. If there is somebody I can go to in a day who can lift me up, then I had better go to that person instead of sitting around and waiting for good people to come to me, waiting for accidents to happen. That's something I can change. And there is no harm in changing that. So the emphasis here is on change.

I thought, "How come, Jess, you haven't talked about acceptance hardly at all? When are you going to do that?" The answer is I'm not talking acceptance that much. I have talked a lot about acceptance in the sense of giving up control, getting out of the driver's seat, taking life the way it is. The laws of life are the way they are. They will not bend for you or me. Our job is to get in harmony with life, it's not going to get in harmony with us. And in that sense, that is indirect acceptance. But it is up to us to move. This is a path that has to be walked. It has been becoming increasingly clear to me that there is a lot of moving we can do. There are a lot of things that we can change. And an awful lot of them we can do now, tonight, tomorrow.

"How do we get energy into our system?" Vince has got a magnificent energy generator. What is it? It's going to his friends and it's giving in love and friendliness, because the more he gives away, the more he gets back. It isn't one for one, he isn't dependent on results. But the more you give away the more you have. So the way to add to the store of energy that you now have is to see your need for energy intake, gasoline to run your car.

Another reason for mutuality is like cars going to gas stations. The more gas stations I have in my life for my car, the longer the trip I can take, the farther I can travel, the more frequently I can go someplace, the more miles I can put on.

When we see the system that way, then we see what makes some old people never get old. About the only way you can kill them is with a bullet. A man I know is ninety-two and is still doing some of his farm work. You can't do that unless you've got a reasonably happy heart. He has found a way to get the energy into his system. Now, he maybe never had to face some of the problems that I've had. Maybe he wasn't as screwed up as I was. But I don't know what the situation is. That's his problem and I've got mine. I know what my dilemma is, I assure you. And I know the urgency of it. So I better do something about it instead of sitting around and saying, "Why was I born unlucky and him lucky? How come he has got all of these great things and he doesn't seem to have to do all of the funny things that I've had to do. He doesn't need to see life as a kind of constant struggle for survival the way that I do." I don't know the answer to that. Very often when you talk to some of these oldsters who are good at living, the sweet ones, they know so much more about this kind of stuff that I'm talking about than I'll ever know. And that's how come they got to be oldsters. They learned the hard way, too. It just looks easy to me, now that they've learned their lessons so well.

There was a story that I was reading about a guy who was running a country grain elevator in Iowa. He really screwed up. He was betting on the futures market and it turned around and went the wrong way on him. He was a million and a half dollars short on his accounts. He took his car and ran it into a railroad train so he would be sure to be killed. He had a fairly good insurance policy to wipe out most of his family obligations. But here was still all the money he owed those farmers and a lot of them settled for a third. That's the kind of thing you do when you need commotion and dust stirred up in your life. But when you value life, and really want to live, you don't do dumb things like that.

The way a guy put it once to me, it's as if you hear some rich relative who had developed a liking for you had just died someplace. Filed at the recorder's office in the town where he died was the paper giving you his money. You wouldn't go into the recorder's office and beg, "Please. Please give me this money." You would